D1234232

Writings of
Emma Goldman

Essays on Anarchism, Feminism, Socialism and Communism

by Emma Goldman

Red and Black Publishers, St Petersburg, Florida

Library of Congress Cataloging-in-Publication Data

Goldman, Emma, 1869-1940.
  Writings of Emma Goldman : essays on anarchism, feminism, socialism and communism / by Emma Goldman.
     pages cm
  ISBN 978-1-61001-031-3
1. Anarchism--United States--History. 2. Feminism--United States--History. 3. Women and socialism--United States--History. 4. Anarchism. 5. Feminism. 6. Women and socialism. 7. Communism. 8. Goldman, Emma, 1869-1940. I. Title.
  HX843.G65 2013
  335'.83092--dc23
                          2012051803

Red and Black Publishers, PO Box 7542, St Petersburg, Florida, 33734
Contact us at: info@RedandBlackPublishers.com
    Printed and manufactured in the United States of America

Contents

Anarchy and the Sex Question

The Alarm, September 27, 1896.

The workingman, whose strength and muscles are so admired by the pale, puny off-springs of the rich, yet whose labour barely brings him enough to keep the wolf of starvation from the door, marries only to have a wife and house-keeper, who must slave from morning till night, who must make every effort to keep down expenses. Her nerves are so tired by the continual effort to make the pitiful wages of her husband support both of them that she grows irritable and no longer is successful in concealing her want of affection for her lord and master, who, alas! soon comes to the conclusion that his hopes and plans have gone astray, and so practically begins to think that marriage is a failure.

The Chain Grows Heavier And Heavier

As the expenses grow larger instead of smaller, the wife, who has lost all of the little strength she had at marriage, likewise feels herself betrayed, and the constant fretting and dread of starvation consumes her beauty in a short time after marriage. She grows despondent, neglects her household duties, and as there are no ties of love and sympathy between herself and her husband to give them strength to face the misery and poverty of their lives, instead of clinging to each other, they become more and more estranged, more and more impatient with each other's faults.

The man cannot, like the millionaire, go to his club, but he goes to a saloon and tries to drown his misery in a glass of beer or whiskey. The unfortunate partner of his misery, who is too honest to seek forgetfulness in the arms of a lover, and who is too poor to allow herself any legitimate recreation or amusement, remains amid the squalid, half-kept surroundings she calls home, and bitterly bemoans the folly that made her a poor man's wife.

Yet there is no way for them to part from each other.

But They Must Wear It.

However galling the chain which has been put around their necks by the law and Church may be, it may not be broken unless those two persons decide to permit it to be severed.

Should the law be merciful enough to grant them liberty, every detail of their private life must be dragged to light. The woman is condemned by public opinion and her whole life is ruined. The fear of this disgrace often causes her to break down under the heavy weight of married life without daring to enter a single protest against the outrageous system that has crushed her and so many of her sisters.

The rich endure it to avoid scandal — the poor for the sake of their children and the fear of public opinion. Their lives are one long continuation of hypocrisy and deceit.

The woman who sells her favours is at liberty to leave the man who purchases them at any time, "while the respectable wife" cannot free herself from a union which is galling to her.

All unnatural unions which are not hallowed by love are prostitution, whether sanctioned by the Church and society or not. Such unions cannot have other than a degrading influence both upon the morals and health of society.

The System Is To Blame

The system which forces women to sell their womanhood and independence to the highest bidder is a branch of the same evil system which gives to a few the right to live on the wealth produced by their fellow-men, 99 percent of whom must toil and slave early and late for barely enough to keep soul and body together, while the fruits of their labour are absorbed by a few idle vampires who are surrounded by every luxury wealth can purchase.

Look for a moment at two pictures of this nineteenth century social system.

Look at the homes of the wealthy, those magnificent palaces whose costly furnishings would put thousands of needy men and women in comfortable circumstances. Look at the dinner parties of these sons and daughters of wealth, a single course of which would feed hundreds of starving ones to whom a full meal of bread washed down by water is a luxury. Look upon these votaries of fashion as they spend their days devising new means of selfish enjoyment — theatres, balls, concerts, yachting, rushing from one part of the globe to another in their mad search for gaiety and pleasure. And then turn a moment and look at those who produce the wealth that pays for these excessive, unnatural enjoyments.

The Other Picture

Look at them herded together in dark, damp cellars, where they never get a breath of fresh air, clothed in rags, carrying their loads of misery from the cradle to the grave, their children running around the streets, naked, starved, without anyone to give them a loving word or tender care, growing up in ignorance and superstition, cursing the day of their birth.

Look at these two startling contrasts, you moralists and philanthropists, and tell me who is to be blamed for it! Those who are driven to prostitution, whether legal or otherwise, or those who drive their victims to such demoralisation?

The cause lies not in prostitution, but in society itself; in the system of inequality of private property and in the State and

Church. In the system of legalized theft, murder and violation of the innocent women and helpless children.

The Cure For The Evil.

Not until this monster is destroyed will we get rid of the disease which exists in the Senate and all public offices; in the houses of the rich as well as in the miserable barracks of the poor. Mankind must become conscious of their strength and capabilities, they must be free to commence a new life, a better and nobler life.

Prostitution will never be suppressed by the means employed by the Rev. Dr. Parkhurst and other reformers. It will exist as long as the system exists which breeds it.

When all these reformers unite their efforts with those who are striving to abolish the system which begets crime of every description and erect one which is based upon perfect equity—a system which guarantees every member, man, woman or child, the full fruits of their labour and a perfectly equal right to enjoy the gifts of nature and to attain the highest knowledge—woman will be self-supporting and independent. Her health no longer crushed by endless toil and slavery no longer will she be the victim of man, while man will no longer be possessed of unhealthy, unnatural passions and vices.

An Anarchist's Dream

Each will enter the marriage state with physical strength and moral confidence in each other. Each will love and esteem the other, and will help in working not only for their own welfare, but, being happy themselves, they will desire also the universal happiness of humanity. The offspring of such unions will be strong and healthy in mind and body and will honour and respect their parents, not because it is their duty to do so, but because the parents deserve it. They will be instructed and cared for by the whole community and will be free to follow their own inclinations, and there will be no necessity to teach them sychophancy and the base art of preying upon their fellow-beings. Their aim in life will be, not to obtain power over their brothers, but to win the respect and esteem of every member of the community.

Anarchist Divorce.

Should the union of a man and woman prove unsatisfactory and distasteful to them they will in a quiet, friendly manner, separate and not debase the several relations of marriage by continuing an uncongenial union.

If, instead of persecuting the victims, the reformers of the day will unite their efforts to eradicate the cause, prostitution will no longer disgrace humanity.

To suppress one class and protect another is worse than folly. It is criminal. Do not turn away your heads, you moral man and woman.

Do not allow your prejudice to influence you: look at the question from an unbiased standpoint.

Instead of exerting your strength uselessly, join hands and assist to abolish the corrupt, diseased system.

If married life has not robbed you of honour and self-respect, if you have love for those you call your children, you must, for your own sake as well as theirs, seek emancipation and establish liberty. Then, and not until then, will the evils of matrimony cease.

Anarchy Defended by Anarchists

with Johann Most

Metropolitan Magazine, October 1896.

To most Americans Anarchy is an evil-sounding word — another name for wickedness, perversity, and chaos. Anarchists are looked upon as a herd of uncombed, unwashed, and vile ruffians, bent on killing the rich and dividing their capital. Anarchy, however, to its followers actually signifies a social theory which regards the union of order with the absence of all government of man by man; in short, it means perfect individual liberty.

If the meaning of Anarchy has so far been interpreted as a state of the greatest disorder, it is because people have been taught that their affairs are regulated, that they are ruled wisely, and that authority is a necessity.

In by-gone centuries any person who asserted that mankind could get along without the aid of worldly and spiritual authority was considered a madman, and was either placed in a lunatic asylum or burned at the stake; whereas today hundreds of thousands of men and women are infidels who scorn the idea of a supernatural Being.

The freethinkers of today, for instance, still believe in the necessity of the State, which protects society; they do not desire to know the history of our barbarian institutions. They do not understand that government did not and cannot exist without oppression; that every government has committed dark deeds and great crimes against society. The development of government has been in the order, despotism, monarchy, oligarchy, plutocracy; but it has always been a tyranny.

It cannot be denied that there are a large number of wise and well-meaning people who are anxious to better the present conditions, but they have not sufficiently emancipated themselves from the prejudices and superstitions of the dark ages to understand the true inwardness of the institution called government.

"How can we get along without government?" ask these people. "If our government is bad let us try to have a good one, but we must have government by all means!"

The trouble is that there is no such thing as good government, because its very existence is based upon the submission of one class to the dictatorship of another. "But men must be governed," some remark; "they must be guided by laws." Well, if men are children who must be led, who then is so perfect, so wise, so faultless as to be able to govern and guide his fellows?

We assert that men can and should govern themselves individually. If men are still immature, rulers are the same. Should one man, or a small number of men, lead all the blind millions who compose a nation?

"But we must have some authority, at least," said an American friend to us. Certainly we must, and we have it, too; it is the inevitable power of natural laws, which manifests itself in the physical and social world. We may or may not understand these laws, but we must obey them as they are a part of our existence; we are the absolute slaves of these laws, but in such slavery there is no humiliation. Slavery as it exists today means an external master, a lawmaker outside of those he controls; while the natural laws are not outside of us — they are in us; we live, we breathe, we think, we move only through these laws; they are therefore not our enemies but our benefactors.

Are the laws made by man, the laws on our statute books, in conformity with the laws of Nature? No one, we think, can have the temerity to assert that they are.

It is because the laws prescribed to us by men are not in conformity with the laws of Nature that mankind suffers from so much ill. It is absurd to talk of human happiness so long as men are not free.

We do not wonder that some people are so bitterly opposed to Anarchy and its exponents, because it demands changes so radical of existing notions, while the latter offend rather than conciliate by the zealousness of their propaganda.

Patience and resignation are preached to the poor, promising them a reward in the hereafter. What matters it to the wretched outcast who has no place to call his own, who is craving for a piece of bread, that the doors of Heaven are wider open for him than for the rich? In the face of the great misery of the masses such promises seem bitter irony.

I have met very few intelligent women and men who honestly and conscientiously could defend existing governments; they even agreed with me on many points, but they were lacking in moral courage when it came to the point, to step to the front and declare themselves openly in sympathy with anarchistic principles.

We who have chosen the path laid down for us by our convictions oppose the organization called the State, on principle, claiming the equal right of all to work and enjoy life.

When once free from the restrictions of extraneous authority, men will enter into free relations; spontaneous organizations will spring up in all parts of the world, and everyone will contribute to his and the common welfare as much labor as he or she is capable of, and consume according to their needs. All modern technical inventions and discoveries will be employed to make work easy and pleasant, and science, culture, and art will be freely used to perfect and elevate the human race, while woman will be coequal with man.

"This is all well said," replies someone, "but people are not angels, men are selfish."

What about? Selfishness is not a crime; it only becomes a crime when conditions are such as to give an individual the opportunity to satisfy his selfishness to the detriment of others. In an anarchistic society everyone will seek to satisfy his ego; but as Mother Nature has so arranged things that only those survive who have the aid of their neighbors, man, in order to satisfy his ego, will extend his aid to those who will aid him, and then selfishness will no more be a curse but a blessing.

A dagger in one hand, a torch in the other, and all his pockets brimful with dynamite bombs — that is the picture of the Anarchist such as it has been drawn by his enemies. They look at him simply as a mixture of a fool and a knave, whose sole purpose is a universal topsy-turvy, and whose only means to that purpose is to slay anyone and everyone who differs from him. The picture is an ugly caricature, but its general acceptance is not to be wondered at, considering how persistently the idea has been drummed into the mind of the public. However, we believe Anarchy — which is freedom of each individual from harmful constraint by others, whether these others be individuals or an organized government — cannot be brought about without violence, and this violence is the same which won at Thermopylae and Marathon.

The popular demand for freedom is stronger and clearer than it has ever been before, and the conditions for reaching the goal are more favorable. It is evident that through the whole course of history runs an evolution before which slavery of any kind, compulsion under any form, must break down, and from which freedom, full and unlimited freedom, for all and from all must come.

From this it follows that Anarchism cannot be a retrograde movement, as has been insinuated, for the Anarchists march in the van and not in the rear of the army of freedom.

We consider it absolutely necessary that the mass of the people should never for a moment forget the gigantic contest that must come before their ideas can be realized, and therefore they use every means at their disposal — the speech, the press, the deed — to hasten the revolutionary development.

The weal of mankind, as the future will and must make plain, depends upon communism. The system of communism logically excludes any and every relation between master and servant, and means really Anarchism, and the way to this goal leads through a social revolution.

As for the violence which people take as the characteristic mark of the Anarchist, it cannot and it shall not be denied that most Anarchists feel convinced that "violence" is not any more reprehensible toward carrying out their designs than it is when used by an oppressed people to obtain freedom. The uprising of the oppressed has always been condemned by tyrants: Persia was astounded at Greece, Rome at the Caudine Forks, and England at Bunker Hill. Can Anarchy expect less, or demand victories without striving for them?

What I Believe

New York World, July 19, 1908.

"What I believe" has many times been the target of hack writers. Such blood-curdling and incoherent stories have been circulated about me, it is no wonder that the average human being has palpitation of the heart at the very mention of the name Emma Goldman. It is too bad that we no longer live in the times when witches were burned at the stake or tortured to drive the evil spirit out of them. For, indeed, Emma Goldman is a witch! True, she does not eat little children, but she does many worse things. She manufactures bombs and gambles in crowned heads. B-r-r!

Such is the impression the public has of myself and my beliefs. It is therefore very much to the credit of *The World* that it gives its readers at least an opportunity to learn what my beliefs really are.

The student of the history of progressive thought is well aware that every idea in its early stages has been misrepresented, and the adherents of such ideas have been maligned and persecuted. One need not go back two thousand years to the time when those who believed in the gospel of Jesus were thrown into the arena or hunted into dungeons to realize how little great beliefs or earnest believers are understood. The history of progress is written in the blood of men and women who have dared to espouse an unpopular cause, as, for instance, the black man's right to his body, or woman's right to her soul. If, then, from time immemorial, the New has met with opposition and condemnation, why should my beliefs be exempt from a crown of thorns?

"What I believe" is a process rather than a finality. Finalities are for gods and governments, not for the human intellect. While it may be true that Herbert Spencer's formulation of liberty is the most important on the subject, as a political basis of society, yet life is something more than formulas. In the battle for freedom, as Ibsen has so well pointed out, it is the struggle for, not so much the attainment of, liberty, that develops all that is strongest, sturdiest and finest in human character.

Anarchism is not only a process, however, that marches on with "sombre steps," coloring all that is positive and constructive in organic development. It is a conspicuous protest of the most militant type. It is so absolutely uncompromising, insisting and permeating a force as to overcome the most stubborn assault and to withstand the criticism of those who really constitute the last trumpets of a decaying age.

Anarchists are by no means passive spectators in the theatre of social development; on the contrary, they have some very positive notions as regards aims and methods.

That I may make myself as clear as possible without using too much space, permit me to adopt the topical mode of treatment of "What I Believe":

I. As To Property

"Property" means dominion over things and the denial to others of the use of those things. So long as production was not equal to the normal demand, institutional property may have had some *raison d'être*. One has only to consult economics, however, to know that the productivity of labor within the last few decades has increased so tremendously as to exceed normal demand a hundred-fold, and to make property not only a hindrance to human well-being, but an obstacle, a deadly barrier, to all progress. It is the private dominion over things that condemns millions of people to be mere nonentities, living corpses without originality or power of initiative, human machines of flesh and blood, who pile up mountains of wealth for others and pay for it with a gray, dull and wretched existence for themselves. I believe that there can be no real wealth, social wealth, so long as it rests on human lives — young lives, old lives, and lives in the making.

It is conceded by all radical thinkers that the fundamental cause of this terrible state of affairs is (1) that man must sell his labor; (2) that his inclination and judgment are subordinated to the will of a master.

Anarchism is the only philosophy that can and will do away with this humiliating and degrading situation. It differs from all other theories inasmuch as it points out that man's development, his physical well-being, his latent qualities and innate disposition alone must determine the character and conditions of his work. Similarly will one's physical and mental appreciations and his soul cravings decide how much he shall consume. To make this a reality will, I believe, be possible only in a society based on voluntary co-operation of productive groups, communities and societies loosely federated together, eventually developing into a free communism, actuated by a solidarity of interests. There can be no freedom in the large sense of the word, no harmonious development, so long as mercenary and commercial considerations play an important part in the determination of personal conduct.

II. As To Government

I believe government, organized authority, or the State is necessary only to maintain or protect property and monopoly. It has proven efficient in that function only. As a promoter of individual liberty, human well-being and social harmony, which alone constitute real order, government stands condemned by all the great men of the world.

I therefore believe, with my fellow-Anarchists, that the statutory regulations, legislative enactments, constitutional provisions, are invasive. They never yet induced man to do anything he could and would not do by virtue of his intellect or temperament, nor prevented anything that man was impelled to do by the same dictates. Millet's pictorial description of "The Man with the Hoe," Meunier's masterpieces of the miners that have aided in lifting labor from its degrading position, Gorki's descriptions of the underworld, Ibsen's psychological analysis of human life, could never have been induced by government any more than the spirit which impels a man to save a drowning child or a crippled woman from a burning building has ever been called into operation by statutory regulations or the policeman's club. I believe—indeed, I know—that whatever is fine and beautiful in the human expresses and asserts itself in spite of government, and not because of it.

The Anarchists are therefore justified in assuming that Anarchism—the absence of government—will insure the widest and greatest scope for unhampered human development, the cornerstone of true social progress and harmony.

As to the stereotyped argument that government acts as a check on crime and vice, even the makers of law no longer believe it. This country spends millions of dollars for the maintenance of her "criminals" behind prison bars, yet crime is on the increase. Surely this state of affairs is not owing to an insufficiency of laws! Ninety percent of all crimes are property crimes, which have their root in our economic iniquities. So long as these latter continue to exist we might convert every lamp-post into a gibbet without having the least effect on the crime in our midst. Crimes resulting from heredity can certainly never be cured by law. Surely we are learning even today that such crimes can effectively be treated only by the best modern medical methods at our command, and, above all, by the spirit of a deeper sense of fellowship, kindness and understanding.

III. As To Militarism

I should not treat of this subject separately, since it belongs to the paraphernalia of government, if it were not for the fact that those who are most vigorously opposed to my beliefs on the ground that the latter stand for force are the advocates of militarism.

The fact is that Anarchists are the only true advocates of peace, the only people who call a halt to the growing tendency of militarism, which is fast making of this erstwhile free country an imperialistic and despotic power.

The military spirit is the most merciless, heartless and brutal in existence. It fosters an institution for which there is not even a pretense of justification. The soldier, to quote Tolstoi, is a professional man-killer. He does not kill for the love of it, like a savage, or in a passion, like a homicide. He is a cold-blooded, mechanical, obedient tool of his military superiors. He is ready to cut throats or scuttle a ship at the command of his ranking officer, without knowing or, perhaps, caring how, why or wherefore. I am supported in this contention by no less a military light than Gen. Funston. I quote from the latter's communication to the *New York Evening Post* of June 30, dealing with the case of Private William Buwalda, which caused such a stir all through the Northwest. "The first duty of an officer or enlisted man," says our noble warrior, "is unquestioning obedience and loyalty to the government to which he has sworn allegiance; it makes no difference whether he approves of that government or not."

How can we harmonize the principle of "unquestioning obedience" with the principle of "life, liberty and the pursuit of happiness"? The deadly power of militarism has never before been so effectually demonstrated in this country as in the recent condemnation by court-martial of William Buwalda, of San Francisco, Company A, Engineers, to five years in military prison. Here was a man who had a record of fifteen years of continuous service. "His character and conduct were unimpeachable," we are told by Gen. Funston, who, in consideration of it, reduced Buwalda's sentence to three years.

Yet the man is thrown suddenly out of the army, dishonored, robbed of his chances of a pension and sent to prison. What was his crime? Just listen, ye free-born Americans! William Buwalda attended a public meeting, and after the lecture he shook hands with the speaker. Gen. Funston, in his letter to the *Post*, to which I have already referred above, asserts that Buwalda's action was a "great military offense, infinitely worse than desertion." In another public statement which the General made in Portland, Ore., he said that "Buwalda's was a serious crime, equal to treason."

It is quite true that the meeting had been arranged by Anarchists. Had the Socialists issued the call, Gen. Funston informs us, there would have been no objection to Buwalda's presence. Indeed, the General says, "I would not have the slightest hesitancy about attending a Socialist meeting myself." But to attend an Anarchist meeting with Emma Goldman as speaker — could there be anything more "treasonable"?

For this horrible crime a man, a free-born American citizen, who has given this country the best fifteen years of his life, and whose character and conduct during that time were "unimpeachable," is now languishing in a prison, dishonored, disgraced and robbed of a livelihood.

Can there be anything more destructive of the true genius of liberty than the spirit that made Buwalda's sentence possible — the spirit of unquestioning obedience? Is it for this that the American people have in the last few years sacrificed four hundred million dollars and their hearts' blood?

I believe that militarism — a standing army and navy in any country — is indicative of the decay of liberty and of the destruction of all that is best and finest in our nation. The steadily growing clamor for more battleships and an increased army on the ground that these guarantee us peace is as absurd as the argument that the peaceful man is he who goes well armed.

The same lack of consistency is displayed by those peace pretenders who oppose Anarchism because it supposedly teaches violence, and who would yet be delighted over the possibility of the American nation soon being able to hurl dynamite bombs upon defenseless enemies from flying machines.

I believe that militarism will cease when the liberty-loving spirits of the world say to their masters: "Go and do your own killing. We have sacrificed ourselves and our loved ones long enough fighting your battles. In return you have made parasites and criminals of us in times of peace and brutalized us in times of war. You have separated us from our brothers and have made of the world a human slaughterhouse. No, we will not do your killing or fight for the country that you have stolen from us."

Oh, I believe with all my heart that human brotherhood and solidarity will clear the horizon from the terrible red streak of war and destruction.

IV. As To Free Speech And Press

The Buwalda case is only one phase of the larger question of free speech, free press and the right of free assembly.

Many good people imagine that the principles of free speech or press can be exercised properly and with safety within the limits of constitutional guarantees. That is the only excuse, it seems to me, for the terrible apathy and indifference to the onslaught upon free speech and press that we have witnessed in this county within the last few months.

I believe that free speech and press mean that I may say and write what I please. This right, when regulated by constitutional provisions, legislative enactments, almighty decisions of the Postmaster General or the policeman's club, becomes a farce. I am well aware that I will be warned of consequences if we remove the chains from speech and press. I believe, however, that the cure of consequences resulting from the unlimited exercise of expression is to allow more expression.

Mental shackles have never yet stemmed the tide of progress, whereas premature social explosions have only too often been brought about through a wave of repression.

Will our governors never learn that countries like England, Holland, Norway, Sweden and Denmark, with the largest freedom of expression, have been freest from "consequences"? Whereas Russia, Spain, Italy, France and, alas! even America, have raised these "consequences" to the most pressing political factor. Ours is supposed to be a country ruled by the majority, yet every policeman who is not vested with power by the majority can break up a meeting, drag the lecturer off the platform and club the audience out of the hall in true Russian fashion. The Postmaster General, who is not an elective officer, has the power to suppress publications and confiscate mail. From his decision there is no more appeal than from that of the Russian Czar. Truly, I believe we need a new Declaration of Independence. Is there no modern Jefferson or Adams?

V. As To The Church

At the recent convention of the political remnants of a once revolutionary idea it was voted that religion and vote getting have nothing to do with each other. Why should they? "So long as man is willing to delegate to the devil the care of his soul, he might, with the same consistency, delegate to the politician the care of his rights. That religion is a private affair has long been settled by the Marxian Socialists of Germany. Our American Marxians, poor of blood and originality, must needs go to Germany for their wisdom. That wisdom has served as a capital whip to lash the several millions of people into the well-disciplined army of Socialism. It might do the same here. For goodness' sake, let's not offend respectability, let's not hurt the religious feelings of the people."

Religion is a superstition that originated in man's mental inability to solve natural phenomena. The Church is an organized institution that has always been a stumbling block to progress.

Organized churchism has stripped religion of its naïveté and primitiveness. It has turned religion into a nightmare that oppresses the human soul and holds the mind in bondage. "The Dominion of Darkness", as the last true Christian, Leo Tolstoi, calls the Church, has been a foe of human development and free thought, and as such it has no place in the life of a truly free people.

VI. As To Marriage And Love

I believe these are probably the most tabooed subjects in this country. It is almost impossible to talk about them without scandalizing the cherished propriety of a lot of good folk. No wonder so much ignorance prevails relative to these questions. Nothing short of an open, frank, and intelligent discussion will purify the air from the hysterical, sentimental rubbish that is shrouding these vital subjects, vital to individual as well as social well-being.

Marriage and love are not synonymous; on the contrary, they are often antagonistic to each other. I am aware of the fact that some marriages are actuated by love, but the narrow, material confines of marriage, as it is, speedily crush the tender flower of affection.

Marriage is an institution which furnishes the State and Church with a tremendous revenue and the means of prying into that phase of life which refined people have long considered their own, their very own most sacred affair. Love is that most powerful factor of human relationship which from time immemorial has defied all man-made laws and broken through the iron bars of conventions in Church and morality. Marriage is often an economic arrangement purely, furnishing the woman with a life-long life insurance policy and the man with a perpetuator of his kind or a pretty toy. That is, marriage, or the training thereto, prepares the woman for the life of a parasite, a dependent, helpless servant, while it furnishes the man the right of a chattel mortgage over a human life.

How can such a condition of affairs have anything in common with love? — with the element that would forego all the wealth of money and power and live in its own world of untrammeled human expression? But this is not the age of romanticism, of Romeo and Juliet, Faust and Marguerite, of moonlight ecstasies, of flowers and songs. Ours is a practical age. Our first consideration is an income. So much the worse for us if we have reached the era when the soul's highest flights are to be checked. No race can develop without the love element.

But if two people are to worship at the shrine of love, what is to become of the golden calf, marriage? "It is the only security for the woman, for the child, the family, the State." But it is no security to love; and without love no true home can or does exist. Without love no child should be born; without love no true woman can be related to a man. The fear that love is not sufficient material safety for the child is out of date. I believe when woman signs her own emancipation, her first declaration of independence will consist in admiring and loving a man for the qualities of his heart and mind and not for the quantities in his pocket. The second declaration will be that she has the right to follow that love without let or hindrance from the outside world. The third and most important declaration will be the absolute right to free motherhood.

In such a mother and an equally free father rests the safety of the child. They have the strength, the sturdiness, the harmony to create an atmosphere wherein alone the human plant can grow into an exquisite flower.

VII. As To Acts Of Violence

And now I have come to that point in my beliefs about which the greatest misunderstanding prevails in the minds of the American public. "Well, come, now, don't you propagate violence, the killing of crowned heads and Presidents?" Who says that I do? Have you heard me, has anyone heard me? Has anyone seen it printed in our literature? No, but the papers say so, everybody says so; consequently it must be so. Oh, for the accuracy and logic of the dear public!

I believe that Anarchism is the only philosophy of peace, the only theory of the social relationship that values human life above everything else. I know that some Anarchists have committed acts of violence, but it is the terrible economic inequality and great political injustice that prompt such acts, not Anarchism. Every institution today rests on violence; our very atmosphere is saturated with it. So long as such a state exists we might as well strive to stop the rush of Niagara as hope to do away with violence. I have already stated that countries with some measure of freedom of expression have had few or no acts of violence. What is the moral? Simply this: No act committed by an Anarchist has been for personal gain, aggrandizement or profit, but rather a conscious protest against some repressive, arbitrary, tyrannical measure from above.

President Carnot, of France, was killed by Caserio in response to Carnot's refusal to commute the death sentence of Vaillant, for whose life the entire literary, scientific and humanitarian world of France had pleaded.

Bresci went to Italy on his own money, earned in the silk weaving mills of Paterson, to call King Humberto to the bar of justice for his order to shoot defenseless women and children during a bread riot. Angelino executed Prime Minister Canovas for the latter's resurrection of the Spanish inquisition at Montjuich Prison. Alexander Berkman attempted the life of Henry C. Frick during the Homestead strike only because of his intense sympathy for the eleven strikers killed by Pinkertons and for the widows and orphans evicted by Frick from their wretched little homes that were owned by Mr. Carnegie.

Every one of these men not only made his reasons known to the world in spoken or written statements, showing the cause that led to his act, proving that the unbearable economic and political pressure, the suffering and despair of their fellow-men, women and children prompted the acts, and not the philosophy of Anarchism. They came openly, frankly and ready to stand the consequences, ready to give their own lives.

In diagnosing the true nature of our social disease I cannot condemn those who, through no fault of their own, are suffering from a wide-spread malady.

I do not believe that these acts can, or ever have been intended to, bring about the social reconstruction. That can only be done, first, by a broad and wide education as to man's place in society and his proper relation to his fellows; and, second, through example. By example I mean the actual living of a truth once recognized, not the mere theorizing of its life element. Lastly, and the most powerful weapon, is the conscious, intelligent, organized, economic protest of the masses through direct action and the general strike.

The general contention that Anarchists are opposed to organization, and hence stand for chaos, is absolutely groundless. True, we do not believe in the compulsory, arbitrary side of organization that would compel people of antagonistic tastes and interests into a body and hold them there by coercion. Organization as the result of natural blending of common interests, brought about through voluntary adhesion, Anarchists do not only not oppose, but believe in organization as the only possible basis of social life.

It is the harmony of organic growth which produces variety of color and form — the complete whole we admire in the flower. Analogously will the organized activity of free human beings endowed with the spirit of solidarity result in the perfection of social harmony — which is Anarchism. Indeed, only Anarchism makes non-authoritarian organization a reality, since it abolishes the existing antagonism between individuals and classes.

A New Declaration of Independence

Mother Earth, July 1909

When, in the course of human development, existing institutions prove inadequate to the needs of man, when they serve merely to enslave, rob, and oppress mankind, the people have the eternal right to rebel against, and overthrow, these institutions.

The mere fact that these forces—inimical to life, liberty, and the pursuit of happiness—are legalized by statute laws, sanctified by divine rights, and enforced by political power, in no way justifies their continued existence.

We hold these truths to be self-evident: that all human beings, irrespective of race, color, or sex, are born with the equal right to share at the table of life; that to secure this right, there must be established among men economic, social, and political freedom; we hold further that government exists but to maintain special privilege and property rights; that it coerces man into submission and therefore robs him of dignity, self-respect, and life.

The history of the American kings of capital and authority is the history of repeated crimes, injustice, oppression, outrage, and abuse, all aiming at the suppression of individual liberties and the exploitation of the people. A vast country, rich enough to supply all her children with all possible comforts, and insure well-being to all, is in the hands of a few, while the nameless millions are at the mercy of ruthless wealth gatherers, unscrupulous lawmakers, and corrupt politicians. Sturdy sons of America are forced to tramp the country in a fruitless search for bread, and many of her daughters are driven into the street, while thousands of tender children are daily sacrificed on the altar of Mammon. The reign of these kings is holding mankind in slavery, perpetuating poverty and disease, maintaining crime and corruption; it is fettering the spirit of liberty, throttling the voice of justice, and degrading and oppressing humanity. It is engaged in continual war and slaughter, devastating the country and destroying the best and finest qualities of man; it nurtures superstition and ignorance, sows prejudice and strife, and turns the human family into a camp of Ishmaelites.

We, therefore, the liberty-loving men and women, realizing the great injustice and brutality of this state of affairs, earnestly and boldly do hereby declare; That each and every individual is and ought to be free to own himself and to enjoy the full fruit of his labor; that man is absolved from all allegiance to the kings of authority and capital; that he has, by the very fact of his being, free access to the land and all means of production, and entire liberty of disposing of the fruits of his efforts; that each and every individual has the unquestionable and unabridgeable right of free and voluntary association with other equally sovereign individuals for economic, political, social, and all other purposes, and that to achieve this end man must emancipate himself from the sacredness of property, the respect for man-made law, the fear of the Church, the cowardice of public opinion, the stupid arrogance of national, racial, religious, and sex superiority, and from the narrow puritanical conception of human life. And for the support of this *Declaration*, and with a firm reliance on the harmonious blending of man's social and individual tendencies, the lovers of liberty joyfully consecrate their uncompromising devotion, their energy and intelligence, their solidarity and their lives.

This *Declaration* was written at the request of a certain newspaper, which subsequently refused to publish it, though the article was already in composition.

The Tragedy of Woman's Emancipation

Anarchism and Other Essays, 1910

I begin with an admission: Regardless of all political and economic theories, treating of the fundamental differences between various groups within the human race, regardless of class and race distinctions, regardless of all artificial boundary lines between woman's rights and man's rights, I hold that there is a point where these differentiations may meet and grow into one perfect whole.

With this I do not mean to propose a peace treaty. The general social antagonism which has taken hold of our entire public life today, brought about through the force of opposing and contradictory interests, will crumble to pieces when the reorganization of our social life, based upon the principles of economic justice, shall have become a reality.

Peace or harmony between the sexes and individuals does not necessarily depend on a superficial equalization of human beings; nor does it call for the elimination of individual traits and peculiarities. The problem that confronts us today, and which the nearest future is to solve, is how to be one's self and yet in oneness with others, to feel deeply with all human beings and still retain one's own characteristic qualities. This seems to me to be the basis upon which the mass and the individual, the true democrat and the true individuality, man and woman, can meet without antagonism and opposition. The motto should not be: "Forgive one another"; rather, "Understand one another." The oft-quoted sentence of Madame de Staël: "To understand everything means to forgive everything," has never particularly appealed to me; it has the odor of the confessional; to forgive one's fellow-being conveys the idea of pharisaical superiority. To understand one's fellow-being suffices. The admission partly represents the fundamental aspect of my views on the emancipation of woman and its effect upon the entire sex.

Emancipation should make it possible for woman to be human in the truest sense. Everything within her that craves assertion and activity should reach its fullest expression; all artificial barriers should be broken, and the road towards greater freedom cleared of every trace of centuries of submission and slavery.

This was the original aim of the movement for woman's emancipation. But the results so far achieved have isolated woman and have robbed her of the fountain springs of that happiness which is so essential to her. Merely external emancipation has made of the modern woman an artificial being, who reminds one of the products of French arboriculture with its arabesque trees and shrubs, pyramids, wheels, and wreaths; anything, except the forms which would be reached by the expression of her own inner qualities. Such artificially grown plants of the female sex are to be found in large numbers, especially in the so-called intellectual sphere of our life.

Liberty and equality for woman! What hopes and aspirations these words awakened when they were first uttered by some of the noblest and bravest souls of those days. The sun in all his light and glory was to rise upon a new world; in this world woman was to be free to direct her own destiny — an aim certainly worthy of the great enthusiasm, courage, perseverance, and ceaseless effort of the tremendous host of pioneer men and women, who staked everything against a world of prejudice and ignorance.

My hopes also move towards that goal, but I hold that the emancipation of woman, as interpreted and practically applied today, has failed to reach that great end. Now, woman is confronted with the necessity of emancipating herself from emancipation, if she really desires to be free. This may sound paradoxical, but is, nevertheless, only too true.

What has she achieved through her emancipation? Equal suffrage in a few States. Has that purified our political life, as many well-meaning advocates predicted? Certainly not. Incidentally, it is really time that persons with plain, sound judgment should cease to talk about corruption in politics in a boarding school tone. Corruption of politics has nothing to do with the morals, or the laxity of morals, of various political personalities. Its cause is altogether a material one. Politics is the reflex of the business and industrial world, the mottos of which are: "To take is more blessed than to give"; "buy cheap and sell dear"; "one soiled hand washes the other." There is no hope even that woman, with her right to vote, will ever purify politics.

Emancipation has brought woman economic equality with man; that is, she can choose her own profession and trade; but as her past and present physical training has not equipped her with the necessary strength to compete with man, she is often compelled to exhaust all her energy, use up her vitality, and strain every nerve in order to reach the market value. Very few ever succeed, for it is a fact that women teachers, doctors, lawyers, architects, and engineers are neither met with the same confidence as their male colleagues, nor receive equal remuneration. And those that do reach that enticing equality, generally do so at the expense of their physical and psychical well-being. As to the great mass of working girls and women, how much independence is gained if the narrowness and lack of freedom of the home is exchanged for the narrowness and lack of freedom of the factory, sweat-shop, department store, or office? In addition is the burden which is laid on many women of looking after a "home, sweet home" — cold, dreary, disorderly, uninviting — after a day's hard work. Glorious independence! No wonder that hundreds of girls are so willing to accept the first offer of marriage, sick and tired of their "independence" behind the counter, at the sewing or typewriting machine. They are just as ready to marry as girls of the middle class, who long to throw off the yoke of parental supremacy. A so-called independence which leads only to earning the merest subsistence is not so enticing, not so ideal, that one could expect woman to sacrifice everything for it. Our highly praised independence is, after all, but a slow process of dulling and stifling woman's nature, her love instinct, and her mother instinct.

Nevertheless, the position of the working girl is far more natural and human than that of her seemingly more fortunate sister in the more cultured professional walks of life; teachers, physicians, lawyers, engineers, etc., who have to make a dignified, proper appearance, while the inner life is growing empty and dead.

The narrowness of the existing conception of woman's independence and emancipation; the dread of love for a man who is not her social equal; the fear that love will rob her of her freedom and independence; the horror that love or the joy of motherhood will only hinder her in the full exercise of her profession — all these together make of the emancipated modern woman a compulsory vestal, before whom life, with its great clarifying sorrows and its deep, entrancing joys, rolls on without touching or gripping her soul.

Emancipation, as understood by the majority of its adherents and exponents, is of too narrow a scope to permit the boundless love and ecstasy contained in the deep emotion of the true woman, sweetheart, mother, in freedom.

The tragedy of the self-supporting or economically free woman does not lie in too many, but in too few experiences. True, she surpasses her sister of past generations in knowledge of the world and human nature; it is just because of this that she feels deeply the lack of life's essence, which alone can enrich the human soul, and without which the majority of women have become mere professional automatons.

That such a state of affairs was bound to come was foreseen by those who realized that, in the domain of ethics, there still remained many decaying ruins of the time of the undisputed superiority of man; ruins that are still considered useful. And, what is more important, a goodly number of the emancipated are unable to get along without them. Every movement that aims at the destruction of existing institutions and the replacement thereof with something more advanced, more perfect, has followers who in theory stand for the most radical ideas, but who, nevertheless, in their everyday practice, are like the average Philistine, feigning respectability and clamoring for the good opinion of their opponents. There are, for example, Socialists, and even Anarchists, who stand for the idea that property is robbery, yet who will grow indignant if anyone owe them the value of a half-dozen pins.

The same Philistine can be found in the movement for woman's emancipation. Yellow journalists and milk-and-water *litterateurs* have painted pictures of the emancipated woman that make the hair of the good citizen and his dull companion stand up on end. Every member of the woman's rights movement was pictured as a George Sand in her absolute disregard of morality. Nothing was sacred to her. She had no respect for the ideal relation between man and woman. In short, emancipation stood only for a reckless life of lust and sin; regardless of society, religion, and morality. The exponents of woman's rights were highly indignant at such misrepresentation, and, lacking humor, they exerted all their energy to prove that they were not at all as bad as they were painted, but the very reverse. Of course, as long as woman was the slave of man, she could not be good and pure, but now that she was free and independent she would prove how good she could be and that her influence would have a purifying effect on all institutions in society. True, the movement for woman's rights has broken many old fetters, but it has also forged new ones. The great movement of true emancipation has not met with a great race of women who could look liberty in the face. Their narrow, Puritanical vision banished man, as a disturber and doubtful character, out of their emotional life. Man was not to be tolerated at any price, except perhaps as the father of a child, since a child could not very well come to life without a father. Fortunately, the most rigid Puritans never will be strong enough to kill the innate craving for motherhood. But woman's freedom is closely allied with man's freedom, and many of my so-called emancipated sisters seem to overlook the fact that a child born in freedom needs the love and devotion of each human being about him, man as well as woman. Unfortunately, it is this narrow conception of human relations that has brought about a great tragedy in the lives of the modern man and woman.

About fifteen years ago appeared a work from the pen of the brilliant Norwegian Laura Marholm, called "Woman, a Character Study". She was one of the first to call attention to the emptiness and narrowness of the existing conception of woman's emancipation, and its tragic effect upon the inner life of woman. In her work Laura Marholm speaks of the fate of several gifted women of international fame: the genius Eleonora Duse; the great mathematician and writer Sonya Kovalevskaia; the artist and poet of nature Marie Bashkirtzeff, who died so young. Through each description of the lives of these women of such extraordinary mentality runs a marked trail of unsatisfied craving for a full, rounded, complete, and beautiful life, and the unrest and loneliness resulting from the lack of it. Through these masterly psychological sketches one cannot help but see that the higher the mental development of woman, the less possible it is for her to meet a congenial mate who will see in her not only sex, but also the human being, the friend, the comrade and strong individuality, who cannot and ought not lose a single trait of her character.

The average man with his self-sufficiency, his ridiculously superior airs of patronage towards the female sex, is an impossibility for woman as depicted in the "Character Study" by Laura Marholm. Equally impossible for her is the man who can see in her nothing more than her mentality and her genius, and who fails to awaken her woman nature.

A rich intellect and a fine soul are usually considered necessary attributes of a deep and beautiful personality. In the case of the modern woman, these attributes serve as a hindrance to the complete assertion of her being. For over a hundred years the old form of marriage, based on the Bible, "till death doth part," has been denounced as an institution that stands for the sovereignty of the man over the woman, of her complete submission to his whims and commands, and absolute dependence on his name and support. Time and again it has been conclusively proved that the old matrimonial relation restricted woman to the function of man's servant and the bearer of his children. And yet we find many emancipated women who prefer marriage, with all its deficiencies, to the narrowness of an unmarried life: narrow and unendurable because of the chains of moral and social prejudice that cramp and bind her nature.

The explanation of such inconsistency on the part of many advanced women is to be found in the fact that they never truly understood the meaning of emancipation. They thought that all that was needed was independence from external tyrannies; the internal tyrants, far more harmful to life and growth—ethical and social conventions—were left to take care of themselves; and they have taken care of themselves. They seem to get along as beautifully in the heads and hearts of the most active exponents of woman's emancipation, as in the heads and hearts of our grandmothers.

These internal tyrants, whether they be in the form of public opinion or what will mother say, or brother, father, aunt, or relative of any sort; what will Mrs. Grundy, Mr. Comstock, the employer, the Board of Education, say? All these busybodies, moral detectives, jailers of the human spirit, what will they say? Until woman has learned to defy them all, to stand firmly on her own ground and to insist upon her own unrestricted freedom, to listen to the voice of her nature, whether it call for life's greatest treasure, love for a man, or her most glorious privilege, the right to give birth to a child, she cannot call herself emancipated. How many emancipated women are brave enough to acknowledge that the voice of love is calling, wildly beating against their breasts, demanding to be heard, to be satisfied.

The French writer Jean Reibrach, in one of his novels, "New Beauty", attempts to picture the ideal, beautiful, emancipated woman. This ideal is embodied in a young girl, a physician. She talks very cleverly and wisely of how to feed infants; she is kind, and administers medicines free to poor mothers. She converses with a young man of her acquaintance about the sanitary conditions of the future, and how various bacilli and germs shall be exterminated by the use of stone walls and floors, and by the doing away with rugs and hangings. She is, of course, very plainly and practically dressed, mostly in black. The young man, who, at their first meeting, was overawed by the wisdom of his emancipated friend, gradually learns to understand her, and recognizes one fine day that he loves her. They are young, and she is kind and beautiful, and though always in rigid attire, her appearance is softened by a spotlessly clean white collar and cuffs. One would expect that he would tell her of his love, but he is not one to commit romantic absurdities. Poetry and the enthusiasm of love cover their blushing faces before the pure beauty of the lady. He silences the voice of his nature, and remains correct. She, too, is always exact, always rational, always well behaved. I fear if they had formed a union, the young man would have risked freezing to death. I must confess that I can see nothing beautiful in this new beauty, who is as cold as the stone walls and floors she dreams of. Rather would I have the love songs of romantic ages, rather Don Juan and Madame Venus, rather an elopement by ladder and rope on a moonlit night, followed by the father's curse, mother's moans, and the moral comments of neighbors, than correctness and propriety measured by yardsticks. If love does not know how to give and take without restrictions, it is not love, but a transaction that never fails to lay stress on a plus and a minus.

The greatest shortcoming of the emancipation of the present day lies in its artificial stiffness and its narrow respectabilities, which produce an emptiness in woman's soul that will not let her drink from the fountain of life. I once remarked that there seemed to be a deeper relationship between the old-fashioned mother and hostess, ever on the alert for the happiness of her little ones and the comfort of those she loved, and the truly new woman, than between the latter and her average emancipated sister. The disciples of emancipation pure and simple declared me a heathen, fit only for the stake. Their blind zeal did not let them see that my comparison between the old and the new was merely to prove that a goodly number of our grandmothers had more blood in their veins, far more humor and wit, and certainly a greater amount of naturalness, kind-heartedness, and simplicity, than the majority of our emancipated professional women who fill the colleges, halls of learning, and various offices. This does not mean a wish to return to the past, nor does it condemn woman to her old sphere, the kitchen and the nursery.

Salvation lies in an energetic march onward towards a brighter and clearer future. We are in need of unhampered growth out of old traditions and habits. The movement for woman's emancipation has so far made but the first step in that direction. It is to be hoped that it will gather strength to make another. The right to vote, or equal civil rights, may be good demands, but true emancipation begins neither at the polls nor in courts. It begins in woman's soul. History tells us that every oppressed class gained true liberation from its masters through its own efforts. It is necessary that woman learn that lesson, that she realize that her freedom will reach as far as her power to achieve her freedom reaches. It is, therefore, far more important for her to begin with her inner regeneration, to cut loose from the weight of prejudices, traditions, and customs. The demand for equal rights in every vocation of life is just and fair; but, after all, the most vital right is the right to love and be loved. Indeed, if partial emancipation is to become a complete and true emancipation of woman, it will have to do away with the ridiculous notion that to be loved, to be sweetheart and mother, is synonymous with being slave or subordinate. It will have to do away with the absurd notion of the dualism of the sexes, or that man and woman represent two antagonistic worlds.

Pettiness separates; breadth unites. Let us be broad and big. Let us not overlook vital things because of the bulk of trifles confronting us. A true conception of the relation of the sexes will not admit of conqueror and conquered; it knows of but one great thing: to give of one's self boundlessly, in order to find one's self richer, deeper, better. That alone can fill the emptiness, and transform the tragedy of woman's emancipation into joy, limitless joy.

Anarchism: What It Really Stands For

Anarchism and Other Essays, 1911

ANARCHY
Ever reviled, accursed, ne'er understood,
Thou art the grisly terror of our age.
"Wreck of all order," cry the multitude,
"Art thou, and war and murder's endless rage."
O, let them cry. To them that ne'er have striven
The truth that lies behind a word to find,
To them the word's right meaning was not given.
They shall continue blind among the blind.
But thou, O word, so clear, so strong, so pure,
Thou sayest all which I for goal have taken.
I give thee to the future! Thine secure
When each at least unto himself shall waken.
Comes it in sunshine? In the tempest's thrill?
I cannot tell–but it the earth shall see!
I am an Anarchist! Wherefore I will
Not rule, and also ruled I will not be!
    — *John Henry Mackay*

The history of human growth and development is at the same time the history of the terrible struggle of every new idea heralding the approach of a brighter dawn. In its tenacious hold on tradition, the Old has never hesitated to make use of the foulest and cruelest means to stay the advent of the New, in whatever form or period the latter may have asserted itself. Nor need we retrace our steps into the distant past to realize the enormity of opposition, difficulties, and hardships placed in the path of every progressive idea. The rack, the thumbscrew, and the knout are still with us; so are the convict's garb and the social wrath, all conspiring against the spirit that is serenely marching on.

Anarchism could not hope to escape the fate of all other ideas of innovation. Indeed, as the most revolutionary and uncompromising innovator, Anarchism must needs meet with the combined ignorance and venom of the world it aims to reconstruct.

To deal even remotely with all that is being said and done against Anarchism would necessitate the writing of a whole volume. I shall therefore meet only two of the principal objections. In so doing, I shall attempt to elucidate what Anarchism really stands for.

The strange phenomenon of the opposition to Anarchism is that it brings to light the relation between so-called intelligence and ignorance. And yet this is not so very strange when we consider the relativity of all things. The ignorant mass has in its favor that it makes no pretense of knowledge or tolerance. Acting, as it always does, by mere impulse, its reasons are like those of a child. "Why?" "Because." Yet the opposition of the uneducated to Anarchism deserves the same consideration as that of the intelligent man.

What, then, are the objections? First, Anarchism is impractical, though a beautiful ideal. Second, Anarchism stands for violence and destruction, hence it must be repudiated as vile and dangerous. Both the intelligent man and the ignorant mass judge not from a thorough knowledge of the subject, but either from hearsay or false interpretation.

A practical scheme, says Oscar Wilde, is either one already in existence, or a scheme that could be carried out under the existing conditions; but it is exactly the existing conditions that one objects to, and any scheme that could accept these conditions is wrong and foolish. The true criterion of the practical, therefore, is not whether the latter can keep intact the wrong or foolish; rather is it whether the scheme has vitality enough to leave the stagnant waters of the old, and build, as well as sustain, new life. In the light of this conception, Anarchism is indeed practical. More than any other idea, it is helping to do away with the wrong and foolish; more than any other idea, it is building and sustaining new life.

The emotions of the ignorant man are continuously kept at a pitch by the most blood-curdling stories about Anarchism. Not a thing too outrageous to be employed against this philosophy and its exponents. Therefore Anarchism represents to the unthinking what the proverbial bad man does to the child—a black monster bent on swallowing everything; in short, destruction and violence.

Destruction and violence! How is the ordinary man to know that the most violent element in society is ignorance; that its power of destruction is the very thing Anarchism is combating? Nor is he aware that Anarchism, whose roots, as it were, are part of nature's forces, destroys, not healthful tissue, but parasitic growths that feed on the life's essence of society. It is merely clearing the soil from weeds and sagebrush, that it may eventually bear healthy fruit.

Someone has said that it requires less mental effort to condemn than to think. The widespread mental indolence, so prevalent in society, proves this to be only too true. Rather than to go to the bottom of any given idea, to examine into its origin and meaning, most people will either condemn it altogether, or rely on some superficial or prejudicial definition of non-essentials.

Anarchism urges man to think, to investigate, to analyze every proposition; but that the brain capacity of the average reader be not taxed too much, I also shall begin with a definition, and then elaborate on the latter.

Anarchism: The philosophy of a new social order based on liberty unrestricted by man-made law; the theory that all forms of government rest on violence, and are therefore wrong and harmful, as well as unnecessary.

The new social order rests, of course, on the materialistic basis of life; but while all Anarchists agree that the main evil today is an economic one, they maintain that the solution of that evil can be brought about only through the consideration of *every phase* of life — individual, as well as the collective; the internal, as well as the external phases.

A thorough perusal of the history of human development will disclose two elements in bitter conflict with each other; elements that are only now beginning to be understood, not as foreign to each other, but as closely related and truly harmonious, if only placed in proper environment: the individual and social instincts. The individual and society have waged a relentless and bloody battle for ages, each striving for supremacy, because each was blind to the value and importance of the other. The individual and social instincts — the one a most potent factor for individual endeavor, for growth, aspiration, self-realization; the other an equally potent factor for mutual helpfulness and social well-being.

The explanation of the storm raging within the individual, and between him and his surroundings, is not far to seek. The primitive man, unable to understand his being, much less the unity of all life, felt himself absolutely dependent on blind, hidden forces ever ready to mock and taunt him. Out of that attitude grew the religious concepts of man as a mere speck of dust dependent on superior powers on high, who can only be appeased by complete surrender. All the early sagas rest on that idea, which continues to be the *leitmotiv* of the biblical tales dealing with the relation of man to God, to the State, to society. Again and again the same motif, *man is nothing, the powers are everything.* Thus Jehovah would only endure man on condition of complete surrender. Man can have all the glories of the earth, but he must not become conscious of himself. The State, society, and moral laws all sing the same refrain: Man can have all the glories of the earth, but he must not become conscious of himself.

Anarchism is the only philosophy which brings to man the consciousness of himself; which maintains that God, the State, and society are non-existent, that their promises are null and void, since they can be fulfilled only through man's subordination. Anarchism is therefore the teacher of the unity of life; not merely in nature, but in man. There is no conflict between the individual and the social instincts, any more than there is between the heart and the lungs: the one the receptacle of a precious life essence, the other the repository of the element that keeps the essence pure and strong. The individual is the heart of society, conserving the essence of social life; society is the lungs which are distributing the element to keep the life essence — that is, the individual — pure and strong.

"The one thing of value in the world," says Emerson, "is the active soul; this every man contains within him. The soul active sees absolute truth and utters truth and creates." In other words, the individual instinct is the thing of value in the world. It is the true soul that sees and creates the truth alive, out of which is to come a still greater truth, the re-born social soul.

Anarchism is the great liberator of man from the phantoms that have held him captive; it is the arbiter and pacifier of the two forces for individual and social harmony. To accomplish that unity, Anarchism has declared war on the pernicious influences which have so far prevented the harmonious blending of individual and social instincts, the individual and society.

Religion, the dominion of the human mind; Property, the dominion of human needs; and Government, the dominion of human conduct, represent the stronghold of man's enslavement and all the horrors it entails. Religion! How it dominates man's mind, how it humiliates and degrades his soul. God is everything, man is nothing, says religion. But out of that nothing God has created a kingdom so despotic, so tyrannical, so cruel, so terribly exacting that naught but gloom and tears and blood have ruled the world since gods began. Anarchism rouses man to rebellion against this black monster. Break your mental fetters, says Anarchism to man, for not until you think and judge for yourself will you get rid of the dominion of darkness, the greatest obstacle to all progress.

Property, the dominion of man's needs, the denial of the right to satisfy his needs. Time was when property claimed a divine right, when it came to man with the same refrain, even as religion, "Sacrifice! Abnegate! Submit!" The spirit of Anarchism has lifted man from his prostrate position. He now stands erect, with his face toward the light. He has learned to see the insatiable, devouring, devastating nature of property, and he is preparing to strike the monster dead.

"Property is robbery," said the great French Anarchist Proudhon. Yes, but without risk and danger to the robber. Monopolizing the accumulated efforts of man, property has robbed him of his birthright, and has turned him loose a pauper and an outcast. Property has not even the time-worn excuse that man does not create enough to satisfy all needs. The A B C student of economics knows that the productivity of labor within the last few decades far exceeds normal demand. But what are normal demands to an abnormal institution? The only demand that property recognizes is its own gluttonous appetite for greater wealth, because wealth means power; the power to subdue, to crush, to exploit, the power to enslave, to outrage, to degrade. America is particularly boastful of her great power, her enormous national wealth. Poor America, of what avail is all her wealth, if the individuals comprising the nation are wretchedly poor? If they live in squalor, in filth, in crime, with hope and joy gone, a homeless, soilless army of human prey.

It is generally conceded that unless the returns of any business venture exceed the cost, bankruptcy is inevitable. But those engaged in the business of producing wealth have not yet learned even this simple lesson. Every year the cost of production in human life is growing larger (50,000 killed, 100,000 wounded in America last year); the returns to the masses, who help to create wealth, are ever getting smaller. Yet America continues to be blind to the inevitable bankruptcy of our business of production. Nor is this the only crime of the latter. Still more fatal is the crime of turning the producer into a mere particle of a machine, with less will and decision than his master of steel and iron. Man is being robbed not merely of the products of his labor, but of the power of free initiative, of originality, and the interest in, or desire for, the things he is making.

Real wealth consists in things of utility and beauty, in things that help to create strong, beautiful bodies and surroundings inspiring to live in. But if man is doomed to wind cotton around a spool, or dig coal, or build roads for thirty years of his life, there can be no talk of wealth. What he gives to the world is only gray and hideous things, reflecting a dull and hideous existence — too weak to live, too cowardly to die. Strange to say, there are people who extol this deadening method of centralized production as the proudest achievement of our age. They fail utterly to realize that if we are to continue in machine subserviency, our slavery is more complete than was our bondage to the King. They do not want to know that centralization is not only the death-knell of liberty, but also of health and beauty, of art and science, all these being impossible in a clock-like, mechanical atmosphere.

Anarchism cannot but repudiate such a method of production: its goal is the freest possible expression of all the latent powers of the individual. Oscar Wilde defines a perfect personality as "one who develops under perfect conditions, who is not wounded, maimed, or in danger." A perfect personality, then, is only possible in a state of society where man is free to choose the mode of work, the conditions of work, and the freedom to work. One to whom the making of a table, the building of a house, or the tilling of the soil, is what the painting is to the artist and the discovery to the scientist — the result of inspiration, of intense longing, and deep interest in work as a creative force. That being the ideal of Anarchism, its economic arrangements must consist of voluntary productive and distributive associations, gradually developing into free communism, as the best means of producing with the least waste of human energy. Anarchism, however, also recognizes the right of the individual, or numbers of individuals, to arrange at all times for other forms of work, in harmony with their tastes and desires.

Such free display of human energy being possible only under complete individual and social freedom, Anarchism directs its forces against the third and greatest foe of all social equality; namely, the State, organized authority, or statutory law — the dominion of human conduct.

Just as religion has fettered the human mind, and as property, or the monopoly of things, has subdued and stifled man's needs, so has the State enslaved his spirit, dictating every phase of conduct. "All government in essence," says Emerson, "is tyranny." It matters not whether it is government by divine right or majority rule. In every instance its aim is the absolute subordination of the individual.

Referring to the American government, the greatest American Anarchist, David Thoreau, said: "Government, what is it but a tradition, though a recent one, endeavoring to transmit itself unimpaired to posterity, but each instance losing its integrity; it has not the vitality and force of a single living man. Law never made man a whit more just; and by means of their respect for it, even the well disposed are daily made agents of injustice."

Indeed, the keynote of government is injustice. With the arrogance and self-sufficiency of the King who could do no wrong, governments ordain, judge, condemn, and punish the most insignificant offenses, while maintaining themselves by the greatest of all offenses, the annihilation of individual liberty. Thus Ouida is right when she maintains that "the State only aims at instilling those qualities in its public by which its demands are obeyed, and its exchequer is filled. Its highest attainment is the reduction of mankind to clockwork. In its atmosphere all those finer and more delicate liberties, which require treatment and spacious expansion, inevitably dry up and perish. The State requires a taxpaying machine in which there is no hitch, an exchequer in which there is never a deficit, and a public, monotonous, obedient, colorless, spiritless, moving humbly like a flock of sheep along a straight high road between two walls."

Yet even a flock of sheep would resist the chicanery of the State, if it were not for the corruptive, tyrannical, and oppressive methods it employs to serve its purposes. Therefore Bakunin repudiates the State as synonymous with the surrender of the liberty of the individual or small minorities — the destruction of social relationship, the curtailment, or complete denial even, of life itself, for its own aggrandizement. The State is the altar of political freedom and, like the religious altar, it is maintained for the purpose of human sacrifice.

In fact, there is hardly a modern thinker who does not agree that government, organized authority, or the State, is necessary *only* to maintain or protect property and monopoly. It has proven efficient in that function only.

Even George Bernard Shaw, who hopes for the miraculous from the State under Fabianism, nevertheless admits that "it is at present a huge machine for robbing and slave-driving of the poor by brute force." This being the case, it is hard to see why the clever prefacer wishes to uphold the State after poverty shall have ceased to exist.

Unfortunately, there are still a number of people who continue in the fatal belief that government rests on natural laws, that it maintains social order and harmony, that it diminishes crime, and that it prevents the lazy man from fleecing his fellows. I shall therefore examine these contentions.

A natural law is that factor in man which asserts itself freely and spontaneously without any external force, in harmony with the requirements of nature. For instance, the demand for nutrition, for sex gratification, for light, air, and exercise, is a natural law. But its expression needs not the machinery of government, needs not the club, the gun, the handcuff, or the prison. To obey such laws, if we may call it obedience, requires only spontaneity and free opportunity. That governments do not maintain themselves through such harmonious factors is proven by the terrible array of violence, force, and coercion all governments use in order to live. Thus Blackstone is right when he says, "Human laws are invalid, because they are contrary to the laws of nature."

Unless it be the order of Warsaw after the slaughter of thousands of people, it is difficult to ascribe to governments any capacity for order or social harmony. Order derived through submission and maintained by terror is not much of a safe guaranty; yet that is the only "order" that governments have ever maintained. True social harmony grows naturally out of solidarity of interests. In a society where those who always work never have anything, while those who never work enjoy everything, solidarity of interests is non-existent; hence social harmony is but a myth. The only way organized authority meets this grave situation is by extending still greater privileges to those who have already monopolized the earth, and by still further enslaving the disinherited masses. Thus the entire arsenal of government—laws, police, soldiers, the courts, legislatures, prisons—is strenuously engaged in "harmonizing" the most antagonistic elements in society.

The most absurd apology for authority and law is that they serve to diminish crime. Aside from the fact that the State is itself the greatest criminal, breaking every written and natural law, stealing in the form of taxes, killing in the form of war and capital punishment, it has come to an absolute standstill in coping with crime. It has failed utterly to destroy or even minimize the horrible scourge of its own creation.

Crime is naught but misdirected energy. So long as every institution of today, economic, political, social, and moral, conspires to misdirect human energy into wrong channels; so long as most people are out of place doing the things they hate to do, living a life they loathe to live, crime will be inevitable, and all the laws on the statutes can only increase, but never do away with, crime. What does society, as it exists today, know of the process of despair, the poverty, the horrors, the fearful struggle the human soul must pass on its way to crime and degradation. Who that knows this terrible process can fail to see the truth in these words of Peter Kropotkin:

"Those who will hold the balance between the benefits thus attributed to law and punishment and the degrading effect of the latter on humanity; those who will estimate the torrent of depravity poured abroad in human society by the informer, favored by the Judge even, and paid for in clinking cash by governments, under the pretext of aiding to unmask crime; those who will go within prison walls and there see what human beings become when deprived of liberty, when subjected to the care of brutal keepers, to coarse, cruel words, to a thousand stinging, piercing humiliations, will agree with us that the entire apparatus of prison and punishment is an abomination which ought to be brought to an end."

The deterrent influence of law on the lazy man is too absurd to merit consideration. If society were only relieved of the waste and expense of keeping a lazy class, and the equally great expense of the paraphernalia of protection this lazy class requires, the social tables would contain an abundance for all, including even the occasional lazy individual. Besides, it is well to consider that laziness results either from special privileges, or physical and mental abnormalities. Our present insane system of production fosters both, and the most astounding phenomenon is that people should want to work at all now. Anarchism aims to strip labor of its deadening, dulling aspect, of its gloom and compulsion. It aims to make work an instrument of joy, of strength, of color, of real harmony, so that the poorest sort of a man should find in work both recreation and hope.

To achieve such an arrangement of life, government, with its unjust, arbitrary, repressive measures, must be done away with. At best it has but imposed one single mode of life upon all, without regard to individual and social variations and needs. In destroying government and statutory laws, Anarchism proposes to rescue the self-respect and independence of the individual from all restraint and invasion by authority. Only in freedom can man grow to his full stature. Only in freedom will he learn to think and move, and give the very best in him. Only in freedom will he realize the true force of the social bonds which knit men together, and which are the true foundation of a normal social life.

But what about human nature? Can it be changed? And if not, will it endure under Anarchism?

Poor human nature, what horrible crimes have been committed in thy name! Every fool, from king to policeman, from the flatheaded parson to the visionless dabbler in science, presumes to speak authoritatively of human nature. The greater the mental charlatan, the more definite his insistence on the wickedness and weaknesses of human nature. Yet, how can any one speak of it today, with every soul in a prison, with every heart fettered, wounded, and maimed?

John Burroughs has stated that experimental study of animals in captivity is absolutely useless. Their character, their habits, their appetites undergo a complete transformation when torn from their soil in field and forest. With human nature caged in a narrow space, whipped daily into submission, how can we speak of its potentialities?

Freedom, expansion, opportunity, and, above all, peace and repose, alone can teach us the real dominant factors of human nature and all its wonderful possibilities.

Anarchism, then, really stands for the liberation of the human mind from the dominion of religion; the liberation of the human body from the dominion of property; liberation from the shackles and restraint of government. Anarchism stands for a social order based on the free grouping of individuals for the purpose of producing real social wealth; an order that will guarantee to every human being free access to the earth and full enjoyment of the necessities of life, according to individual desires, tastes, and inclinations.

This is not a wild fancy or an aberration of the mind. It is the conclusion arrived at by hosts of intellectual men and women the world over; a conclusion resulting from the close and studious observation of the tendencies of modern society:

individual liberty and economic equality, the twin forces for the birth of what is fine and true in man.

As to methods. Anarchism is not, as some may suppose, a theory of the future to be realized through divine inspiration. It is a living force in the affairs of our life, constantly creating new conditions. The methods of Anarchism therefore do not comprise an iron-clad program to be carried out under all circumstances. Methods must grow out of the economic needs of each place and clime, and of the intellectual and temperamental requirements of the individual. The serene, calm character of a Tolstoy will wish different methods for social reconstruction than the intense, overflowing personality of a Michael Bakunin or a Peter Kropotkin. Equally so it must be apparent that the economic and political needs of Russia will dictate more drastic measures than would England or America. Anarchism does not stand for military drill and uniformity; it does, however, stand for the spirit of revolt, in whatever form, against everything that hinders human growth. All Anarchists agree in that, as they also agree in their opposition to the political machinery as a means of bringing about the great social change.

"All voting," says Thoreau, "is a sort of gaming, like checkers, or backgammon, a playing with right and wrong; its obligation never exceeds that of expediency. Even voting for the right thing is doing nothing for it. A wise man will not leave the right to the mercy of chance, nor wish it to prevail through the power of the majority." A close examination of the machinery of politics and its achievements will bear out the logic of Thoreau.

What does the history of parliamentarism show? Nothing but failure and defeat, not even a single reform to ameliorate the economic and social stress of the people. Laws have been passed and enactments made for the improvement and protection of labor. Thus it was proven only last year that Illinois, with the most rigid laws for mine protection, had the greatest mine disasters. In States where child labor laws prevail, child exploitation is at its highest, and though with us the workers enjoy full political opportunities, capitalism has reached the most brazen zenith.

Even were the workers able to have their own representatives, for which our good Socialist politicians are clamoring, what chances are there for their honesty and good faith? One has but to bear in mind the process of politics to realize that its path of good intentions is full of pitfalls: wire-pulling, intriguing, flattering, lying, cheating; in fact, chicanery of every description, whereby the political aspirant can achieve success. Added to that is a complete demoralization of character and conviction, until nothing is left that would make one hope for anything from such a human derelict. Time and time again the people were foolish enough to trust, believe, and support with their last farthing aspiring politicians, only to find themselves betrayed and cheated.

It may be claimed that men of integrity would not become corrupt in the political grinding mill. Perhaps not; but such men would be absolutely helpless to exert the slightest influence in behalf of labor, as indeed has been shown in numerous instances. The State is the economic master of its servants. Good men, if such there be, would either remain true to their political faith and lose their economic support, or they would cling to their economic master and be utterly unable to do the slightest good. The political arena leaves one no alternative, one must either be a dunce or a rogue.

The political superstition is still holding sway over the hearts and minds of the masses, but the true lovers of liberty will have no more to do with it. Instead, they believe with Stirner that man has as much liberty as he is willing to take. Anarchism therefore stands for direct action, the open defiance of, and resistance to, all laws and restrictions, economic, social, and moral. But defiance and resistance are illegal. Therein lies the salvation of man. Everything illegal necessitates integrity, self-reliance, and courage. In short, it calls for free, independent spirits, for "men who are men, and who have a bone in their backs which you cannot pass your hand through."

Universal suffrage itself owes its existence to direct action. If not for the spirit of rebellion, of the defiance on the part of the American revolutionary fathers, their posterity would still wear the King's coat. If not for the direct action of a John Brown and his comrades, America would still trade in the flesh of the black man. True, the trade in white flesh is still going on; but that, too, will have to be abolished by direct action. Trade-unionism, the economic arena of the modern gladiator, owes its existence to direct action. It is but recently that law and government have attempted to crush the trade-union movement, and condemned the exponents of man's right to organize to prison as conspirators. Had they sought to assert their cause through begging, pleading, and compromise, trade-unionism would today be a negligible quantity. In France, in Spain, in Italy, in Russia, nay even in England (witness the growing rebellion of English labor unions), direct, revolutionary, economic action has become so strong a force in the battle for industrial liberty as to make the world realize the tremendous importance of labor's power. The General Strike, the supreme expression of the economic consciousness of the workers, was ridiculed in America but a short time ago. Today every great strike, in order to win, must realize the importance of the solidaric general protest.

Direct action, having proven effective along economic lines, is equally potent in the environment of the individual. There a hundred forces encroach upon his being, and only persistent resistance to them will finally set him free. Direct action against the authority in the shop, direct action against the authority of the law, direct action against the invasive, meddlesome authority of our moral code, is the logical, consistent method of Anarchism.

Will it not lead to a revolution? Indeed, it will. No real social change has ever come about without a revolution. People are either not familiar with their history, or they have not yet learned that revolution is but thought carried into action.

Anarchism, the great leaven of thought, is today permeating every phase of human endeavor. Science, art, literature, the drama, the effort for economic betterment, in fact every individual and social opposition to the existing disorder of things, is illumined by the spiritual light of Anarchism. It is the philosophy of the sovereignty of the individual. It is the theory of social harmony. It is the great, surging, living truth that is reconstructing the world, and that will usher in the Dawn.

Woman Suffrage

Anarchism and Other Essays, 1911.

We boast of the age of advancement, of science, and progress. Is it not strange, then, that we still believe in fetish worship? True, our fetishes have different form and substance, yet in their power over the human mind they are still as disastrous as were those of old.

Our modern fetish is universal suffrage. Those who have not yet achieved that goal fight bloody revolutions to obtain it, and those who have enjoyed its reign bring heavy sacrifice to the altar of this omnipotent deity. Woe to the heretic who dare question that divinity!

Woman, even more than man, is a fetish worshipper, and though her idols may change, she is ever on her knees, ever holding up her hands, ever blind to the fact that her god has feet of clay. Thus woman has been the greatest supporter of all deities from time immemorial. Thus, too, she has had to pay the price that only gods can exact—her freedom, her heart's blood, her very life.

Nietzsche's memorable maxim, "When you go to woman, take the whip along," is considered very brutal, yet Nietzsche expressed in one sentence the attitude of woman towards her gods.

Religion, especially the Christian religion, has condemned woman to the life of an inferior, a slave. It has thwarted her nature and fettered her soul, yet the Christian religion has no greater supporter, none more devout, than woman. Indeed, it is safe to say that religion would have long ceased to be a factor in the lives of the people, if it were not for the support it receives from woman. The most ardent churchworkers, the most tireless missionaries the world over, are women, always sacrificing on the altar of the gods that have chained her spirit and enslaved her body.

The insatiable monster, war, robs woman of all that is dear and precious to her. It exacts her brothers, lovers, sons, and in return gives her a life of loneliness and despair. Yet the greatest supporter and worshiper of war is woman. She it is who instills the love of conquest and power into her children; she it is who whispers the glories of war into the ears of her little ones, and who rocks her baby to sleep with the tunes of trumpets and the noise of guns. It is woman, too, who crowns the victor on his return from the battlefield. Yes, it is woman who pays the highest price to that insatiable monster, war.

Then there is the home. What a terrible fetish it is! How it saps the very life-energy of woman—this modern prison with golden bars. Its shining aspect blinds woman to the price she would have to pay as wife, mother, and housekeeper. Yet woman clings tenaciously to the home, to the power that holds her in bondage.

It may be said that because woman recognizes the awful toll she is made to pay to the Church, State, and the home, she wants suffrage to set herself free. That may be true of the few; the majority of suffragists repudiate utterly such blasphemy. On the contrary, they insist always that it is woman suffrage which will make her a better Christian and home keeper, a staunch citizen of the State. Thus suffrage is only a means of strengthening the omnipotence of the very Gods that woman has served from time immemorial.

What wonder, then, that she should be just as devout, just as zealous, just as prostrate before the new idol, woman suffrage. As of old, she endures persecution, imprisonment, torture, and all forms of condemnation, with a smile on her face. As of old, the most enlightened, even, hope for a miracle from the twentieth-century deity — suffrage. Life, happiness, joy, freedom, independence — all that, and more, is to spring from suffrage. In her blind devotion woman does not see what people of intellect perceived fifty years ago: that suffrage is an evil, that it has only helped to enslave people, that it has but closed their eyes that they may not see how craftily they were made to submit.

Woman's demand for equal suffrage is based largely on the contention that woman must have the equal right in all affairs of society. No one could, possibly, refute that, if suffrage were a right. Alas, for the ignorance of the human mind, which can see a right in an imposition. Or is it not the most brutal imposition for one set of people to make laws that another set is coerced by force to obey? Yet woman clamors for that "golden opportunity" that has wrought so much misery in the world, and robbed man of his integrity and self-reliance; an imposition which has thoroughly corrupted the people, and made them absolute prey in the hands of unscrupulous politicians.

The poor, stupid, free American citizen! Free to starve, free to tramp the highways of this great country, he enjoys universal suffrage, and, by that right, he has forged chains about his limbs. The reward that he receives is stringent labor laws prohibiting the right of boycott, of picketing, in fact, of everything, except the right to be robbed of the fruits of his labor. Yet all these disastrous results of the twentieth-century fetish have taught woman nothing. But, then, woman will purify politics, we are assured.

Needless to say, I am not opposed to woman suffrage on the conventional ground that she is not equal to it. I see neither physical, psychological, nor mental reasons why woman should not have the equal right to vote with man. But that can not possibly blind me to the absurd notion that woman will accomplish that wherein man has failed. If she would not make things worse, she certainly could not make them better. To assume, therefore, that she would succeed in purifying something which is not susceptible of purification, is to credit her with supernatural powers. Since woman's greatest misfortune has been that she was looked upon as either angel or devil, her true salvation lies in being placed on earth; namely, in being considered human, and therefore subject to all human follies and mistakes. Are we, then, to believe that two errors will make a right? Are we to assume that the poison already inherent in politics will be decreased, if women were to enter the political arena? The most ardent suffragists would hardly maintain such a folly.

As a matter of fact, the most advanced students of universal suffrage have come to realize that all existing systems of political power are absurd, and are completely inadequate to meet the pressing issues of life. This view is also borne out by a statement of one who is herself an ardent believer in woman suffrage, Dr. Helen L. Sumner. In her able work on "Equal Suffrage", she says: "In Colorado, we find that equal suffrage serves to show in the most striking way the essential rottenness and degrading character of the existing system." Of course, Dr. Sumner has in mind a particular system of voting, but the same applies with equal force to the entire machinery of the representative system. With such a basis, it is difficult to understand how woman, as a political factor, would benefit either herself or the rest of mankind.

But, say our suffrage devotees, look at the countries and States where female suffrage exists. See what woman has accomplished — in Australia, New Zealand, Finland, the Scandinavian countries, and in our own four States, Idaho, Colorado, Wyoming, and Utah. Distance lends enchantment — or, to quote a Polish formula — "it is well where we are not." Thus one would assume that those countries and States are unlike other countries or States, that they have greater freedom, greater social and economic equality, a finer appreciation of human life, deeper understanding of the great social struggle, with all the vital questions it involves for the human race.

The women of Australia and New Zealand can vote, and help make the laws. Are the labor conditions better there than they are in England, where the suffragettes are making such a heroic struggle? Does there exist a greater motherhood, happier and freer children than in England? Is woman there no longer considered a mere sex commodity? Has she emancipated herself from the Puritanical double standard of morality for men and women? Certainly none but the ordinary female stump politician will dare answer these questions in the affirmative. If that be so, it seems ridiculous to point to Australia and New Zealand as the Mecca of equal suffrage accomplishments.

On the other hand, it is a fact to those who know the real political conditions in Australia, that politics have gagged labor by enacting the most stringent labor laws, making strikes without the sanction of an arbitration committee a crime equal to treason.

Not for a moment do I mean to imply that woman suffrage is responsible for this state of affairs. I do mean, however, that there is no reason to point to Australia as a wonder-worker of woman's accomplishment, since her influence has been unable to free labor from the thralldom of political bossism.

Finland has given woman equal suffrage; nay, even the right to sit in Parliament. Has that helped to develop a greater heroism, an intenser zeal than that of the women of Russia? Finland, like Russia, smarts under the terrible whip of the bloody Tsar. Where are the Finnish Perovskaias, Spiridonovas, Figners, Breshkovskaias? Where are the countless numbers of Finnish young girls who cheerfully go to Siberia for their cause? Finland is sadly in need of heroic liberators. Why has the ballot not created them? The only Finnish avenger of his people was a man, not a woman, and he used a more effective weapon than the ballot.

As to our own States where women vote, and which are constantly being pointed out as examples of marvels, what has been accomplished there through the ballot that women do not to a large extent enjoy in other States; or that they could not achieve through energetic efforts without the ballot?

True, in the suffrage States women are guaranteed equal rights to property; but of what avail is that right to the mass of women without property, the thousands of wage workers, who live from hand to mouth? That equal suffrage did not, and cannot, affect their condition is admitted even by Dr. Sumner, who certainly is in a position to know. As an ardent suffragist, and having been sent to Colorado by the Collegiate Equal Suffrage League of New York State to collect material in favor of suffrage, she would be the last to say anything derogatory; yet we are informed that "equal suffrage has but slightly affected the economic conditions of women. That women do not receive equal pay for equal work, and that, though woman in Colorado has enjoyed school suffrage since 1876, women teachers are paid less than in California." On the other hand, Miss Sumner fails to account for the fact that although women have had school suffrage for thirty-four years, and equal suffrage since 1894, the census in Denver alone a few months ago disclosed the fact of fifteen thousand defective school children. And that, too, with mostly women in the educational department, and also notwithstanding that women in Colorado have passed the "most stringent laws for child and animal protection." The women of Colorado "have taken great interest in the State institutions for the care of dependent, defective, and delinquent children." What a horrible indictment against woman's care and interest, if one city has fifteen thousand defective children. What about the glory of woman suffrage, since it has failed utterly in the most important social issue, the child? And where is the superior sense of justice that woman was to bring into the political field? Where was it in 1903, when the mine owners waged a guerilla war against the Western Miners' Union; when General Bell established a reign of terror, pulling men out of bed at night, kidnapping them across the border line, throwing them into bull pens, declaring "to hell with the Constitution, the club is the Constitution"? Where were the women politicians then, and why did they not exercise the power of their vote? But they did. They helped to defeat the most fair-minded and liberal man, Governor Waite. The latter had to make way for the tool of the mine kings, Governor Peabody, the enemy of labor, the Tsar of Colorado. "Certainly male suffrage could have done nothing worse." Granted. Wherein, then, are the advantages to woman and society from woman suffrage? The oft-repeated assertion that woman will purify politics is also but a myth. It is not borne out by the people who know the political conditions of Idaho, Colorado, Wyoming, and Utah.

Woman, essentially a purist, is naturally bigoted and relentless in her effort to make others as good as she thinks they ought to be. Thus, in Idaho, she has disfranchised her sister of the street, and declared all women of "lewd character" unfit to vote. "Lewd" not being interpreted, of course, as prostitution in marriage. It goes without saying that illegal prostitution and gambling have been prohibited. In this regard the law must needs be of feminine gender: it always prohibits. Therein all laws are wonderful. They go no further, but their very tendencies open all the floodgates of hell. Prostitution and gambling have never done a more flourishing business than since the law has been set against them.

In Colorado, the Puritanism of woman has expressed itself in a more drastic form. "Men of notoriously unclean lives, and men connected with saloons, have been dropped from politics since women have the vote." Could Brother Comstock do more? Could all the Puritan fathers have done more? I wonder how many women realize the gravity of this would-be feat. I wonder if they understand that it is the very thing which, instead of elevating woman, has made her a political spy, a contemptible pry into the private affairs of people, not so much for the good of the cause, but because, as a Colorado woman said, "they like to get into houses they have never been in, and find out all they can, politically and otherwise." Yes, and into the human soul and its minutest nooks and corners. For nothing satisfies the craving of most women so much as scandal. And when did she ever enjoy such opportunities as are hers, the politician's?

"Notoriously unclean lives, and men connected with the saloons." Certainly, the lady vote gatherers can not be accused of much sense of proportion. Granting even that these busybodies can decide whose lives are clean enough for that eminently clean atmosphere, politics, must it follow that saloon-keepers belong to the same category? Unless it be American hypocrisy and bigotry, so manifest in the principle of Prohibition, which sanctions the spread of drunkenness among men and women of the rich class, yet keeps vigilant watch on the only place left to the poor man. If no other reason, woman's narrow and purist attitude toward life makes her a greater danger to liberty wherever she has political power. Man has long overcome the superstitions that still engulf woman. In the economic competitive field, man has been compelled to exercise efficiency, judgment, ability, competency. He therefore had neither time nor inclination to measure everyone's morality with a Puritanic yardstick. In his political activities, too, he has not gone about blindfolded. He knows that quantity and not quality is the material for the political grinding mill, and, unless he is a sentimental reformer or an old fossil, he knows that politics can never be anything but a swamp.

Women who are at all conversant with the process of politics know the nature of the beast, but in their self-sufficiency and egotism they make themselves believe that they have but to pet the beast, and he will become as gentle as a lamb, sweet and pure. As if women have not sold their votes, as if women politicians cannot be bought! If her body can be bought in return for material consideration, why not her vote? That it is being done in Colorado and in other States, is not denied even by those in favor of woman suffrage.

As I have said before, woman's narrow view of human affairs is not the only argument against her as a politician superior to man. There are others. Her life-long economic parasitism has utterly blurred her conception of the meaning of equality. She clamors for equal rights with man, yet we learn that "few women care to canvas in undesirable districts." How little equality means to them compared with the Russian women, who face hell itself for their ideal!

Woman demands the same rights as man, yet she is indignant that her presence does not strike him dead: he smokes, keeps his hat on, and does not jump from his seat like a flunkey. These may be trivial things, but they are nevertheless the key to the nature of American suffragists. To be sure, their English sisters have outgrown these silly notions. They have shown themselves equal to the greatest demands on their character and power of endurance. All honor to the heroism and sturdiness of the English suffragettes. Thanks to their energetic, aggressive methods, they have proved an inspiration to some of our own lifeless and spineless ladies. But after all, the suffragettes, too, are still lacking in appreciation of real equality. Else how is one to account for the tremendous, truly gigantic effort set in motion by those valiant fighters for a wretched little bill which will benefit a handful of propertied ladies, with absolutely no provision for the vast mass of working women? True, as politicians they must be opportunists, must take half-measures if they can not get all. But as intelligent and liberal women they ought to realize that if the ballot is a weapon, the disinherited need it more than the economically superior class, and that the latter already enjoy too much power by virtue of their economic superiority.

The brilliant leader of the English suffragettes, Mrs. Emmeline Pankhurst, herself admitted, when on her American lecture tour, that there can be no equality between political superiors and inferiors. If so, how will the workingwomen of England, already inferior economically to the ladies who are benefited by the Shackleton bill, be able to work with their political superiors, should the bill pass? Is it not probable that the class of Annie Keeney, so full of zeal, devotion, and martyrdom, will be compelled to carry on their backs their female political bosses, even as they are carrying their economic masters. They would still have to do it, were universal suffrage for men and women established in England. No matter what the workers do, they are made to pay, always. Still, those who believe in the power of the vote show little sense of justice when they concern themselves not at all with those whom, as they claim, it might serve most.

The American suffrage movement has been, until very recently, altogether a parlor affair, absolutely detached from the economic needs of the people. Thus Susan B. Anthony, no doubt an exceptional type of woman, was not only indifferent but antagonistic to labor; nor did she hesitate to manifest her antagonism when, in 1869, she advised women to take the places of striking printers in New York. I do not know whether her attitude had changed before her death.

There are, of course, some suffragists who are affiliated with workingwomen—the Women's Trade Union League, for instance; but they are a small minority, and their activities are essentially economic. The rest look upon toil as a just provision of Providence. What would become of the rich, if not for the poor? What would become of these idle, parasitic ladies, who squander more in a week than their victims earn in a year, if not for the eighty million wage-workers? Equality, who ever heard of such a thing?

Few countries have produced such arrogance and snobbishness as America. Particularly is this true of the American woman of the middle class. She not only considers herself the equal of man, but his superior, especially in her purity, goodness, and morality. Small wonder that the American suffragist claims for her vote the most miraculous powers. In her exalted conceit she does not see how truly enslaved she is, not so much by man, as by her own silly notions and traditions. Suffrage can not ameliorate that sad fact; it can only accentuate it, as indeed it does.

One of the great American women leaders claims that woman is entitled not only to equal pay, but that she ought to be legally entitled even to the pay of her husband. Failing to support her, he should be put in convict stripes, and his earnings in prison be collected by his equal wife. Does not another brilliant exponent of the cause claim for woman that her vote will abolish the social evil, which has been fought in vain by the collective efforts of the most illustrious minds the world over? It is indeed to be regretted that the alleged creator of the universe has already presented us with his wonderful scheme of things, else woman suffrage would surely enable woman to outdo him completely.

Nothing is so dangerous as the dissection of a fetish. If we have outlived the time when such heresy was punishable by the stake, we have not outlived the narrow spirit of condemnation of those who dare differ with accepted notions. Therefore I shall probably be put down as an opponent of woman. But that can not deter me from looking the question squarely in the face. I repeat what I have said in the beginning: I do not believe that woman will make politics worse; nor can I believe that she could make it better. If, then, she cannot improve on man's mistakes, why perpetrate the latter?

History may be a compilation of lies; nevertheless, it contains a few truths, and they are the only guide we have for the future. The history of the political activities of men proves that they have given him absolutely nothing that he could not have achieved in a more direct, less costly, and more lasting manner. As a matter of fact, every inch of ground he has gained has been through a constant fight, a ceaseless struggle for self-assertion, and not through suffrage. There is no reason whatever to assume that woman, in her climb to emancipation, has been, or will be, helped by the ballot.

In the darkest of all countries, Russia, with her absolute despotism, woman has become man's equal, not through the ballot, but by her will to be and to do. Not only has she conquered for herself every avenue of learning and vocation, but she has won man's esteem, his respect, his comradeship; aye, even more than that: she has gained the admiration, the respect of the whole world. That, too, not through suffrage, but by her wonderful heroism, her fortitude, her ability, willpower, and her endurance in her struggle for liberty. Where are the women in any suffrage country or State that can lay claim to such a victory? When we consider the accomplishments of woman in America, we find also that something deeper and more powerful than suffrage has helped her in the march to emancipation.

It is just sixty-two years ago since a handful of women at the Seneca Falls Convention set forth a few demands for their right to equal education with men, and access to the various professions, trades, etc. What wonderful accomplishments, what wonderful triumphs! Who but the most ignorant dare speak of woman as a mere domestic drudge? Who dare suggest that this or that profession should not be open to her? For over sixty years she has molded a new atmosphere and a new life for herself. She has become a world-power in every domain of human thought and activity. And all that without suffrage, without the right to make laws, without the "privilege" of becoming a judge, a jailer, or an executioner.

Yes, I may be considered an enemy of woman; but if I can help her see the light, I shall not complain.

The misfortune of woman is not that she is unable to do the work of a man, but that she is wasting her life-force to outdo him, with a tradition of centuries which has left her physically incapable of keeping pace with him. Oh, I know some have succeeded, but at what cost, at what terrific cost! The import is not the kind of work woman does, but rather the quality of the work she furnishes. She can give suffrage or the ballot no new quality, nor can she receive anything from it that will enhance her own quality. Her development, her freedom, her independence, must come from and through herself. First, by asserting herself as a personality, and not as a sex commodity. Second, by refusing the right to anyone over her body; by refusing to bear children, unless she wants them; by refusing to be a servant to God, the State, society, the husband, the family, etc., by making her life simpler, but deeper and richer. That is, by trying to learn the meaning and substance of life in all its complexities, by freeing herself from the fear of public opinion and public condemnation. Only that, and not the ballot, will set woman free, will make her a force hitherto unknown in the world, a force for real love, for peace, for harmony; a force of divine fire, of life-giving; a creator of free men and women.

Patriotism, a Menace to Liberty

Anarchism and Other Essays, 1911

What is patriotism? Is it love of one's birthplace, the place of childhood's recollections and hopes, dreams and aspirations? Is it the place where, in childlike naivete, we would watch the fleeting clouds, and wonder why we, too, could not run so swiftly? The place where we would count the milliard glittering stars, terror-stricken lest each one "an eye should be," piercing the very depths of our little souls? Is it the place where we would listen to the music of the birds, and long to have wings to fly, even as they, to distant lands? Or the place where we would sit at mother's knee, enraptured by wonderful tales of great deeds and conquests? In short, is it love for the spot, every inch representing dear and precious recollections of a happy, joyous, and playful childhood?

If that were patriotism, few American men of today could be called upon to be patriotic, since the place of play has been turned into factory, mill, and mine, while deafening sounds of machinery have replaced the music of the birds. Nor can we longer hear the tales of great deeds, for the stories our mothers tell today are but those of sorrow, tears, and grief.

What, then, is patriotism? "Patriotism, sir, is the last resort of scoundrels," said Dr. Johnson. Leo Tolstoy, the greatest anti-patriot of our times, defines patriotism as the principle that will justify the training of wholesale murderers; a trade that requires better equipment for the exercise of man-killing than the making of such necessities of life as shoes, clothing, and houses; a trade that guarantees better returns and greater glory than that of the average workingman.

Gustave Hervé, another great anti-patriot, justly calls patriotism a superstition—one far more injurious, brutal, and inhumane than religion. The superstition of religion originated in man's inability to explain natural phenomena. That is, when primitive man heard thunder or saw the lightning, he could not account for either, and therefore concluded that back of them must be a force greater than himself. Similarly he saw a supernatural force in the rain, and in the various other changes in nature. Patriotism, on the other hand, is a superstition artificially created and maintained through a network of lies and falsehoods; a superstition that robs man of his self-respect and dignity, and increases his arrogance and conceit.

Indeed, conceit, arrogance, and egotism are the essentials of patriotism. Let me illustrate. Patriotism assumes that our globe is divided into little spots, each one surrounded by an iron gate. Those who have had the fortune of being born on some particular spot, consider themselves better, nobler, grander, more intelligent than the living beings inhabiting any other spot. It is, therefore, the duty of everyone living on that chosen spot to fight, kill, and die in the attempt to impose his superiority upon all the others.

The inhabitants of the other spots reason in like manner, of course, with the result that, from early infancy, the mind of the child is poisoned with bloodcurdling stories about the Germans, the French, the Italians, Russians, etc. When the child has reached manhood, he is thoroughly saturated with the belief that he is chosen by the Lord himself to defend his country against the attack or invasion of any foreigner. It is for that purpose that we are clamoring for a greater army and navy, more battleships and ammunition. It is for that purpose that America has within a short time spent four hundred million dollars. Just think of it—four hundred million dollars taken from the produce of the people. For surely it is not the rich who contribute to patriotism. They are cosmopolitans, perfectly at home in every land. We in America know well the truth of this. Are not our rich Americans Frenchmen in France, Germans in Germany, or Englishmen in England? And do they not squander with cosmopolitan grace fortunes coined by American factory children and cotton slaves? Yes, theirs is the patriotism that will make it possible to send messages of condolence to a despot like the Russian Tsar when any mishap befalls him, as President Roosevelt did in the name of his people, when Sergius was punished by the Russian revolutionists.

It is a patriotism that will assist the arch-murderer, Diaz, in destroying thousands of lives in Mexico, or that will even aid in arresting Mexican revolutionists on American soil and keep them incarcerated in American prisons, without the slightest cause or reason.

But, then, patriotism is not for those who represent wealth and power. It is good enough for the people. It reminds one of the historic wisdom of Frederick the Great, the bosom friend of Voltaire, who said: "Religion is a fraud, but it must be maintained for the masses."

That patriotism is rather a costly institution, no one will doubt after considering the following statistics. The progressive increase of the expenditures for the leading armies and navies of the world during the last quarter of a century is a fact of such gravity as to startle every thoughtful student of economic problems. It may be briefly indicated by dividing the time from 1881 to 1905 into five-year periods, and noting the disbursements of several great nations for army and navy purposes during the first and last of those periods. From the first to the last of the periods noted the expenditures of Great Britain increased from $2,101,848,936 to $4,143,226,885, those of France from $3,324,500,000 to $3,455,109,900, those of Germany from $725,000,200 to $2,700,375,600, those of the United States from \$1,275,500,750 to \$2,650,900,450, those of Russia from \$1,900,975,500 to \$5,250,445,100, those of Italy from \$1,600,975,750 to \$1,755,500,100, and those of Japan from \$182,900,500 to \$700,925,475.

The military expenditures of each of the nations mentioned increased in each of the five-year periods under review. During the entire interval from 1881 to 1905 Great Britain's outlay for her army increased fourfold, that of the United States was tripled, Russia's was doubled, that of Germany increased 35 percent, that of France about 15 percent, and that of Japan nearly 500 percent If we compare the expenditures of these nations upon their armies with their total expenditures for all the twenty-five years ending with l905, the proportion rose as follows:

In Great Britain from 20 percent to 37; in the United States from 15 to 23; in France from 16 to 18; in Italy from 12 to 15; in Japan from 12 to 14. On the other hand, it is interesting to note that the proportion in Germany decreased from about 58 percent to 25, the decrease being due to the enormous increase in the imperial expenditures for other purposes, the fact being that the army expenditures for the period of 190l-5 were higher than for any five-year period preceding. Statistics show that the countries in which army expenditures are greatest, in proportion to the total national revenues, are Great Britain, the United States, Japan, France, and Italy, in the order named.

The showing as to the cost of great navies is equally impressive. During the twenty-five years ending with 1905 naval expenditures increased approximately as follows: Great Britain, 300 percent; France 60 percent; Germany 600 percent; the United States 525 percent; Russia 300 percent; Italy 250 percent; and Japan, 700 percent. With the exception of Great Britain, the United States spends more for naval purposes than any other nation, and this expenditure bears also a larger proportion to the entire national disbursements than that of any other power. In the period 1881-5, the expenditure for the United States navy was \$6.20 out of each \$100 appropriated for all national purposes; the amount rose to \$6.60 for the next five-year period, to $8.10 for the next, to $11.70 for the next, and to $16.40 for 1901-5. It is morally certain that the outlay for the current period of five years will show a still further increase.

The rising cost of militarism may be still further illustrated by computing it as a per capita tax on population. From the first to the last of the five-year periods taken as the basis for the comparisons here given, it has risen as follows: In Great Britain, from $18.47 to $52.50; in France, from $19.66 to $23.62; in Germany, from $10.17 to $15.51; in the United States, from $5.62 to $13.64; in Russia, from $6.14 to $8.37; in Italy, from $9.59 to $11.24, and in Japan from 86 cents to $3.11.

It is in connection with this rough estimate of cost per capita that the economic burden of militarism is most appreciable. The irresistible conclusion from available data is that the increase of expenditure for army and navy purposes is rapidly surpassing the growth of population in each of the countries considered in the present calculation. In other words, a continuation of the increased demands of militarism threatens each of those nations with a progressive exhaustion both of men and resources.

The awful waste that patriotism necessitates ought to be sufficient to cure the man of even average intelligence from this disease. Yet patriotism demands still more. The people are urged to be patriotic and for that luxury they pay, not only by supporting their "defenders," but even by sacrificing their own children. Patriotism requires allegiance to the flag, which means obedience and readiness to kill father, mother, brother, sister.

The usual contention is that we need a standing army to protect the country from foreign invasion. Every intelligent man and woman knows, however, that this is a myth maintained to frighten and coerce the foolish. The governments of the world, knowing each other's interests, do not invade each other. They have learned that they can gain much more by international arbitration of disputes than by war and conquest. Indeed, as Carlyle said, "War is a quarrel between two thieves too cowardly to fight their own battle; therefore they take boys from one village and another village, stick them into uniforms, equip them with guns, and let them loose like wild beasts against each other."

It does not require much wisdom to trace every war back to a similar cause. Let us take our own Spanish-American war, supposedly a great and patriotic event in the history of the United States. How our hearts burned with indignation against the atrocious Spaniards! True, our indignation did not flare up spontaneously. It was nurtured by months of newspaper agitation, and long after Butcher Weyler had killed off many noble Cubans and outraged many Cuban women. Still, in justice to the American Nation be it said, it did grow indignant and was willing to fight, and that it fought bravely. But when the smoke was over, the dead buried, and the cost of the war came back to the people in an increase in the price of commodities and rent—that is, when we sobered up from our patriotic spree—it suddenly dawned on us that the cause of the Spanish-American war was the consideration of the price of sugar; or, to be more explicit, that the lives, blood, and money of the American people were used to protect the interests of American capitalists, which were threatened by the Spanish government. That this is not an exaggeration, but is based on absolute facts and figures, is best proven by the attitude of the American government to Cuban labor. When Cuba was firmly in the clutches of the United States, the very soldiers sent to liberate Cuba were ordered to shoot Cuban workingmen during the great cigarmakers' strike, which took place shortly after the war.

Nor do we stand alone in waging war for such causes. The curtain is beginning to be lifted on the motives of the terrible Russo-Japanese war, which cost so much blood and tears. And we see again that back of the fierce Moloch of war stands the still fiercer god of Commercialism. Kuropatkin, the Russian Minister of War during the Russo-Japanese struggle, has revealed the true secret behind the latter. The Tsar and his Grand Dukes, having invested money in Korean concessions, the war was forced for the sole purpose of speedily accumulating large fortunes.

The contention that a standing army and navy is the best security of peace is about as logical as the claim that the most peaceful citizen is he who goes about heavily armed. The experience of every-day life fully proves that the armed individual is invariably anxious to try his strength. The same is historically true of governments. Really peaceful countries do not waste life and energy in war preparations, with the result that peace is maintained.

However, the clamor for an increased army and navy is not due to any foreign danger. It is owing to the dread of the growing discontent of the masses and of the international spirit among the workers. It is to meet the internal enemy that the Powers of various countries are preparing themselves; an enemy, who, once awakened to consciousness, will prove more dangerous than any foreign invader.

The powers that have for centuries been engaged in enslaving the masses have made a thorough study of their psychology. They know that the people at large are like children whose despair, sorrow, and tears can be turned into joy with a little toy. And the more gorgeously the toy is dressed, the louder the colors, the more it will appeal to the million-headed child.

An army and navy represents the people's toys. To make them more attractive and acceptable, hundreds and thousands of dollars are being spent for the display of these toys. That was the purpose of the American government in equipping a fleet and sending it along the Pacific coast, that every American citizen should be made to feel the pride and glory of the United States. The city of San Francisco spent one hundred thousand dollars for the entertainment of the fleet; Los Angeles, sixty thousand; Seattle and Tacoma, about one hundred thousand. To entertain the fleet, did I say? To dine and wine a few superior officers, while the "brave boys" had to mutiny to get sufficient food. Yes, two hundred and sixty thousand dollars were spent on fireworks, theatre parties, and revelries, at a time when men, women, and children through the breadth and length of the country were starving in the streets; when thousands of unemployed were ready to sell their labor at any price.

Two hundred and sixty thousand dollars! What could not have been accomplished with such an enormous sum? But instead of bread and shelter, the children of those cities were taken to see the fleet, that it may remain, as one of the newspapers said, "a lasting memory for the child."

A wonderful thing to remember, is it not? The implements of civilized slaughter. If the mind of the child is to be poisoned with such memories, what hope is there for a true realization of human brotherhood?

We Americans claim to be a peace-loving people. We hate bloodshed; we are opposed to violence. Yet we go into spasms of joy over the possibility of projecting dynamite bombs from flying machines upon helpless citizens. We are ready to hang, electrocute, or lynch anyone, who, from economic necessity, will risk his own life in the attempt upon that of some industrial magnate. Yet our hearts swell with pride at the thought that America is becoming the most powerful nation on earth, and that it will eventually plant her iron foot on the necks of all other nations.

Such is the logic of patriotism.

Considering the evil results that patriotism is fraught with for the average man, it is as nothing compared with the insult and injury that patriotism heaps upon the soldier himself—that poor, deluded victim of superstition and ignorance. He, the savior of his country, the protector of his nation—what has patriotism in store for him? A life of slavish submission, vice, and perversion, during peace; a life of danger, exposure, and death, during war.

While on a recent lecture tour in San Francisco, I visited the Presidio, the most beautiful spot overlooking the Bay and Golden Gate Park. Its purpose should have been playgrounds for children, gardens and music for the recreation of the weary. Instead it is made ugly, dull, and gray by barracks—barracks wherein the rich would not allow their dogs to dwell. In these miserable shanties soldiers are herded like cattle; here they waste their young days, polishing the boots and brass buttons of their superior officers. Here, too, I saw the distinction of classes: sturdy sons of a free Republic, drawn up in line like convicts, saluting every passing shrimp of a lieutenant. American equality, degrading manhood and elevating the uniform!

Barrack life further tends to develop tendencies of sexual perversion. It is gradually producing along this line results similar to European military conditions. Havelock Ellis, the noted writer on sex psychology, has made a thorough study of the subject. I quote: "Some of the barracks are great centers of male prostitution.... The number of soldiers who prostitute themselves is greater than we are willing to believe. It is no exaggeration to say that in certain regiments the presumption is in favor of the venality of the majority of the men.... On summer evenings Hyde Park and the neighborhood of Albert Gate are full of guardsmen and others plying a lively trade, and with little disguise, in uniform or out.... In most cases the proceeds form a comfortable addition to Tommy Atkins' pocket money."

To what extent this perversion has eaten its way into the army and navy can best be judged from the fact that special houses exist for this form of prostitution. The practice is not limited to England; it is universal. "Soldiers are no less sought after in France than in England or in Germany, and special houses for military prostitution exist both in Paris and the garrison towns."

Had Mr. Havelock Ellis included America in his investigation of sex perversion, he would have found that the same conditions prevail in our army and navy as in those of other countries. The growth of the standing army inevitably adds to the spread of sex perversion; the barracks are the incubators.

Aside from the sexual effects of barrack life, it also tends to unfit the soldier for useful labor after leaving the army. Men, skilled in a trade, seldom enter the army or navy, but even they, after a military experience, find themselves totally unfitted for their former occupations. Having acquired habits of idleness and a taste for excitement and adventure, no peaceful pursuit can content them. Released from the army, they can turn to no useful work. But it is usually the social riff-raff, discharged prisoners and the like, whom either the struggle for life or their own inclination drives into the ranks. These, their military term over, again turn to their former life of crime, more brutalized and degraded than before. It is a well-known fact that in our prisons there is a goodly number of ex-soldiers; while, on the other hand, the army and navy are to a great extent plied with ex-convicts.

Of all the evil results I have just described none seems to me so detrimental to human integrity as the spirit patriotism has produced in the case of Private William Buwalda. Because he foolishly believed that one can be a soldier and exercise his rights as a man at the same time, the military authorities punished him severely. True, he had served his country fifteen years, during which time his record was unimpeachable. According to Gen. Funston, who reduced Buwalda's sentence to three years, "the first duty of an officer or an enlisted man is unquestioned obedience and loyalty to the government, and it makes no difference whether he approves of that government or not." Thus Funston stamps the true character of allegiance. According to him, entrance into the army abrogates the principles of the Declaration of Independence.

What a strange development of patriotism that turns a thinking being into a loyal machine!

In justification of this most outrageous sentence of Buwalda, Gen. Funston tells the American people that the soldier's action was "a serious crime equal to treason." Now, what did this "terrible crime" really consist of? Simply in this: William Buwalda was one of fifteen hundred people who attended a public meeting in San Francisco; and, oh, horrors, he shook hands with the speaker, Emma Goldman. A terrible crime, indeed, which the General calls "a great military offense, infinitely worse than desertion."

Can there be a greater indictment against patriotism than that it will thus brand a man a criminal, throw him into prison, and rob him of the results of fifteen years of faithful service?

Buwalda gave to his country the best years of his life and his very manhood. But all that was as nothing. Patriotism is inexorable and, like all insatiable monsters, demands all or nothing. It does not admit that a soldier is also a human being, who has a right to his own feelings and opinions, his own inclinations and ideas. No, patriotism can not admit of that. That is the lesson which Buwalda was made to learn; made to learn at a rather costly, though not at a useless, price. When he returned to freedom, he had lost his position in the army, but he regained his self-respect. After all, that is worth three years of imprisonment.

A writer on the military conditions of America, in a recent article, commented on the power of the military man over the civilian in Germany. He said, among other things, that if our Republic had no other meaning than to guarantee all citizens equal rights, it would have just cause for existence. I am convinced that the writer was not in Colorado during the patriotic regime of General Bell. He probably would have changed his mind had he seen how, in the name of patriotism and the Republic, men were thrown into bull-pens, dragged about, driven across the border, and subjected to all kinds of indignities. Nor is that Colorado incident the only one in the growth of military power in the United States. There is hardly a strike where troops and militia do not come to the rescue of those in power, and where they do not act as arrogantly and brutally as do the men wearing the Kaiser's uniform. Then, too, we have the Dick military law. Had the writer forgotten that?

A great misfortune with most of our writers is that they are absolutely ignorant on current events, or that, lacking honesty, they will not speak of these matters. And so it has come to pass that the Dick military law was rushed through Congress with little discussion and still less publicity—a law which gives the President the power to turn a peaceful citizen into a bloodthirsty man-killer, supposedly for the defense of the country, in reality for the protection of the interests of that particular party whose mouthpiece the President happens to be.

Our writer claims that militarism can never become such a power in America as abroad, since it is voluntary with us, while compulsory in the Old World. Two very important facts, however, the gentleman forgets to consider. First, that conscription has created in Europe a deep-seated hatred of militarism among all classes of society. Thousands of young recruits enlist under protest and, once in the army, they will use every possible means to desert. Second, that it is the compulsory feature of militarism which has created a tremendous anti-militarist movement, feared by European Powers far more than anything else. After all, the greatest bulwark of capitalism is militarism. The very moment the latter is undermined, capitalism will totter. True, we have no conscription; that is, men are not usually forced to enlist in the army, but we have developed a far more exacting and rigid force—necessity. Is it not a fact that during industrial depressions there is a tremendous increase in the number of enlistments? The trade of militarism may not be either lucrative or honorable, but it is better than tramping the country in search of work, standing in the bread line, or sleeping in municipal lodging houses. After all, it means thirteen dollars per month, three meals a day, and a place to sleep. Yet even necessity is not sufficiently strong a factor to bring into the army an element of character and manhood. No wonder our military authorities complain of the "poor material" enlisting in the army and navy. This admission is a very encouraging sign. It proves that there is still enough of the spirit of independence and love of liberty left in the average American to risk starvation rather than don the uniform.

Thinking men and women the world over are beginning to realize that patriotism is too narrow and limited a conception to meet the necessities of our time. The centralization of power has brought into being an international feeling of solidarity among the oppressed nations of the world; a solidarity which represents a greater harmony of interests between the workingman of America and his brothers abroad than between the American miner and his exploiting compatriot; a solidarity which fears not foreign invasion, because it is bringing all the workers to the point when they will say to their masters, "Go and do your own killing. We have done it long enough for you." This solidarity is awakening the consciousness of even the soldiers, they, too, being flesh of the flesh of the great human family. A solidarity that has proven infallible more than once during past struggles, and which has been the impetus inducing the Parisian soldiers, during the Commune of 1871, to refuse to obey when ordered to shoot their brothers. It has given courage to the men who mutinied on Russian warships during recent years. It will eventually bring about the uprising of all the oppressed and downtrodden against their international exploiters.

The proletariat of Europe has realized the great force of that solidarity and has, as a result, inaugurated a war against patriotism and its bloody spectre, militarism. Thousands of men fill the prisons of France, Germany, Russia, and the Scandinavian countries, because they dared to defy the ancient superstition. Nor is the movement limited to the working class; it has embraced representatives in all stations of life, its chief exponents being men and women prominent in art, science, and letters.

America will have to follow suit. The spirit of militarism has already permeated all walks of life. Indeed, I am convinced that militarism is growing a greater danger here than anywhere else, because of the many bribes capitalism holds out to those whom it wishes to destroy.

The beginning has already been made in the schools. Evidently the government holds to the Jesuitical conception, "Give me the child mind, and I will mould the man." Children are trained in military tactics, the glory of military achievements extolled in the curriculum, and the youthful minds perverted to suit the government. Further, the youth of the country is appealed to in glaring posters to join the army and navy. "A fine chance to see the world!" cries the governmental huckster. Thus innocent boys are morally shanghaied into patriotism, and the military Moloch strides conquering through the Nation.

The American workingman has suffered so much at the hands of the soldier, State and Federal, that he is quite justified in his disgust with, and his opposition to, the uniformed parasite. However, mere denunciation will not solve this great problem. What we need is a propaganda of education for the soldier: anti-patriotic literature that will enlighten him as to the real horrors of his trade, and that will awaken his consciousness to his true relation to the man to whose labor he owes his very existence. It is precisely this that the authorities fear most. It is already high treason for a soldier to attend a radical meeting. No doubt they will also stamp it high treason for a soldier to read a radical pamphlet. But, then, has not authority from time immemorial stamped every step of progress as treasonable? Those, however, who earnestly strive for social reconstruction can well afford to face all that; for it is probably even more important to carry the truth into the barracks than into the factory. When we have undermined the patriotic lie, we shall have cleared the path for that great structure wherein all nationalities shall be united into a universal brotherhood—a truly *free society*.

Psychology of Political Violence

1911

To analyze the psychology of political violence is not only extremely difficult, but also very dangerous. If such acts are treated with understanding, one is immediately accused of eulogizing them. If, on the other hand, human sympathy is expressed for the *Attentater* (a revolutionist committing an act of political violence) one risks being considered a possible accomplice. Yet it is only intelligence and sympathy that can bring us closer to the source of human suffering, and teach us the ultimate way out of it.

The primitive man, ignorant of natural forces, dreaded their approach, hiding from the perils they threatened. As man learned to understand Nature's phenomena, he realized that though these may destroy life and cause great loss, they also bring relief. To the earnest student it must be apparent that the accumulated forces in our social and economic life, culminating in a political act of violence, are similar to the terrors of the atmosphere, manifested in storm and lightning.

To thoroughly appreciate the truth of this view, one must feel intensely the indignity of our social wrongs; one's very being must throb with the pain, the sorrow, the despair millions of people are daily made to endure. Indeed, unless we have become a part of humanity, we cannot even faintly understand the just indignation that accumulates in a human soul, the burning, surging passion that makes the storm inevitable.

The ignorant mass looks upon the man who makes a violent protest against our social and economic iniquities as upon a wild beast, a cruel, heartless monster, whose joy it is to destroy life and bathe in blood; or at best, as upon an irresponsible lunatic.

Yet nothing is further from the truth. As a matter of fact, those who have studied the character and personality of these men, or who have come in close contact with them, are agreed that it is their super-sensitiveness to the wrong and injustice surrounding them which compels them to pay the toll of our social crimes. The most noted writers and poets, discussing the psychology of political offenders, have paid them the highest tribute. Could anyone assume that these men had advised violence, or even approved of the acts? Certainly not. Theirs was the attitude of the social student, of the man who knows that beyond every violent act there is a vital cause.

Bjornstjerne Bjornson, in the second part of "Beyond Human Power", emphasizes the fact that it is among the Anarchists that we must look for the modern martyrs who pay for their faith with their blood, and who welcome death with a smile, because they believe, as truly as Christ did, that their martyrdom will redeem humanity.

Francois Coppee, the French novelist, thus expresses himself regarding the psychology of the *Attentater*:

"The reading of the details of Vaillant's execution left me in a thoughtful mood. I imagined him expanding his chest under the ropes, marching with firm step, stiffening his will, concentrating all his energy, and, with eyes fixed upon the knife, hurling finally at society his cry of malediction. And, in spite of me, another spectacle rose suddenly before my mind. I saw a group of men and women pressing against each other in the middle of the oblong arena of the circus, under the gaze of thousands of eyes, while from all the steps of the immense amphitheater went up the terrible cry, *Ad leones!* and, below, the opening cages of the wild beasts.

"I did not believe the execution would take place. In the first place, no victim had been struck with death, and it had long been the custom not to punish an abortive crime with the last degree of severity. Then, this crime, however terrible in intention, was disinterested, born of an abstract idea. The man's past, his abandoned childhood, his life of hardship, pleaded also in his favor. In the independent press generous voices were raised in his behalf, very loud and eloquent. 'A purely literary current of opinion' some have said, with no little scorn. It is, on the contrary, an honor to the men of art and thought to have expressed once more their disgust at the scaffold."

Again Zola, in *Germinal and Paris*, describes the tenderness and kindness, the deep sympathy with human suffering, of these men who close the chapter of their lives with a violent outbreak against our system.

Last, but not least, the man who probably better than anyone else understands the psychology of the *Attentator* is M. Hamon, the author of the brilliant work, *Une Psychologie du Militaire Professionel*, who has arrived at these suggestive conclusions:

"The positive method confirmed by the rational method enables us to establish an ideal type of Anarchist, whose mentality is the aggregate of common psychic characteristics. Every Anarchist partakes sufficiently of this ideal type to make it possible to differentiate him from other men. The typical Anarchist, then, may be defined as follows: A man perceptible by the spirit of revolt under one or more of its forms— opposition, investigation, criticism, innovation—endowed with a strong love of liberty, egoistic or individualistic, and possessed of great curiosity, a keen desire to know. These traits are supplemented by an ardent love of others, a highly developed moral sensitiveness, a profound sentiment of justice, and imbued with missionary zeal."

To the above characteristics, says Alvin F. Sanborn, must be added these sterling qualities: a rare love of animals, surpassing sweetness in all the ordinary relations of life, exceptional sobriety of demeanor, frugality and regularity, austerity, even, of living, and courage beyond compare.

"There is a truism that the man in the street seems always to forget, when he is abusing the Anarchists, or whatever party happens to be his *bete noire* for the moment, as the cause of some outrage just perpetrated. This indisputable fact is that homicidal outrages have, from time immemorial, been the reply of goaded and desperate classes, and goaded and desperate individuals, to wrongs from their fellow-men, which they felt to be intolerable. Such acts are the violent recoil from violence, whether aggressive or repressive; they are the last desperate struggle of outraged and exasperated human nature for breathing space and life. And their cause lies not in any special conviction, but in the depths of that human nature itself. The whole course of history, political and social, is strewn with evidence of this fact. To go no further, take the three most notorious examples of political parties goaded into violence during the last fifty years: the Mazzinians in Italy, the Fenians in Ireland, and the Terrorists in Russia. Were these people Anarchists? No. Did they all three even hold the same political opinions? No. The Mazzinians were Republicans, the Fenians political separatists, the Russians Social Democrats or Constitutionalists. But all were driven by desperate circumstances into this terrible form of revolt. And when we turn from parties to individuals who have acted in like manner, we stand appalled by the number of human beings goaded and driven by sheer desperation into conduct obviously violently opposed to their social instincts. Now that Anarchism has become a living force in society, such deeds have been sometimes committed by Anarchists, as well as by others. For no new faith, even the most essentially peaceable and humane the mind of man has yet accepted, but at its first coming has brought upon earth not peace, but a sword; not because of anything violent or anti-social in the doctrine itself; simply because of the ferment any new and creative idea excites in men's minds, whether they accept or reject it. And a conception of Anarchism which, on one hand, threatens every vested interest, and, on the other, holds out a vision of a free and noble life to be won by a struggle against existing wrongs, is certain to rouse the fiercest opposition, and bring the whole repressive force of ancient evil into violent contact with the tumultuous outburst of a new hope.

"Under miserable conditions of life, shy vision of the possibility of better things makes the present misery more intolerable, and spurs those who suffer to the most energetic struggles to improve their lot, and if these struggles only immediately result in sharper misery, the outcome is sheer desperation. In our present society, for instance, an exploited wage worker, who catches a glimpse of what work and life might and ought to be, finds the toilsome routine and the squalor of his existence almost intolerable; and even when he has the resolution and courage to continue steadily working his best, and waiting until new ideas have so permeated society as to pave the way for better times, the mere fact that he has such ideas and tries to spread them, brings him into difficulties with his employers. How many thousands of Socialists, and above all Anarchists, have lost work and even the chance of work, solely on the ground of their opinions. It is only the specially gifted craftsman, who, if he be a zealous propagandist, can hope to retain permanent employment. And what happens to a man with his brain working actively with a ferment of new ideas, with a vision before his eyes of a new hope dawning for toiling and agonizing men, with the knowledge that his suffering and that of his fellows in misery is not caused by the cruelty of fate, but by the injustice of other human beings—what happens to such a man when he sees those dear to him starving, when he himself is starved? Some natures in such a plight, and those by no means the least social or the least sensitive, will become violent, and will even feel that their violence is social and not anti-social, that in striking when and how they can, they are striking, not for themselves, but for human nature, outraged and despoiled in their persons and in those of their fellow sufferers. And are we, who ourselves are not in this horrible predicament, to stand by and coldly condemn these piteous victims of the Furies and Fates? Are we to decry as miscreants these human beings who act with heroic self-devotion, sacrificing their lives in protest, where less social and less energetic natures would lie down and grovel in abject submission to injustice and wrong? Are we to join the ignorant and brutal outcry which stigmatizes such men as monsters of wickedness, gratuitously running amok in a harmonious and innocently peaceful society? No! We hate murder with a hatred that may seem absurdly exaggerated to apologists for Matabele massacres, to callous acquiescers in hangings and bombardments, but we decline in such cases of homicide, or attempted homicide, as those of which we are treating, to be guilty of the cruel injustice of flinging the whole responsibility of the deed upon the immediate perpetrator. The guilt of these homicides lies upon every man and woman who, intentionally or by cold indifference, helps to keep up social conditions that drive human beings to despair. The man who flings his whole life into the attempt, at the cost of his own life, to protest against the wrongs of his fellow-men, is a saint compared to the active and passive upholders of cruelty and injustice, even if his protest destroy other lives besides his own. Let him who is without sin in society cast the first stone at such an one."

That every act of political violence should nowadays be attributed to Anarchists is not at all surprising. Yet it is a fact known to almost everyone familiar with the Anarchist movement that a great number of acts for which Anarchists had to suffer, either originated with the capitalist press or were instigated, if not directly perpetrated, by the police.

For a number of years acts of violence had been committed in Spain, for which the Anarchists were held responsible, hounded like wild beasts, and thrown into prison. Later it was disclosed that the perpetrators of these acts were not Anarchists, but members of the police department. The scandal became so widespread that the conservative Spanish papers demanded the apprehension and punishment of the gang-leader, Juan Rull, who was subsequently condemned to death and executed. The sensational evidence, brought to light during the trial, forced Police Inspector Momento to exonerate completely the Anarchists from any connection with the acts committed during a long period. This resulted in the dismissal of a number of police officials, among them Inspector Tressols, who, in revenge, disclosed the fact that behind the gang of police bomb-throwers were others of far higher position, who provided them with funds and protected them.

This is one of the many striking examples of how Anarchist conspiracies are manufactured.

That the American police can perjure themselves with the same ease, that they are just as merciless, just as brutal and cunning as their European colleagues, has been proved on more than one occasion. We need only recall the tragedy of the eleventh of November, 1887, known as the Haymarket Riot.

No one who is at all familiar with the case can possibly doubt that the Anarchists, judicially murdered in Chicago, died as victims of a lying, bloodthirsty press and of a cruel police conspiracy. Has not Judge Gary himself said: "Not because you have caused the Haymarket bomb, but because you are Anarchists, you are on trial."

The impartial and thorough analysis by Governor Altgeld of that blotch on the American escutcheon verified the brutal frankness of Judge Gary. It was this that induced Altgeld to pardon the three Anarchists, thereby earning the lasting esteem of every liberty-loving man and woman in the world.

When we approach the tragedy of September sixth, 1901, we are confronted by one of the most striking examples of how little social theories are responsible for an act of political violence. "Leon Czolgosz, an Anarchist, incited to commit the act by Emma Goldman." To be sure, has she not incited violence even before her birth, and will she not continue to do so beyond death? Everything is possible with the Anarchists.

Today, even, nine years after the tragedy, after it was proved a hundred times that Emma Goldman had nothing to do with the event, that no evidence whatsoever exists to indicate that Czolgosz ever called himself an Anarchist, we are confronted with the same lie, fabricated by the police and perpetuated by the press. No living soul ever heard Czolgosz make that statement, nor is there a single written word to prove that the boy ever breathed the accusation. Nothing but ignorance and insane hysteria, which have never yet been able to solve the simplest problem of cause and effect.

The President of a free Republic killed! What else can be the cause, except that the *Attentäter* must have been insane, or that he was incited to the act.

A free Republic! How a myth will maintain itself, how it will continue to deceive, to dupe, and blind even the comparatively intelligent to its monstrous absurdities. A free Republic! And yet within a little over thirty years a small band of parasites have successfully robbed the American people, and trampled upon the fundamental principles, laid down by the fathers of this country, guaranteeing to every man, woman, and child "life, liberty, and the pursuit of happiness." For thirty years they have been increasing their wealth and power at the expense of the vast mass of workers, thereby enlarging the army of the unemployed, the hungry, homeless, and friendless portion of humanity, who are tramping the country from east to west, from north to south, in a vain search for work. For many years the home has been left to the care of the little ones, while the parents are exhausting their life and strength for a mere pittance. For thirty years the sturdy sons of America have been sacrificed on the battlefield of industrial war, and the daughters outraged in corrupt factory surroundings. For long and weary years this process of undermining the nation's health, vigor, and pride, without much protest from the disinherited and oppressed, has been going on. Maddened by success and victory, the money powers of this "free land of ours" became more and more audacious in their heartless, cruel efforts to compete with the rotten and decayed European tyrannies for supremacy of power.

In vain did a lying press repudiate Leon Czolgosz as a foreigner. The boy was a product of our own free American soil, that lulled him to sleep with, "My country, 'tis of thee, Sweet land of liberty". Who can tell how many times this American child had gloried in the celebration of the Fourth of July, or of Decoration Day, when he faithfully honored the Nation's dead? Who knows but that he, too, was willing to "fight for his country and die for her liberty," until it dawned upon him that those he belonged to have no country, because they have been robbed of all that they have produced; until he realized that the liberty and independence of his youthful dreams was but a farce. Poor Leon Czdgosz, your crime consisted of too sensitive a social consciousness. Unlike your ideal-less and brainless American brothers, your ideals soared above the belly and the bank account. No wonder you impressed the one human being among all the infuriated mob at your trial—a newspaper woman—as a visionary, totally oblivious to your surroundings. Your large, dreamy eyes must have beheld a new and glorious dawn.

Now, to a recent instance of police-manufactured Anarchist plots. In that bloodstained city, Chicago, the life of Chief of Police Shippy was attempted by a young man named Averbuch. Immediately the cry was sent to the four corners of the world that Averbuch was an Anarchist, and that the Anarchists were responsible for the act. Everyone who was at all known to entertain Anarchist ideas was closely watched, a number of people arrested, the library of an Anarchist group confiscated, and all meetings made impossible. It goes without saying that, as on various previous occasions, I must needs be held responsible for the act. Evidently the American police credit me with occult powers. I did not know Averbuch; in fact, had never before heard his name, and the only way I could have possibly "conspired" with him was in my astral body. But, then, the police are not concerned with logic or justice. What they seek is a target, to mask their absolute ignorance of the cause, of the psychology of a political act. Was Averbuch an Anarchist? There is no positive proof of it. He had been but three months in the country, did not know the language, and, as far as I could ascertain, was quite unknown to the Anarchists of Chicago.

What led to his act? Averbuch, like most young Russian immigrants, undoubtedly believed in the mythical liberty of America. He received his first baptism by the policeman's club during the brutal dispersement of the unemployed parade. He further experienced American equality and opportunity in the vain efforts to find an economic master. In short, a three months' sojourn in the glorious land brought him face to face with the fact that the disinherited are in the same position the world over. In his native land he probably learned that necessity knows no law — there was no difference between a Russian and an American policeman.

The question to the intelligent social student is not whether the acts of Czolgosz or Averbuch were practical, any more than whether the thunderstorm is practical. The thing that will inevitably impress itself on the thinking and feeling man and woman is that the sight of brutal clubbing of innocent victims in a so-called free Republic, and the degrading, soul-destroying economic struggle, furnish the spark that kindles the dynamic force in the overwrought, outraged souls of men like Czolgosz or Averbuch. No amount of persecution, of hounding, of repression, can stay this social phenomenon.

But, it is often asked, have not acknowledged Anarchists committed acts of violence? Certainly they have, always however ready to shoulder the responsibility. My contention is that they were impelled, not by the teachings of Anarchism, but by the tremendous pressure of conditions, making life unbearable to their sensitive natures. Obviously, Anarchism, or any other social theory, making man a conscious social unit, will act as a leaven for rebellion. This is not a mere assertion, but a fact verified by all experience. A close examination of the circumstances bearing upon this question will further clarify my position.

Let us consider some of the most important Anarchist acts within the last two decades. Strange as it may seem, one of the most significant deeds of political violence occurred here in America, in connection with the Homestead strike of 1892.

During that memorable time the Carnegie Steel Company organized a conspiracy to crush the Amalgamated Association of Iron and Steel Workers. Henry Clay Frick, then Chairman of the Company, was intrusted with that democratic task. He lost no time in carrying out the policy of breaking the Union, the policy which he had so successfully practiced during his reign of terror in the coke regions. Secretly, and while peace negotiations were being purposely prolonged, Frick supervised the military preparations, the fortification of the Homestead Steel Works, the erection of a high board fence, capped with barbed wire and provided with loopholes for sharpshooters. And then, in the dead of night, he attempted to smuggle his army of hired Pinkerton thugs into Homestead, which act precipitated the terrible carnage of the steel workers. Not content with the death of eleven victims, killed in the Pinkerton skirmish, Henry Clay Frick, good Christian and free American, straightway began the hounding down of the helpless wives and orphans, by ordering them out of the wretched Company houses.

The whole country was aroused over these inhuman outrages. Hundreds of voices were raised in protest, calling on Frick to desist, not to go too far. Yes, hundreds of people protested — as one objects to annoying flies. Only one there was who actively responded to the outrage at Homestead — Alexander Berkman. Yes, he was an Anarchist. He gloried in that fact, because it was the only force that made the discord between his spiritual longing and the world without at all bearable. Yet not Anarchism, as such, but the brutal slaughter of the eleven steel workers was the urge for Alexander Berkman's act, his attempt on the life of Henry Clay Frick.

The record of European acts of political violence affords numerous and striking instances of the influence of environment upon sensitive human beings.

The court speech of Vaillant, who, in 1894, exploded a bomb in the Paris Chamber of Deputies, strikes the true keynote of the psychology of such acts:

"Gentlemen, in a few minutes you are to deal your blow, but in receiving your verdict I shall have at least the satisfaction of having wounded the existing society, that cursed society in which one may see a single man spending, uselessly, enough to feed thousands of families; an infamous society which permits a few individuals to monopolize all the social wealth, while there are hundreds of thousands of unfortunates who have not even the bread that is not refused to dogs, and while entire families are committing suicide for want of the necessities of life.

"Ah, gentlemen, if the governing classes could go down among the unfortunates! But no, they prefer to remain deaf to their appeals. It seems that a fatality impels them, like the royalty of the eighteenth century, toward the precipice which will engulf them; for woe be to those who remain deaf to the cries of the starving, woe to those who, believing themselves of superior essence, assume the right to exploit those beneath them! There comes a time when the people no longer reason; they rise like a hurricane, and pass away like a torrent. Then we see bleeding heads impaled on pikes.

"Among the exploited, gentlemen, there are two classes of individuals: Those of one class, not realizing what they are and what they might be, take life as it comes, believe that they are born to be slaves, and content themselves with the little that is given them in exchange for their labor. But there are others, on the contrary, who think, who study, and who, looking about them, discover social iniquities. Is it their fault if they see clearly and suffer at seeing others suffer? Then they throw themselves into the struggle, and make themselves the bearers of the popular claims.

"Gentlemen, I am one of these last. Wherever have gone, I have seen unfortunates bent beneath the yoke of capital. Everywhere I have seen the same wounds causing tears of blood to flow, even in the remoter parts of the inhabited districts of South America, where I had the right to believe that he who was weary of the pains of civilization might rest in the shade of the palm trees and there study nature. Well, there even, more than elsewhere, I have seen capital come, like a vampire, to suck the last drop of blood of the unfortunate pariahs.

"Then I came back to France, where it was reserved for me to see my family suffer atrociously. This was the last drop in the cup of my sorrow. Tired of leading this life of suffering and cowardice, I carried this bomb to those who are primarily responsible for social sufferings.

"I am reproached with the wounds of those who were hit by my projectiles. Permit me to point out in passing that, if the bourgeois had not massacred or caused massacres during the Revolution, it is probable that they would still be under the yoke of the nobility. On the other hand, figure up the dead and wounded of Tonquin, Madagascar, Dahomey, adding thereto the thousands, yes, millions of unfortunates who die in the factories, the mines, and wherever the grinding power of capital is felt. Add also those who die of hunger, and all this with the assent of our Deputies. Besides all this, of how little weight are the reproaches now brought against me!

"It is true that one does not efface the other; but, after all, are we not acting on the defensive when we respond to the blows which we receive from above? I know very well that I shall be told that I ought to have confined myself to speech for the vindication of the people's claims. But what can you expect! It takes a loud voice to make the deaf hear. Too long have they answered our voices by imprisonment, the rope, rifle volleys. Make no mistake; the explosion of my bomb is not only the cry of the rebel Vaillant, but the cry of an entire class which vindicates its rights, and which will soon add acts to words. For, be sure of it, in vain will they pass laws. The ideas of the thinkers will not halt; just as, in the last century, all the governmental forces could not prevent the Diderots and the Voltaires from spreading emancipating ideas among the people, so all the existing governmental forces will not prevent the Reclus, the Darwins, the Spencers, the Ibsens, the Mirabeaus, from spreading the ideas of justice and liberty which will annihilate the prejudices that hold the mass in ignorance. And these ideas, welcomed by the unfortunate, will flower in acts of revolt as they have done in me, until the day when the disappearance of authority shall permit all men to organize freely according to their choice, when we shall each be able to enjoy the product of his labor, and when those moral maladies called prejudices shall vanish, permitting human beings to live in harmony, having no other desire than to study the sciences and love their fellows.

"I conclude, gentlemen, by saying that a society in which one sees such social inequalities as we see all about us, in which we see every day suicides caused by poverty, prostitution flaring at every street corner, a society whose principal monuments are barracks and prisons—such a society must be transformed as soon as possible, on pain of being eliminated, and that speedily, from the human race. Hail to him who labors, by no matter what means, for this transformation! It is this idea that has guided me in my duel with authority, but as in this duel I have only wounded my adversary, it is now its turn to strike me.

"Now, gentlemen, to me it matters little what penalty you may inflict, for, looking at this assembly with the eyes of reason, I can not help smiling to see you, atoms lost in matter, and reasoning only because you possess a prolongation of the spinal marrow, assume the right to judge one of your fellows.

"Ah! gentlemen, how little a thing is your assembly and your verdict in the history of humanity; and human history, in its turn, is likewise a very little thing in the whirlwind which bears it through immensity, and which is destined to disappear, or at least to be transformed, in order to begin again the same history and the same facts, a veritably perpetual play of cosmic forces renewing and transferring themselves forever."

Will anyone say that Vaillant was an ignorant, vicious man, or a lunatic? Was not his mind singularly clear, analytic? No wonder that the best intellectual forces of France spoke in his behalf, and signed the petition to President Carnot, asking him to commute Vaillant's death sentence.

Carnot would listen to no entreaty; he insisted on more than a pound of flesh, he wanted Vaillant's life, and then the inevitable happened: President Carnot was killed. On the handle of the stiletto used by the *Attentater* was engraved, significantly, *Vaillant* !

Santa Caserio was an Anarchist. He could have gotten away, saved himself; but he remained, he stood the consequences.

His reasons for the act are set forth in so simple, dignified, and childlike manner that one is reminded of the touching tribute paid Caserio by his teacher, of the little village school, Ada Negri, the Italian poet, who spoke of him as a sweet, tender plant, of too fine and sensitive texture to stand the cruel strain of the world.

"Gentlemen of the Jury! I do not propose to make a defense, but only an explanation of my deed.

"Since my early youth I began to learn that present society is badly organized, so badly that every day many wretched men commit suicide, leaving women and children in the most terrible distress. Workers, by thousands, seek for work and cannot find it. Poor families beg for food and shiver with cold; they suffer the greatest misery; the little ones ask their miserable mothers for food, and the mothers cannot give them, because they have nothing. The few things which the home contained have already been sold or pawned. All they can do is beg alms; often they are arrested as vagabonds.

"I went away from my native place because I was frequently moved to tears at seeing little girls of eight or ten years obliged to work fifteen hours a day for the paltry pay of twenty centimes. Young women of eighteen or twenty also work fifteen hours daily, for a mockery of remuneration. And that happens not only to my fellow countrymen, but to all the workers, who sweat the whole day long for a crust of bread, while their labor produces wealth in abundance. The workers are obliged to live under the most wretched conditions, and their food consists of a little bread, a few spoonfuls of rice, and water; so by the time they are thirty or forty years old, they are exhausted, and go to die in the hospitals. Besides, in consequence of bad food and overwork, these unhappy creatures are, by hundreds, devoured by pellagra—a disease that, in my country, attacks, as the physicians say, those who are badly fed and lead a life of toil and privation.

"I have observed that there are a great many people who are hungry, and many children who suffer, whilst bread and clothes abound in the towns. I saw many and large shops full of clothing and woolen stuffs, and I also saw warehouses full of wheat and Indian corn, suitable for those who are in want. And, on the other hand, I saw thousands of people who do not work, who produce nothing and live on the labor of others; who spend every day thousands of francs for their amusement; who debauch the daughters of the workers; who own dwellings of forty or fifty rooms; twenty or thirty horses, many servants; in a word, all the pleasures of life.

"I believed in God; but when I saw so great an inequality between men, I acknowledged that it was not God who created man, but man who created God: And I discovered that those who want their property to be respected, have an interest in preaching the existence of paradise and hell, and in keeping the people in ignorance.

"Not long ago, Vaillant threw a bomb in the Chamber of Deputies, to protest against the present system of society. He killed no one, only wounded some persons; yet bourgeois justice sentenced him to death. And not satisfied with the condemnation of the guilty man, they began to pursue the Anarchists, and arrest not only those who had known Vaillant, but even those who had merely been present at any Anarchist lecture.

"The government did not think of their wives and children. It did not consider that the men kept in prison were not the only ones who suffered, and that their little ones cried for bread. Bourgeois justice did not trouble itself about these innocent ones, who do not yet know what society is. It is no fault of theirs that their fathers are in prison; they only want to eat.

"The government went on searching private houses, opening private letters, forbidding lectures and meetings, and practicing the most infamous oppressions against us. Even now, hundreds of Anarchists are arrested for having written an article in a newspaper, or for having expressed an opinion in public.

"Gentlemen of the Jury, you are representatives of bourgeois society. If you want my head, take it; but do not believe that in so doing you will stop the Anarchist propaganda. Take care; for men reap what they have sown."

During a religious procession in 1896 at Barcelona, a bomb was thrown. Immediately three hundred men and women were arrested. Some were Anarchists, but the majority were trade unionists and Socialists. They were thrown into that terrible bastille, Montjuich, and subjected to most horrible tortures. After a number had been killed, or had gone insane, their cases were taken up by the liberal press of Europe, resulting in the release of a few survivors.

The man primarily responsible for this revival of the Inquisition was Canovas del Castillo, Prime Minister of Spain. It was he who ordered the torturing of the victims, their flesh burned, their bones crushed, their tongues cut out. Practiced in the art of brutality during his regime in Cuba, Canovas remained absolutely deaf to the appeals and protests of the awakened civilized conscience.

In 1897 Canovas del Castillo was shot to death by a young Italian, Angiolillo. The latter was an editor in his native land, and his bold utterances soon attracted the attention of the authorities. Persecution began, and Angiolillo fled from Italy to Spain, thence to France and Belgium, finally settling in England. While there he found employment as a compositor, and immediately became the friend of all his colleagues. One of the latter thus described Angiolillo: "His appearance suggested the journalist, rather than the disciple of Guttenberg. His delicate hands, moreover, betrayed the fact that he had not grown up at the 'case.' With his handsome frank face, his soft dark hair, his alert expression, he looked the very type of the vivacious Southerner. Angiolillo spoke Italian, Spanish, and French, but no English; the little French I knew was not sufficient to carry on a prolonged conversation. However, Angiolillo soon began to acquire the English idiom; he learned rapidly, playfully, and it was not long until he became very popular with his fellow compositors. His distinguished and yet modest manner, and his consideration towards his colleagues, won him the hearts of all the boys."

Angiolillo soon became familiar with the detailed accounts in the press. He read of the great wave of human sympathy with the helpless victims at Montjuich. On Trafalgar Square he saw with his own eyes the results of those atrocities, when the few Spaniards who escaped Castillo's clutches came to seek asylum in England. There, at the great meeting, these men opened their shirts and showed the horrible scars of burned flesh. Angiolillo saw, and the effect surpassed a thousand theories; the impetus was beyond words, beyond arguments, beyond himself even.

Senor Antonio Canovas del Castillo, Prime Minister of Spain, sojourned at Santa Agueda. As usual in such cases, all strangers were kept away from his exalted presence. One exception was made, however, in the case of a distinguished looking, elegantly dressed Italian—the representative, it was understood, of an important journal. The distinguished gentleman was Angiolillo.

Senor Canovas, about to leave his house, stepped on the veranda. Suddenly Angiolillo confronted him. A shot rang out, and Canovas was a corpse.

The wife of the Prime Minister rushed upon the scene. "Murderer! Murderer!" she cried, pointing at Angiolillo. The latter bowed. "Pardon, Madame," he said, "I respect you as a lady, but I regret that you were the wife of that man."

Calmly Angiolillo faced death. Death in its most terrible form—for the man whose soul was as a child's.

He was garrotted. His body lay, sun-kissed, till the day hid in twilight. And the people came, and pointing the finger of terror and fear, they said: "There—the criminal—the cruel murderer."

How stupid, how cruel is ignorance! It misunderstands always, condemns always.

A remarkable parallel to the case of Angiolillo is to be found in the act of Gaetano Bresci, whose *Attentat* upon King Umberto made an American city famous.

Bresci came to this country, this land of opportunity, where one has but to try to meet with golden success. Yes, he too would try to succeed. He would work hard and faithfully. Work had no terrors for him, if it would only help him to independence, manhood, self-respect.

Thus full of hope and enthusiasm he settled in Paterson, New Jersey, and there found a lucrative job at six dollars per week in one of the weaving mills of the town. Six whole dollars per week was, no doubt, a fortune for Italy, but not enough to breathe on in the new country. He loved his little home. He was a good husband and devoted father to his *bambinu*, Bianca, whom he adored. He worked and worked for a number of years. He actually managed to save one hundred dollars out of his six dollars per week.

Bresci had an ideal. Foolish, I know, for a workingman to have an ideal — the Anarchist paper published in Paterson, *La Questione Sociale*.

Every week, though tired from work, he would help to set up the paper. Until late hours he would assist, and when the little pioneer had exhausted all resources and his comrades were in despair, Bresci brought cheer and hope, one hundred dollars, the entire savings of years. That would keep the paper afloat.

In his native land people were starving. The crops had been poor, and the peasants saw themselves face to face with famine. They appealed to their good King Umberto; he would help. And he did. The wives of the peasants who had gone to the palace of the King, held up in mute silence their emaciated infants. Surely that would move him. And then the soldiers fired and killed those poor fools.

Bresci, at work in the weaving mill at Paterson, read of the horrible massacre. His mental eye beheld the defenceless women and innocent infants of his native land, slaughtered right before the good King. His soul recoiled in horror. At night he heard the groans of the wounded. Some may have been his comrades, his own flesh. Why, why these foul murders?

The little meeting of the Italian Anarchist group in Paterson ended almost in a fight. Bresci had demanded his hundred dollars. His comrades begged, implored him to give them a respite. The paper would go down if they were to return him his loan. But Bresci insisted on its return.

How cruel and stupid is ignorance. Bresci got the money, but lost the good will, the confidence of his comrades. They would have nothing more to do with one whose greed was greater than his ideals.

On the twenty-ninth of July, 1900, King Umberto was shot at Monzo. The young Italian weaver of Paterson, Gaetano Bresci, had taken the life of the good King.

Paterson was placed under police surveillance, everyone known as an Anarchist hounded and persecuted, and the act of Bresci ascribed to the teachings of Anarchism. As if the teachings of Anarchism in its extremest form could equal the force of those slain women and infants, who had pilgrimed to the King for aid. As if any spoken word, ever so eloquent, could burn into a human soul with such white heat as the life blood trickling drop by drop from those dying forms. The ordinary man is rarely moved either by word or deed; and those whose social kinship is the greatest living force need no appeal to respond — even as does steel to the magnet — to the wrongs and horrors of society.

If a social theory is a strong factor inducing acts of political violence, how are we to account for the recent violent outbreaks in India, where Anarchism has hardly been born. More than any other old philosophy, Hindu teachings have exalted passive resistance, the drifting of life, the Nirvana, as the highest spiritual ideal. Yet the social unrest in India is daily growing, and has only recently resulted in an act of political violence, the killing of Sir Curzon Wyllie by the Hindu, Madar Sol Dhingra.

If such a phenomenon can occur in a country socially and individually permeated for centuries with the spirit of passivity, can one question the tremendous, revolutionizing effect on human character exerted by great social iniquities? Can one doubt the logic, the justice of these words:

"Repression, tyranny, and indiscriminate punishment of innocent men have been the watchwords of the government of the alien domination in India ever since we began the commercial boycott of English goods. The tiger qualities of the British are much in evidence now in India. They think that by the strength of the sword they will keep down India! It is this arrogance that has brought about the bomb, and the more they tyrannize over a helpless and unarmed people, the more terrorism will grow. We may deprecate terrorism as outlandish and foreign to our culture, but it is inevitable as long as this tyranny continues, for it is not the terrorists that are to be blamed, but the tyrants who are responsible for it. It is the only resource for a helpless and unarmed people when brought to the verge of despair. It is never criminal on their part. The crime lies with the tyrant."

Even conservative scientists are beginning to realize that heredity is not the sole factor molding human character. Climate, food, occupation; nay, color, light, and sound must be considered in the study of human psychology.

If that be true, how much more correct is the contention that great social abuses will and must influence different minds and temperaments in a different way.

And how utterly fallacious the stereotyped notion that the teachings of Anarchism, or certain exponents of these teachings, are responsible for the acts of political violence.

Anarchism, more than any other social theory, values human life above things. All Anarchists agree with Tolstoy in this fundamental truth: if the production of any commodity necessitates the sacrifice of human life, society should do without that commodity, but it cannot do without that life. That, however, nowise indicates that Anarchism teaches submission. How can it, when it knows that all suffering, all misery, all ills, result from the evil of submission?

Has not some American ancestor said, many years ago, that resistance to tyranny is obedience to God? And he was not an Anarchist even. I would say that resistance to tyranny is man's highest ideal. So long as tyranny exists, in whatever form, man's deepest aspiration must resist it as inevitably as man must breathe.

Compared with the wholesale violence of capital and government, political acts of violence are but a drop in the ocean. That so few resist is the strongest proof how terrible must be the conflict between their souls and unbearable social iniquities.

High strung, like a violin string, they weep and moan for life, so relentless, so cruel, so terribly inhuman. In a desperate moment the string breaks.

Untuned ears hear nothing but discord. But those who feel the agonized cry understand its harmony; they hear in it the fulfillment of the most compelling moment of human nature.

Such is the psychology of political violence.

Syndicalism: The Modern Menace to Capitalism

1913

In view of the fact that the ideas embodied in Syndicalism have been practised by the workers for the last half century, even if without the background of social consciousness; that in this country five men had to pay with their lives because they advocated Syndicalist methods as the most effective in the struggle of labor against capital; and that, furthermore, Syndicalism has been consciously practised by the workers of France, Italy and Spain since 1395, it is rather amusing to witness some people in America and England now swooping down upon Syndicalism as a perfectly new and never before heard-of proposition.

It is astonishing how very naive Americans are, how crude and immature in matters of international importance. For all his boasted practical aptitude, the average American is the very last to learn of the modern means and tactics employed in the great struggles of his day. Always he lags behind in ideas and methods that the European workers have for years past been applying with great success.

It may be contended, of course, that this is merely a sign of youth on the part of the American. And it is indeed beautiful to possess a young mind, fresh to receive and perceive. But unfortunately the American mind seems never to grow, to mature and crystallize its views.

Perhaps that is why an American revolutionist can at the same time be a politician. That is also the reason why leaders of the Industrial Workers of the World continue in the Socialist party, which is antagonistic to the principles as well as to the activities of the I. W. W. Also why a rigid Marxian may propose that the Anarchists work together with the faction that began its career by a most bitter and malicious persecution of one of the pioneers of Anarchism, Michael Bakunin. In short, to the indefinite, uncertain mind of the American radical the most contradictory ideas and methods are possible. The result is a sad chaos in the radical movement, a sort of intellectual hash, which has neither taste nor character.

Just at present Syndicalism is the pastime of a great many Americans, so-called intellectuals. Not that they know anything about it, except that some great authorities—Sorel, Lagardelle, Berth and others—stand for it: because the American needs the seal of authority, or he would not accept an idea, no matter how true and valuable it might be.

Our bourgeois magazines are full of dissertations on Syndicalism. One of our most conservative colleges has even gone to the extent of publishing a work of one of its students on the subject, which has the approval of a professor. And all this, not because Syndicalism is a force and is being successfully practised by the workers of Europe, but because—as I said before—it has official authoritative sanction.

As if Syndicalism had been discovered by the philosophy of Bergson or the theoretic discourses of Sorel and Berth, and had not existed and lived among the workers long before these men wrote about it. The feature which distinguishes Syndicalism from most philosophies is that it represents the revolutionary philosophy of labor conceived and born in the actual struggle and experience of the workers themselves—not in universities, colleges, libraries, or in the brain of some scientists. The revolutionary philosophy of labor, that is the true and vital meaning of Syndicalism.

Already as far back as 1848 a large section of the workers realized the utter futility of political activity as a means of helping them in their economic struggle. At that time already the demand went forth for direct economic measures, as against the useless waste of energy along political lines. This was the case not only in France, but even prior to that in England, where Robert Owen, the true revolutionary Socialist, propagated similar ideas.

After years of agitation and experiment the idea was incorporated by the first convention of the Internationale, in 1867, in the resolution that the economic emancipation of the workers must be the principal aim of all revolutionists, to which everything else is to be subordinated.

In fact, it was this determined radical stand which eventually brought about the split in the revolutionary movement of that day, and its division into two factions: the one, under Marx and Engels, aiming at political conquest; the other, under Bakunin and the Latin workers, forging ahead along industrial and Syndicalist lines. The further development of those two wings is familiar to every thinking man and woman: the one has gradually centralized into a huge machine, with the sole purpose of conquering political power within the existing capitalist State; the other is becoming an ever more vital revolutionary factor, dreaded by the enemy as the greatest menace to its rule.

It was in the year 1900, while a delegate to the Anarchist Congress in Paris, that I first came in contact with Syndicalism in operation. The Anarchist press had been discussing the subject for years prior to that: therefore we Anarchists knew something about Syndicalism. But those of us who lived in America had to content themselves with the theoretic side of it.

In 1900, however, I saw its effect upon labor in France: the strength, the enthusiasm and hope with which Syndicalism inspired the workers. It was also my good fortune to learn of the man who more than anyone else had directed Syndicalism into definite working channels, Fernand Pelloutier. Unfortunately, I could not meet thus remarkable young man, as he was at that time already very ill with cancer. But wherever I went, with whomever I spoke, the love and devotion for Pelloutier was wonderful, all agreeing that it was he who had gathered the discontented forces in the French labor movement and imbued them with new life and a new purpose, that of Syndicalism.

On my return to America I immediately began to propagate Syndicalist ideas, especially Direct Action and the General Strike. But it was like talking to the Rocky Mountains—no understanding, even among the more radical elements, and complete indifference in labor ranks.

In 1907 I went as a delegate to the Anarchist Congress at Amsterdam and, while in Paris, met the most active Syndicalists in the Confederation Generale du Travail: Pouget, Delesalle, Monatte, and many others. More than that, I had the opportunity to see Syndicalism in daily operation, in its most constructive and inspiring forms.

I allude to this, to indicate that my knowledge of Syndicalism does not come from Sorel, Lagardelle, or Berth, but from actual contact with and observation of the tremendous work carried on by the workers of Paris within the ranks of the Confederation. It would require a volume to explain in detail what Syndicalism is doing for the French workers. In the American press you read only of its resistive methods, of strikes and sabotage, of the conflicts of labor with capital. These are no doubt very important matters, and yet the chief value of Syndicalism lies much deeper. It lies in the constructive and educational effect upon the life and thought of the masses.

The fundamental difference between Syndicalism and the old trade union methods is this: while the old trade unions, without exception, move within the wage system and capitalism, recognizing the latter as inevitable, Syndicalism repudiates and condemns present industrial arrangements as unjust and criminal, and holds out no hope to the worker for lasting results from this system.

Of course Syndicalism, like the old trade unions, fights for immediate gains, but it is not stupid enough to pretend that labor can expect humane conditions from inhuman economic arrangements in society. Thus it merely wrests from the enemy what it can force him to yield; on the whole, however, Syndicalism aims at, and concentrates its energies upon, the complete overthrow of the wage system. Indeed, Syndicalism goes further: it aims to liberate labor from every institution that has not for its object the free development of production for the benefit of all humanity. In short, the ultimate purpose of Syndicalism is to reconstruct society from its present centralized, authoritative and brutal state to one based upon the free, federated grouping of the workers along lines of economic and social liberty.

With this object in view, Syndicalism works in two directions: first, by undermining the existing institutions; secondly, by developing and educating the workers and cultivating their spirit of solidarity, to prepare them for a full, free life, when capitalism shall have been abolished.

Syndicalism is, in essence, the economic expression of Anarchism. That circumstance accounts for the presence of so many Anarchists in the Syndicalist movement. Like Anarchism, Syndicalism prepares the workers along direct economic lines, as conscious factors in the great struggles of today, as well as conscious factors in the task of reconstructing society along autonomous industrial lines, as against the paralyzing spirit of centralization with its bureaucratic machinery of corruption, inherent in all political parties.

Realizing that the diametrically opposed interests of capital and labor can never be reconciled, Syndicalism must needs repudiate the old rusticated, worn-out methods of trade unionism, and declare for an open war against the capitalist regime, as well as against every institution which today supports and protects capitalism.

As a logical sequence Syndicalism, in its daily warfare against capitalism, rejects the contract system, because it does not consider labor and capital equals, hence cannot consent to an agreement which the one has the power to break, while the other must submit to without redress.

For similar reasons Syndicalism rejects negotiations in labor disputes, because such a procedure serves only to give the enemy time to prepare his end of the fight, thus defeating the very object the workers set out to accomplish. Also, Syndicalism stands for spontaneity, both as a preserver of the fighting strength of labor and also because it takes the enemy unawares, hence compels him to a speedy settlement or causes him great loss.

Syndicalism objects to a large union treasury, because money is as corrupting an element in the ranks of labor as it is in those of capitalism. We in America know this to be only too true. If the labor movement in this country were not backed by such large funds, it would not be as conservative as it is, nor would the leaders be so readily corrupted. However, the main reason for the opposition of Syndicalism to large treasuries consists in the fact that they create class distinctions and jealousies within the ranks of labor, so detrimental to the spirit of solidarity. The worker whose organization has a large purse considers himself superior to his poorer brother, just as he regards himself better than the man who earns fifty cents less per day.

The chief ethical value of Syndicalism consists in the stress it lays upon the necessity of labor getting rid of the element of dissension, parasitism and corruption in its ranks. It seeks to cultivate devotion, solidarity and enthusiasm, which are far more essential and vital in the economic struggle than money.

As I have already stated, Syndicalism has grown out of the disappointment of the workers with politics and parliamentary methods. In the course of its development Syndicalism has learned to see in the State—with its mouthpiece, the representative system—one of the strongest supports of capitalism; just as it has learned that the army and the church are the chief pillars of the State.

It is therefore that Syndicalism has turned its back upon parliamentarism and political machines, and has set its face toward the economic arena wherein alone gladiator Labor can meet his foe successfully.

Historic experience sustains the Syndicalists in their uncompromising opposition to parliamentarism. Many had entered political life and, unwilling to be corrupted by the atmosphere, withdrew from office, to devote themselves to the economic struggle—Proudhon, the Dutch revolutionist Nieuwenhuis, John Most and numerous others. While those who remained in the parliamentary quagmire ended by betraying their trust, without having gained anything for labor. But it is unnecessary to discuss here political history. Suffice to say that Syndicalists are anti-parlamentarians as a result of bitter experience.

Equally so has experience determined their anti-military attitude. Time and again has the army been used to shoot down strikers and to inculcate the sickening idea of patriotism, for the purpose of dividing the workers against themselves and helping the masters to the spoils. The inroads that Syndicalist agitation has made into the superstition of patriotism are evident from the dread of the ruling class for the loyalty of the army, and the rigid persecution of the anti-militarists. Naturally—for the ruling class realizes much better than the workers that when the soldiers will refuse to obey their superiors, the whole system of capitalism will be doomed.

Indeed, why should the workers sacrifice their children that the latter may be used to shoot their own parents? Therefore Syndicalism is not merely logical in its anti-military agitation; it is most practical and far-reaching, inasmuch as it robs the enemy of his strongest weapon against labor.

Now, as to the methods employed by Syndicalism—Direct Action, Sabotage, and the General Strike.

Direct Action. Conscious individual or collective effort to protest against, or remedy, social conditions through the systematic assertion of the economic power of the workers.

Sabotage has been decried as criminal, even by so-called revolutionary Socialists. Of course, if you believe that property, which excludes the producer from its use, is justifiable, then sabotage is indeed a crime. But unless a Socialist continues to be under the influence of our bourgeois morality—a morality which enables the few to monopolize the earth at the expense of the many—he cannot consistently maintain that capitalist property is inviolate. Sabotage undermines this form of private possession. Can it therefore be considered criminal? On the contrary, it is ethical in the best sense, since it helps society to get rid of its worst foe, the most detrimental factor of social life.

Sabotage is mainly concerned with obstructing, by every possible method, the regular process of production, thereby demonstrating the determination of the workers to give according to what they receive, and no more. For instance, at the time of the French railroad strike of 1910, perishable goods were sent in slow trains, or in an opposite direction from the one intended. Who but the most ordinary Philistine will call that a crime? If the railway men themselves go hungry, and the "innocent" public has not enough feeling of solidarity to insist that these men should get enough to live on, the public has forfeited the sympathy of the strikers and must take the consequences.

Another form of sabotage consisted, during this strike, in placing heavy boxes on goods marked "Handle with care," cut glass and china and precious wines. From the standpoint of the law this may have been a crime, but from the standpoint of common humanity it was a very sensible thing. The same is true of disarranging a loom in a weaving mill, or living up to the letter of the law with all its red tape, as the Italian railway men did, thereby causing confusion in the railway service. In other words, sabotage is merely a weapon of defense in the industrial warfare, which is the more effective, because it touches capitalism in its most vital spot, the pocket.

By the General Strike, Syndicalism means a stoppage of work, the cessation of labor. Nor need such a strike be postponed until all the workers of a particular place or country are ready for it. As has been pointed out by Pelloutier, Pouget, as well as others, and particularly by recent events in England, the General Strike may be started by one industry and exert a tremendous force. It is as if one man suddenly raised the cry "Stop the thief!" Immediately others will take up the cry, till the air rings with it. The General Strike, initiated by one determined organization, by one industry or by a small, conscious minority among the workers, is the industrial cry of "Stop the thief," which is soon taken up by many other industries, spreading like wildfire in a very short time.

One of the objections of politicians to the General Strike is that the workers also would suffer for the necessaries of life. In the first place, the workers are past masters in going hungry; secondly, it is certain that a General Strike is surer of prompt settlement than an ordinary strike. Witness the transport and miner strikes in England: how quickly the lords of State and capital were forced to make peace! Besides, Syndicalism recognizes the right of the producers to the things which they have created; namely, the right of the workers to help themselves if the strike does not meet with speedy settlement.

When Sorel maintains that the General Strike is an inspiration necessary for the people to give their life meaning, he is expressing a thought which the Anarchists have never tired of emphasizing. Yet I do not hold with Sorel that the General Strike is a "social myth," that may never be realized. I think that the General Strike will become a fact the moment labor understands its full value—its destructive as well as constructive value, as indeed many workers all over the world are beginning to realize.

These ideas and methods of Syndicalism some may consider entirely negative, though they are far from it in their effect upon society today. But Syndicalism has also a directly positive aspect. In fact, much more time and effort is being devoted to that phase than to the others. Various forms of Syndicalist activity are designed to prepare the workers, even within present social and industrial conditions, for the life of a new and better society. To that end the masses are trained in the spirit of mutual aid and brotherhood, their initiative and self-reliance developed, and an esprit de corps maintained whose very soul is solidarity of purpose and the community of interests of the international proletariat.

Chief among these activities are the *mutualites*, or mutual aid societies, established by the French Syndicalists. Their object is, foremost, to secure work for unemployed members, and to further that spirit of mutual assistance which rests upon the consciousness of labor's identity of interests throughout the world.

In his "The Labor Movement in France," Mr. L. Levine states that during the year 1902 over 74,000 workers, out of a total of 99,000 applicants, were provided with work by these societies, without being compelled to submit to the extortion of the employment bureau sharks.

These latter are a source of the deepest degradation, as well as of most shameless exploitation, of the worker. Especially does it hold true of America, where the employment agencies are in many cases also masked detective agencies, supplying workers in need of employment to strike regions, under false promises of steady, remunerative employment.

The French Confederation had long realized the vicious role of employment agencies as leeches upon the jobless worker and nurseries of scabbery. By the threat of a General Strike the French Syndicalists forced the government to abolish the employment bureau sharks, and the workers' own *mutualites* have almost entirely superseded them, to the great economic and moral advantage of labor.

Besides the *mutualites*, the French Syndicalists have established other activities tending to weld labor in closer bonds of solidarity and mutual aid. Among these are the efforts to assist workingmen journeying from place to place. The practical as well as ethical value of such assistance is inestimable. It serves to instill the spirit of fellowship and gives a sense of security in the feeling of oneness with the large family of labor. This is one of the vital effects of the Syndicalist spirit in France and other Latin countries. What a tremendous need there is for just such efforts in this country! Can anyone doubt the significance of the consciousness of working-men coming from

Chicago, for instance, to New York, sure to find there among their comrades welcome lodging and food until they have secured employment? This form of activity is entirely foreign to the labor bodies of this country, and as a result the traveling workman in search of a job—the "blanket stiff"—is constantly at the mercy of the constable and policeman, a victim of the vagrancy laws, and the unfortunate material whence is recruited, through stress of necessity, the army of scabdom.

I have repeatedly witnessed, while at the headquarters of the Confederation, the cases of workingmen who came with their union cards from various parts of France, and even from other countries of Europe, and were supplied with meals and lodging, and encouraged by every evidence of brotherly spirit, and made to feel at home by their fellow workers of the Confederation. It is due, to a great extent, to these activities of the Syndicalists that the French government is forced to employ the army for strikebreaking, because few workers are willing to lend themselves for such service, thanks to the efforts and tactics of Syndicalism.

No less in importance than the mutual aid activities of the Syndicalists is the cooperation established by them between the city and the country, the factory worker and the peasant or farmer, the latter providing the workers with food supplies during strikes, or taking care of the strikers' children. This form of practical solidarity has for the first time been tried in this country during the Lawrence strike, with inspiring results.

And all these Syndicalist activities are permeated with the spirit of educational work, carried on systematically by evening classes on all vital subjects treated from an unbiased, libertarian standpoint—not the adulterated "knowledge" with which the minds are stuffed in our public schools. The scope of the education is truly phenomenal, including sex hygiene, the care of women during pregnancy and confinement, the care of home and children, sanitation and general hygiene; in fact, every branch of human knowledge—science, history, art—receives thorough attention, together with the practical application in the established workingmen's libraries, dispensaries, concerts and festivals, in which the greatest artists and literati of Paris consider it an honor to participate.

One of the most vital efforts of Syndicalism is to prepare the workers, now, for their role in a free society. Thus the Syndicalist organizations supply its members with textbooks on every trade and industry, of a character that is calculated to make the worker an adept in his chosen line, a master of his craft, for the purpose of familiarizing him with all the branches of his industry, so that when labor finally takes over production and distribution, the people will be fully prepared to manage successfully their own affairs.

A demonstration of the effectiveness of this educational campaign of Syndicalism is given by the railroad men of Italy, whose mastery of all the details of transportation is so great that they could offer to the Italian government to take over the railroads of the country and guarantee their operation with greater economy and fewer accidents than is at present done by the government.

Their ability to carry on production has been strikingly proved by the Syndicalists, in connection with the glass blowers' strike in Italy. There the strikers, instead of remaining idle during the progress of the strike, decided themselves to carry on the production of glass. The wonderful spirit of solidarity resulting from the Syndicalist propaganda enabled them to build a glass factory within an incredibly short time. An old building, rented for the purpose and which would have ordinarily required months to be put into proper condition, was turned into a glass factory within a few weeks, by the solidaric efforts of the strikers aided by their comrades who toiled with them after working hours. Then the strikers began operating the glass-blowing factory, and their cooperative plan of work and distribution during the strike has proved so satisfactory in every way that the experimental factory has been made permanent and a part of the glass-blowing industry in Italy is now in the hands of the cooperative organization of the workers.

This method of applied education not only trains the worker in his daily struggle, but serves also to equip him for the battle royal and the future, when he is to assume his place in society as an intelligent, conscious being and useful producer, once capitalism is abolished.

Nearly all leading Syndicalists agree with the Anarchists that a free society can exist only through voluntary association, and that its ultimate success will depend upon the intellectual and moral development of the workers who will supplant the wage system with a new social arrangement, based on solidarity and economic well-being for all. That is Syndicalism, in theory and practice.

The Philosophy of Atheism

Mother Earth, February 1916.

To give an adequate exposition of the Philosophy of Atheism, it would be necessary to go into the historical changes of the belief in a Deity, from its earliest beginning to the present day. But that is not within the scope of the present paper. However, it is not out of place to mention, in passing, that the concept God, Supernatural Power, Spirit, Deity, or in whatever other term the essence of Theism may have found expression, has become more indefinite and obscure in the course of time and progress. In other words, the God idea is growing more impersonal and nebulous in proportion as the human mind is learning to understand natural phenomena and in the degree that science progressively correlates human and social events.

God, today, no longer represents the same forces as in the beginning of His existence; neither does He direct human destiny with the same iron hand as of yore. Rather does the God idea express a sort of spiritualistic stimulus to satisfy the fads and fancies of every shade of human weakness. In the course of human development the God idea has been forced to adapt itself to every phase of human affairs, which is perfectly consistent with the origin of the idea itself.

The conception of gods originated in fear and curiosity. Primitive man, unable to understand the phenomena of nature and harassed by them, saw in every terrifying manifestation some sinister force expressly directed against him; and as ignorance and fear are the parents of all superstition, the troubled fancy of primitive man wove the God idea.

Very aptly, the world-renowned atheist and anarchist, Michael Bakunin, says in his great work *God and the State*: "All religions, with their gods, their demi-gods, and their prophets, their messiahs and their saints, were created by the prejudiced fancy of men who had not attained the full development and full possession of their faculties. Consequently, the religious heaven is nothing but the mirage in which man, exalted by ignorance and faith, discovered his own image, but enlarged and reversed—that is divinised. The history of religions, of the birth, grandeur, and the decline of the gods who had succeeded one another in human belief, is nothing, therefore, but the development of the collective intelligence and conscience of mankind. As fast as they discovered, in the course of their historically progressive advance, either in themselves or in external nature, a quality, or even any great defect whatever, they attributed it to their gods, after having exaggerated and enlarged it beyond measure, after the manner of children, by an act of their religious fancy. . . . With all due respect, then, to the metaphysicians and religious idealists, philosophers, politicians or poets: the idea of God implies the abdication of human reason and justice; it is the most decisive negation of human liberty, and necessarily ends in the enslavement of mankind, both in theory and practice."

Thus the God idea, revived, readjusted, and enlarged or narrowed, according to the necessity of the time, has dominated humanity and will continue to do so until man will raise his head to the sunlit day, unafraid and with an awakened will to himself. In proportion as man learns to realize himself and mold his own destiny theism becomes superfluous. How far man will be able to find his relation to his fellows will depend entirely upon how much he can outgrow his dependence upon God.

Already there are indications that theism, which is the theory of speculation, is being replaced by Atheism, the science of demonstration; the one hangs in the metaphysical clouds of the Beyond, while the other has its roots firmly in the soil. It is the earth, not heaven, which man must rescue if he is truly to be saved.

The decline of theism is a most interesting spectacle, especially as manifested in the anxiety of the theists, whatever their particular brand. They realize, much to their distress, that the masses are growing daily more atheistic, more anti-religious; that they are quite willing to leave the Great Beyond and its heavenly domain to the angels and sparrows; because more and more the masses are becoming engrossed in the problems of their immediate existence.

How to bring the masses back to the God idea, the spirit, the First Cause, etc. — that is the most pressing question to all theists. Metaphysical as all these questions seem to be, they yet have a very marked physical background. Inasmuch as religion, "Divine Truth," rewards and punishments are the trade-marks of the largest, the most corrupt and pernicious, the most powerful and lucrative industry in the world, not excepting the industry of manufacturing guns and munitions. It is the industry of befogging the human mind and stifling the human heart. Necessity knows no law; hence the majority of theists are compelled to take up every subject, even if it has no bearing upon a deity or revelation or the Great Beyond. Perhaps they sense the fact that humanity is growing weary of the hundred and one brands of God.

How to raise this dead level of theistic belief is really a matter of life and death for all denominations. Therefore their tolerance; but it is a tolerance not of understanding, but of weakness. Perhaps that explains the efforts fostered in all religious publications to combine variegated religious philosophies and conflicting theistic theories into one denominational trust. More and more, the various concepts "of the only true God, the only pure spirit, the only true religion" are tolerantly glossed over in the frantic effort to establish a common ground to rescue the modern mass from the "pernicious" influence of atheistic ideas.

It is characteristic of theistic "tolerance" that no one really cares what the people believe in, just so they believe or pretend to believe. To accomplish this end, the crudest and vulgarest methods are being used. Religious endeavor meetings and revivals with Billy Sunday as their champion—methods which must outrage every refined sense, and which in their effect upon the ignorant and curious often tend to create a mild state of insanity not infrequently coupled with erotomania. All these frantic efforts find approval and support from the earthly powers; from the Russian despot to the American President; from Rockefeller and Wanamaker down to the pettiest business man. They know that capital invested in Billy Sunday, the Y.M.C.A., Christian Science, and various other religious institutions will return enormous profits from the subdued, tamed, and dull masses.

Consciously or unconsciously, most theists see in gods and devils, heaven and hell, reward and punishment, a whip to lash the people into obedience, meekness and contentment. The truth is that theism would have lost its footing long before this but for the combined support of Mammon and power. How thoroughly bankrupt it really is, is being demonstrated in the trenches and battlefields of Europe today.

Have not all theists painted their Deity as the god of love and goodness? Yet after thousands of years of such preachments the gods remain deaf to the agony of the human race. Confucius cares not for the poverty, squalor and misery of people of China. Buddha remains undisturbed in his philosophical indifference to the famine and starvation of outraged Hindus; Jahwe continues deaf to the bitter cry of Israel; while Jesus refuses to rise from the dead against his Christians who are butchering each other.

The burden of all song and praise "unto the Highest" has been that God stands for justice and mercy. Yet injustice among men is ever on the increase; the outrages committed against the masses in this country alone would seem enough to overflow the very heavens. But where are the gods to make an end to all these horrors, these wrongs, this inhumanity to man? No, not the gods, but *man* must rise in his mighty wrath. He, deceived by all the deities, betrayed by their emissaries, he, himself, must undertake to usher in justice upon the earth.

The philosophy of Atheism expresses the expansion and growth of the human mind. The philosophy of theism, if we can call it philosophy, is static and fixed. Even the mere attempt to pierce these mysteries represents, from the theistic point of view, non-belief in the all-embracing omnipotence and even a denial of the wisdom of the divine powers outside of man. Fortunately, however, the human mind never was, and never can be, bound by fixities. Hence it is forging ahead in its restless march towards knowledge and life. The human mind is realizing "that the universe is not the result of a creative fiat by some divine intelligence, out of nothing, producing a masterpiece chaotic in perfect operation," but that it is the product of chaotic forces operating through eons of time, of clashes and cataclysms, of repulsion and attraction crystallizing through the principle of selection into what the theists call "the universe guided into order and beauty." As Joseph McCabe well points out in his *Existence of God*: "a law of nature is not a formula drawn up by a legislator, but a mere summary of the observed facts — a 'bundle of facts.' Things do not act in a particular way because there is a law, but we state the 'law' because they act in that way."

The philosophy of Atheism represents a concept of life without any metaphysical Beyond or Divine Regulator. It is the concept of an actual, real world with its liberating, expanding and beautifying possibilities, as against an unreal world, which, with its spirits, oracles, and mean contentment has kept humanity in helpless degradation.

It may seem a wild paradox, and yet it is pathetically true, that this real, visible world and our life should have been so long under the influence of metaphysical speculation, rather than of physical demonstrable forces. Under the lash of the theistic idea, this earth has served no other purpose than as a temporary station to test man's capacity for immolation to the will of God. But the moment man attempted to ascertain the nature of that will, he was told that it was utterly futile for "finite human intelligence" to get beyond the all-powerful infinite will. Under the terrific weight of this omnipotence, man has been bowed into the dust—a will-less creature, broken and sweating in the dark. The triumph of the philosophy of Atheism is to free man from the nightmare of gods; it means the dissolution of the phantoms of the beyond. Again and again the light of reason has dispelled the theistic nightmare, but poverty, misery and fear have recreated the phantoms—though whether old or new, whatever their external form, they differed little in their essence. Atheism, on the other hand, in its philosophic aspect refuses allegiance not merely to a definite concept of God, but it refuses all servitude to the God idea, and opposes the theistic principle as such. Gods in their individual function are not half as pernicious as the principle of theism which represents the belief in a supernatural, or even omnipotent, power to rule the earth and man upon it. It is the absolutism of theism, its pernicious influence upon humanity, its paralyzing effect upon thought and action, which Atheism is fighting with all its power.

The philosophy of Atheism has its root in the earth, in this life; its aim is the emancipation of the human race from all Godheads, be they Judaic, Christian, Mohammedan, Buddhistic, Brahministic, or what not. Mankind has been punished long and heavily for having created its gods; nothing but pain and persecution have been man's lot since gods began. There is but one way out of this blunder: Man must break his fetters which have chained him to the gates of heaven and hell, so that he can begin to fashion out of his reawakened and illumined consciousness a new world upon earth.

Only after the triumph of the Atheistic philosophy in the minds and hearts of man will freedom and beauty be realized. Beauty as a gift from heaven has proved useless. It will, however, become the essence and impetus of life when man learns to see in the earth the only heaven fit for man. Atheism is already helping to free man from his dependence upon punishment and reward as the heavenly bargain-counter for the poor in spirit.

Do not all theists insist that there can be no morality, no justice, honesty or fidelity without the belief in a Divine Power? Based upon fear and hope, such morality has always been a vile product, imbued partly with self-righteousness, partly with hypocrisy. As to truth, justice, and fidelity, who have been their brave exponents and daring proclaimers? Nearly always the godless ones: the Atheists; they lived, fought, and died for them. They knew that justice, truth, and fidelity are not conditioned in heaven, but that they are related to and interwoven with the tremendous changes going on in the social and material life of the human race; not fixed and eternal, but fluctuating, even as life itself. To what heights the philosophy of Atheism may yet attain, no one can prophesy. But this much can already be predicted: only by its regenerating fire will human relations be purged from the horrors of the past

Thoughtful people are beginning to realize that moral precepts, imposed upon humanity through religious terror, have become stereotyped and have therefore lost all vitality. A glance at life today, at its disintegrating character, its conflicting interests with their hatreds, crimes, and greed, suffices to prove the sterility of theistic morality.

Man must get back to himself before he can learn his relation to his fellows. Prometheus chained to the Rock of Ages is doomed to remain the prey of the vultures of darkness. Unbind Prometheus, and you dispel the night and its horrors.

Atheism in its negation of gods is at the same time the strongest affirmation of man, and through man, the eternal yea to life, purpose, and beauty.

Minorities versus Majorities

1917

If I were to give a summary of the tendency of our times, I would say, Quantity. The multitude, the mass spirit, dominates everywhere, destroying quality. Our entire life—production, politics, and education—rests on quantity, on numbers. The worker who once took pride in the thoroughness and quality of his work has been replaced by brainless, incompetent automatons, who turn out enormous quantities of things, valueless to themselves, and generally injurious to the rest of mankind. Thus quantity, instead of adding to life's comforts and peace, has merely increased man's burden.

In politics, naught but quantity counts. In proportion to its increase, however, principles, ideals, justice, and uprightness are completely swamped by the array of numbers. In the struggle for supremacy the various political parties outdo each other in trickery, deceit, cunning, and shady machinations, confident that the one who succeeds is sure to be hailed by the majority as the victor. That is the only god—Success. As to what expense, what terrible cost to character, is of no moment. We have not far to go in search of proof to verify this sad fact.

Never before did the corruption, the complete rottenness of our government, stand so thoroughly exposed; never before were the American people brought face to face with the Judas nature of that political body, which has claimed for years to be absolutely beyond reproach, as the mainstay of our institutions, the true protector of the rights and liberties of the people.

Yet when the crimes of that party became so brazen that even the blind could see them, it needed but to muster up its minions, and its supremacy was assured. Thus the very victims, duped, betrayed, outraged a hundred times, decided, not against, but in favor of the victor. Bewildered, the few asked how could the majority betray the traditions of American liberty? Where was its judgment, its reasoning capacity? That is just it, the majority cannot reason; it has no judgment. Lacking utterly in originality and moral courage, the majority has always placed its destiny in the hands of others. Incapable of standing responsibilities, it has followed its leaders even unto destruction. Dr. Stockman was right: "The most dangerous enemies of truth and justice in our midst are the compact majorities, the damned compact majority." Without ambition or initiative, the compact mass hates nothing so much as innovation. It has always opposed, condemned, and hounded the innovator, the pioneer of a new truth.

The oft-repeated slogan of our time is, among all politicians, the Socialists included, that ours is an era of individualism, of the minority. Only those who do not probe beneath the surface might be led to entertain this view. Have not the few accumulated the wealth of the world? Are they not the masters, the absolute kings of the situation? Their success, however, is due not to individualism, but to the inertia, the cravenness, the utter submission of the mass. The latter wants but to be dominated, to be led, to be coerced. As to individualism, at no time in human history did it have less chance of expression, less opportunity to assert itself in a normal, healthy manner.

The individual educator imbued with honesty of purpose, the artist or writer of original ideas, the independent scientist or explorer, the non-compromising pioneers of social changes, are daily pushed to the wall by men whose learning and creative ability have become decrepit with age.

Educators of Ferrer's type are nowhere tolerated, while the dieticians of predigested food, a la Professors Eliot and Butler, are the successful perpetuators of an age of nonentities, of automatons. In the literary and dramatic world, the Humphrey Wards and Clyde Fitches are the idols of the mass, while but few know or appreciate the beauty and genius of an Emerson, Thoreau, Whitman; an Ibsen, a Hauptmann, a Butler Yeats, or a Stephen Phillips. They are like solitary stars, far beyond the horizon of the multitude.

Publishers, theatrical managers, and critics ask not for the quality inherent in creative art, but will it meet with a good sale, will it suit the palate of the people? Alas, this palate is like a dumping ground; it relishes anything that needs no mental mastication. As a result, the mediocre, the ordinary, the commonplace represents the chief literary output.

Need I say that in art we are confronted with the same sad facts? One has but to inspect our parks and thoroughfares to realize the hideousness and vulgarity of the art manufacture. Certainly, none but a majority taste would tolerate such an outrage on art. False in conception and barbarous in execution, the statuary that infests American cities has as much relation to true art, as a totem to a Michaelangelo. Yet that is the only art that succeeds. The true artistic genius, who will not cater to accepted notions, who exercises originality, and strives to be true to life, leads an obscure and wretched existence. His work may some day become the fad of the mob, but not until his heart's blood had been exhausted; not until the pathfinder has ceased to be, and a throng of an idealless and visionless mob has done to death the heritage of the master.

It is said that the artist of today cannot create because Prometheus-like he is bound to the rock of economic necessity. This, however, is true of art in all ages. Michaelangelo was dependent on his patron saint, no less than the sculptor or painter of today, except that the art connoisseurs of those days were far away from the madding crowd. They felt honored to be permitted to worship at the shrine of the master.

The art protector of our time knows but one criterion, one value — the dollar. He is not concerned about the quality of any great work, but in the quantity of dollars his purchase implies. Thus the financier in Mirbeau's *Les Affaires sont les Affaires* points to some blurred arrangement in colors, saying: "See how great it is; it cost 50,000 francs." Just like our own parvenus. The fabulous figures paid for their great art discoveries must make up for the poverty of their taste.

The most unpardonable sin in society is independence of thought. That this should be so terribly apparent in a country whose symbol is democracy, is very significant of the tremendous power of the majority.

Wendell Phillips said fifty years ago: "In our country of absolute democratic equality, public opinion is not only omnipotent, it is omnipresent. There is no refuge from its tyranny, there is no hiding from its reach, and the result is that if you take the old Greek lantern and go about to seek among a hundred, you will not find a single American who has not, or who does not fancy at least he has, something to gain or lose in his ambition, his social life, or business, from the good opinion and the votes of those around him. And the consequence is that instead of being a mass of individuals, each one fearlessly blurting out his own conviction, as a nation compared to other nations we are a mass of cowards. More than any other people we are afraid of each other." Evidently we have not advanced very far from the condition that confronted Wendell Phillips.

Today, as then, public opinion is the omnipresent tyrant; today, as then, the majority represents a mass of cowards, willing to accept him who mirrors its own soul and mind poverty. That accounts for the unprecedented rise of a man like Roosevelt. He embodies the very worst element of mob psychology. A politician, he knows that the majority cares little for ideals or integrity. What it craves is display. It matters not whether that be a dog show, a prize fight, the lynching of a "nigger," the rounding up of some petty offender, the marriage exposition of an heiress, or the acrobatic stunts of an ex-president. The more hideous the mental contortions, the greater the delight and bravos of the mass. Thus, poor in ideals and vulgar of soul, Roosevelt continues to be the man of the hour.

On the other hand, men towering high above such political pygmies, men of refinement, of culture, of ability, are jeered into silence as mollycoddles. It is absurd to claim that ours is the era of individualism. Ours is merely a more poignant repetition of the phenomenon of all history: every effort for progress, for enlightenment, for science, for religious, political and economic liberty, emanates from the minority, and not from the mass. Today, as ever, the few are misunderstood, hounded, imprisoned, tortured, and killed.

The principle of brotherhood expounded by the agitator of Nazareth preserved the germ of life, of truth and justice, so long as it was the beacon light of the few. The moment the majority seized upon it, that great principle became a shibboleth and harbinger of blood and fire, spreading suffering and disaster. The attack on the omnipotence of Rome, led by the colossal figures of Huss, Calvin, and Luther, was like a sunrise amid the darkness of the night. But so soon as Luther and Calvin turned politicians and began catering to the small potentates, the nobility, and the mob spirit, they jeopardized the great possibilities of the Reformation. They won success and the majority, but that majority proved no less cruel and bloodthirsty in the persecution of thought and reason than was the Catholic monster. Woe to the heretics, to the minority, who would not bow to its dicta. After infinite zeal, endurance, and sacrifice, the human mind is at last free from the religious phantom; the minority has gone on in pursuit of new conquests, and the majority is lagging behind, handicapped by truth grown false with age.

Politically the human race should still be in the most absolute slavery, were it not for the John Balls, the Wat Tylers, the Tells, the innumerable individual giants who fought inch by inch against the power of kings and tyrants. But for individual pioneers the world would have never been shaken to its very roots by that tremendous wave, the French Revolution. Great events are usually preceded by apparently small things. Thus the eloquence and fire of Camille Desmoulins was like the trumpet before Jericho, razing to the ground that emblem of torture, of abuse, of horror, the Bastille.

Always, at every period, the few were the banner bearers of a great idea, of liberating effort. Not so the mass, the leaden weight of which does not let it move. The truth of this is borne out in Russia with greater force than elsewhere. Thousands of lives have already been consumed by that bloody regime, yet the monster on the throne is not appeased. How is such a thing possible when ideas, culture, literature, when the deepest and finest emotions groan under the iron yoke? The majority, that compact, immobile, drowsy mass, the Russian peasant, after a century of struggle, of sacrifice, of untold misery, still believes that the rope which strangles "the man with the white hands" brings luck.

In the American struggle for liberty, the majority was no less of a stumbling block. Until this very day the ideas of Jefferson, of Patrick Henry, of Thomas Paine, are denied and sold by their posterity. The mass wants none of them. The greatness and courage worshipped in Lincoln have been forgotten in the men who created the background for the panorama of that time. The true patron saints of the black men were represented in that handful of fighters in Boston, Lloyd Garrison, Wendell Phillips, Thoreau, Margaret Fuller, and Theodore Parker, whose great courage and sturdiness culminated in that somber giant John Brown. Their untiring zeal, their eloquence and perseverance undermined the stronghold of the Southern lords. Lincoln and his minions followed only when abolition had become a practical issue, recognized as such by all.

About fifty years ago, a meteorlike idea made its appearance on the social horizon of the world, an idea so far-reaching, so revolutionary, so all-embracing, as to spread terror in the hearts of tyrants everywhere. On the other hand, that idea was a harbinger of joy, of cheer, of hope to the millions. The pioneers knew the difficulties in their way, they knew the opposition, the persecution, the hardships that would meet them, but proud and unafraid they started on their march onward, ever onward. Now that idea has become a popular slogan. Almost everyone is a Socialist today: the rich man, as well as his poor victim; the upholders of law and authority, as well as their unfortunate culprits; the freethinker, as well as the perpetuator of religious falsehoods; the fashionable lady, as well as the shirtwaist girl. Why not? Now that the truth of fifty years ago has become a lie, now that it has been clipped of all its youthful imagination, and been robbed of its vigor, its strength, its revolutionary ideal — why not? Now that it is no longer a beautiful vision, but a "practical, workable scheme," resting on the will of the majority, why not? Political cunning ever sings the praise of the mass: the poor majority, the outraged, the abused, the giant majority, if only it would follow us.

Who has not heard this litany before? Who does not know this never-varying refrain of all politicians? That the mass bleeds, that it is being robbed and exploited, I know as well as our vote-baiters. But I insist that not the handful of parasites, but the mass itself is responsible for this horrible state of affairs. It clings to its masters, loves the whip, and is the first to cry Crucify! the moment a protesting voice is raised against the sacredness of capitalistic authority or any other decayed institution. Yet how long would authority and private property exist, if not for the willingness of the mass to become soldiers, policemen, jailers, and hangmen. The Socialist demagogues know that as well as I, but they maintain the myth of the virtues of the majority, because their very scheme of life means the perpetuation of power. And how could the latter be acquired without numbers? Yes, authority, coercion, and dependence rest on the mass, but never freedom or the free unfoldment of the individual, never the birth of a free society.

Not because I do not feel with the oppressed, the disinherited of the earth; not because I do not know the shame, the horror, the indignity of the lives the people lead, do I repudiate the majority as a creative force for good. Oh, no, no! But because I know so well that as a compact mass it has never stood for justice or equality. It has suppressed the human voice, subdued the human spirit, chained the human body. As a mass its aim has always been to make life uniform, gray, and monotonous as the desert. As a mass it will always be the annihilator of individuality, of free initiative, of originality. I therefore believe with Emerson that "the masses are crude, lame, pernicious in their demands and influence, and need not to be flattered, but to be schooled. I wish not to concede anything to them, but to drill, divide, and break them up, and draw individuals out of them. Masses! The calamity are the masses. I do not wish any mass at all, but honest men only, lovely, sweet, accomplished women only."

In other words, the living, vital truth of social and economic well-being will become a reality only through the zeal, courage, the non-compromising determination of intelligent minorities, and not through the mass.

Speech Against Conscription and War

June 14, 1917

THE CHAIRMAN: The next speaker is one who is well known to you. I shall not waste words or time in introducing her but I want to tell you that before she came to the meeting tonight somebody telephoned to her and told her, "If you go to that meeting you will not get home alive." I simply want to introduce a woman who has more courage than half a dozen regiments (tremendous cheering and applause at 9:12 P.M.) I introduce to you—(interrupted by applause and cheers). Some young man said, "Who loves Emma Goldman? We all do." Great cheering and applause.)

EMMA GOLDMAN: This is not the place to applaud or shout Hurrah for Emma Goldman. We have more serious things to talk about and some serious things to do. First of all I wish to say to you, all of you, workers, men and women from the East Side, that I regret deeply that I cannot speak to you in the language I have always spoken from this platform; that I cannot speak to you tonight in Yiddish. I shall speak English because I want those representing the State and Militarism and the Courts and Prisons to understand what I have to say. (Miss Goldman's remarks were so frequently interrupted by cheering and applause that reference to such interruptions will not be made in this report further.) I don't want them to get it secondhand. No language is ever rendered well in translation and I want them to hear what I have to say in the only language they can speak, and speak it poorly.

Friends, tomorrow morning I am sure that you will read the report that a meeting took place on the East Side attended by foreigners, by workmen, and ill-kempt, poorly washed people of the East Side—foreigners who are being jeered at the present time in this country, foreigners who are being ridiculed because they have an idea. Well, friends, if the Americans are to wait until Americans wake up the country they will have to resurrect the Indians who were killed in America and upon whose bodies this so-called democracy was established, because every other American, if you scratch him, you will find him to be an Englishman, Dutchman, Frenchman, Spaniard, a Jew, and a German and a hundred and one other nationalities who sent their young men and their women to this country in the foolish belief that liberty was awaiting them at the American Harbor, Liberty holding a torch. That torch has been burning dimly in the United States for a very long time. It is because the Goddess of Liberty is ashamed of the American people and what they have done in the name of liberty to liberty in the United States. And yet, friends, I am not sorry for the things that are happening in America today. I have come to the conclusion that every nation is like an individual, it must have its own experience and it does not accept the experience of other nations any more than you accept the experience of another individual, for if it were possible for a nation to learn by the bitter and tragic experiences of other nations America today could not be in war and America today could not have inaugurated a reign of terror which is sweeping across the country from one end to another. America had Europe before its face as an example, with all the murders and bloodshed and corpses and millions of lives lost. America had the trenches and the battlefields of the last, nearly, three years of Europe before her. America realized that this war is one of the bloodiest and most criminal wars that has ever been fought by civilized people. America had the lesson that the working people and the sons of working women are being sacrificed in the name of *Kultur* and they want democracy upon the battlefields of Europe, and if America had been a grown man instead of a child it would have learned the lesson that no matter how great the cause it is never great enough to sacrifice millions of people in the trenches and on the battlefield in the name of democracy or liberty.

Evidently, America has to learn a salutary lesson and it is going to pay a terrible price. It is going to shed oceans of blood, it is going to heap mountains of human sacrifices of men of this country who are able to create and produce, to whom the future belongs. They are to be slaughtered in blood and in sacrifice in the name of a thing which has never yet existed in the United States of America, in the name of democracy and liberty.

My friends, there are people who say and tell you that when they prophecy something the prophecy comes true. I am sorry to say that I am one such and I have to say the same. For thirty years we have pointed out to you that this democratic State, which is a government supposedly of the people, by the people and for the people, has now become one of the most imperialistic that the world has ever laid its eyes upon. For twenty-five or thirty years we have told you that the United States of America is appropriating more power every day until the time will come when individual men or women will be nothing but cogs in a machine of this centralized, cruel, blood thirsty government known as the United States. We told you that, and you said "you are alarmists". You said, "you are too extreme, that will never happen in the United States". And here you are, friends. It has happened in the United States. A Czar was imposed upon you without the consent of the people. The people were never asked whether they wanted war. Indeed, the people of America placed Mr. Wilson in the White House and in the Chair of the Presidency because he told the people that he would keep them out of war, and as one of his political advertisements posters were posted all over the city with the picture of a working woman and her children saying, "He has kept us out of war." He promised you heaven, he promised you everything if you would only place him in power. What made you place him in power? You expected peace and not war. The moment you placed him in power, however, he forgot his promises and he is giving you hell. War was imposed upon the people without the people getting a chance to say whether they wanted war or not, and war was imposed upon them, I say, because the gentlemen of power and those who back power want war. And because war has been declared upon you, we are told, we men and women of the United States who work and sweat and toil to sustain these gentlemen of power, we are told that there is a law and we must go to war. If war is necessary, only the people must decide whether they want war or not, and as long as the people have not given their consent I deny that the President of the United States has any right to declare it; I deny that the President or those who back the President have any right to tell the people that they shall take their sons and husbands and brothers and lovers and shall conscript them in order to ship them across the seas for the conquest of militarism and the support of wealth and power in the United States. You say that is a law. I deny your law. I don't believe in it.

The only law that I recognize is the law which ministers to the needs of humanity, which makes men and women finer and better and more humane, the kind of law which teaches children that human life is sacred, and that those who arm for the purpose of taking human life are going to be called before the bar of human justice and not before a wretched little court which is called your law of the United States. And so, friends, the people have not yet decided whether they want war and the people are going to say, ultimately, whether they want war or not.

It is not surprising that President Wilson cannot sense the pulse of time. He has been in colleges too long; he has been too long within closed doors; he has been too long at the historical books. He cannot sense the pulse of time. But I tell you, without wishing to be a prophet, that within the next six months — not years but within the next six months—President Wilson will regret deeply that he ever declared war in the United States.

Of course, friends, of course since the war was declared by a country in whose interest it is that the American boy shall be sacrificed it was not to the interest of that country to put the war to a test and therefore conscription had to be imposed upon you. Don't you know that during the Spanish-American War when the people believed in the war there was no need of asking the young men of the country, at the point of the bayonet and gun and club, to put on an American uniform? They flocked to the war because they believed in it. And whether they were American citizens or were residents of America the people of America were all willing to give their lives for something they considered right and just. But because the people of America do not believe in this war, because the people of America have not been asked whether there shall be war, that is why they do not flock to the colors and that is why you in America are doing as the Russians used to do, as the German Kaiser is doing, as all the imperialistic tyrants are doing. That is why you are going to drag your manhood by force into the uniform. But you are forgetting one thing, gentlemen of the law, you are driving a horse to water but you cannot compel him to drink. You will put the young manhood of America in the uniform, you will drag them to the battlefield and into the trenches, but while they are there, there is going to be a bond of anti-militarism among the people of the world (great applause).

No, friends, you cannot compel human beings to take human life, if you give them the chance to reason and to think, to investigate and to analyze. And that is precisely what the authorities of this country don't want. They don't want you to hear anything about conscription; they don't want you to hear anything about the State Military Census. Why don't they want you to hear anything? If their position were correct and logical, if the State Military Census rested upon the need of the people, if conscription rested upon the desire of the people, all the revolutionists and Emma Goldmans and Alexander Berkmans might talk their heads off and the people would not listen to them. But because the people know that conscription is a crime and oppression and an outrage upon reason, because the people know that the Military State Census was determined upon by one of the most reactionary men, we find Mr. Whitman who is on your backs, whom you supported, whom you gave the possibility to live. And the Military State Census, as you have been told, is going to turn every man of you here into a militiaman and into something who is fighting the Kaiser, because it is just as if the Kaiser wanted you to do a thing so that if you are a soldier and I tell you to shoot your mother and father and brother and sister you must obey orders. With the President is Mr. Whitman saying anything else? And then telling you that when you will become militiamen and you shall be ordered to shoot your brothers and fathers and sisters and mothers in the name of democracy that you are going to carry to the poor unfortunate people of Germany. And so, friends, we are here to tell you before you decide what you are going to do, think twice, and remember it is easy to make a mistake but it is very difficult to undo the mistake. You workmen of the East Side; you who have lived in Russia, you who remember the days when you could not meet unless you had detectives and soldiers and police, look about you. See what you have in the United States. See what you have in America.

If the framers of the Declaration of Independence, if Jefferson or Henry or the others, if they could look down upon the country and see what their offspring has done to it, how they have outraged it, how they have robbed it, how they have polluted it—why, my friends, they would turn in their graves. They would rise again and they would cleanse this country from its internal enemies, and that is the ruling class of the United States. There is a lesson you are going to learn and terrible as it is for us we nevertheless are glad that you will have to learn that lesson.

And now we come down to the tragedy that was committed in the United States Court in the State of New York yesterday, when two boys were sentenced. It is not only a tragedy because they were sentenced. Such things happen every day, hundreds, thousands of innocent working men are sent to the prison and the penitentiary, thousands of unfortunates throughout the world as well as here in so-called free America and nobody ever hears anything about it. It is an ordinary, commonplace thing to do. But the tragedy of yesterday is in the fact that a Judge, supported as you have been told by your money, protected by public opinion, protected by the President, the tragedy of it is that that Judge had the impudence and audacity to insult Kramer and Becker after he gave them the sentence of such horrible dimensions. Think of a man like that who sits there in judgment on other human beings. Think what must be his character, what must be his mind, what must be his soul, if he can spit human beings in the face, only because he has got the power.

But evidently the Judge knows nothing of history, any more than the ruling class knows. Don't you know there was a time when Marie Antoinette, very much surprised that the people had no bread asked, "Why don't they eat cake"? Don't you know what happened to the fair lady of France, Marie Antoinette? Don't you know what happened to the land-owning class of France who said that the people should eat straw? Don't you know what happened to them? The people gave them all the straw they could possibly eat. I consider the action of Judge Mayer an insult and an outrage and I warrant you that he is going to hear about it, not only all over the United States but even from Europe. It may have seemed very insignificant to send two poor workingmen to the penitentiary and to insult them, to send Becker and Kramer, who are both workingmen—that is their crime, they were both honest enough to say they were anarchists. To be condemned in an American Court it is enough that you are an anarchist. The Judge was horrified at the audacity of these people to say it to him, face to face. Don't you know, men, you who are free Americans, the moment you enter an American court you must say, like Dante said, "Ye who enter here leave all hope behind." That is what the American Courts are. And so today you are governed by the bayonet and the police can treat you like dogs. But I say to you, they who live by the sword shall perish by the sword. So I tell you, gentlemen, now is your time. Do whatever you please. But you are forgetting the story and you are forgetting the writing on the wall. You are making a mistake if you think that by sending Kramer and Becker to jail you are going to silence the human voice. You are making a mistake if you believe that by threatening and arresting people you are going to stop the agitation against war. The agitation is in the hearts of the people, the agitation is in the minds of the people, and it only requires the psychological moment to come along, as it did in Russia, and the Judges like Mayer and the other Judges will fly off the bench and into the gutters.

My friends, if we thought for one single minute that the entire agitation is dependent only upon a handful of people we would never bother and endanger your lives, but we know the agitation is in your hearts and souls, we know that the people from the East and West and South and North are opposed to the war, are opposed to conscription, opposed to the Military State Census, and the people will be heard from, I can tell you that. And so, to threaten anyone's life, to say that she will not come back from a meeting alive — how stupid. What is life unless you can live it in freedom and in beauty, and unless you can express yourself, unless you can be true to yourself what is life? I would rather than live the life of a dog, to be compelled to sneak about and slink about, to worry that somebody is looking for you ready to take your life — rather than that I would die the death of a lion any day. Why, what consequence is it if you tell people, we are going to arrest you, Miss Goldman. Just as if arresting Emma Goldman solves all the problems in the world. Prisons have never solved any problems. Guns and bayonets have never solved any problems. Bloodshed has never solved a problem. Never on earth, men and women, have such methods of violence, concentrated and organized violence, ever solved a single problem. Nothing but the human mind, nothing but human emotions, nothing but an intense passion for a great ideal, nothing but perseverance and devotion and strength of character — nothing else ever solved any problem.

And so, men and women, workmen and workwomen, you of the East Side, you who are sweated and bled to create the wealth of this country, you who are being sneered at because you are foreigners—very well, then, if you are good enough to create the wealth of America, if America had to go to Europe for her Art, if America had to go to Europe for her Literature, if America had to go to Europe for her Music and her ideals, by God you will have to go to the foreigners for liberty.

I wish to say here, and I don't say it with any authority and I don't say it as a prophet, I merely tell you—I merely tell you the more people you lock up, the more will be the idealists who will take their place; the more of the human voice you suppress, the greater and louder and the profounder will be the human voice. At present it is a mere rumbling, but that rumbling is increasing in volume, it is growing in depth, it is spreading all over the country until it will be raised into a thunder and people of America will rise and say, we want to be a democracy, to be sure, but we want the kind of democracy which means liberty and opportunity to every man and woman in America. (Great and continued applause).

Address to the Jury

July 9, 1917

Gentlemen of the Jury:

As in the case of my co-defendant, Alexander Berkman, this is also the first time in my life I have ever addressed a jury. I once had occasion to speak to three judges.

On the day after our arrest it was given out by the U.S. Marshal and the District Attorney's office that the "big fish" of the No-Conscription activities had been caught, and that there would be no more trouble-makers and disturbers to interfere with the highly democratic effort of the Government to conscript its young manhood for the European slaughter. What a pity that the faithful servants of the Government, personified in the U.S. Marshal and the District Attorney, should have used such a weak and flimsy net for their big catch. The moment the anglers pulled their heavily laden net ashore, it broke, and all the labor was so much wasted energy.

The methods employed by Marshal McCarthy and his hosts of heroic warriors were sensational enough to satisfy the famous circus men, Barnum & Bailey. A dozen or more heroes dashing up two flights of stairs, prepared to stake their lives for their country, only to discover the two dangerous disturbers and trouble-makers, Alexander Berkman and Emma Goldman, in their separate offices, quietly at work at their desks, wielding not a sword, nor a gun or a bomb, but merely their pens! Verily, it required courage to catch such big fish.

To be sure, two officers equipped with a warrant would have sufficed to carry out the business of arresting the defendants Alexander Berkman and Emma Goldman. Even the police know that neither of them is in the habit of running away or hiding under the bed. But the farce-comedy had to be properly staged if the Marshal and the District Attorney were to earn immortality. Hence the sensational arrest; hence also, the raid upon the offices of *The Blast*, *Mother Earth*, and the No-Conscription League.

In their zeal to save the country from the trouble-makers, the Marshal and his helpers did not even consider it necessary to produce a search warrant. After all, what matters a mere scrap of paper when one is called upon to raid the offices of Anarchists! Of what consequence is the sanctity of property, the right of privacy, to officials in their dealings with Anarchists! In our day of military training for battle, an Anarchist office is an appropriate camping ground. Would the gentlemen who came with Marshal McCarthy have dared to go into the offices of Morgan, or Rockefeller, or of any of those men without a search warrant? They never showed us the search warrant, although we asked them for it. Nevertheless, they turned our office into a battlefield, so that when they were through with it, it looked like invaded Belgium, with the only difference that the invaders were not Prussian barbarians but good American patriots bent on making New York safe for democracy.

The stage having been appropriately set for the three-act comedy, and the first act successfully played by carrying off the villains in a madly dashing automobile — which broke every traffic regulation and barely escaped crushing everyone in its way — the second act proved even more ludicrous. Fifty thousand dollars bail was demanded, and real estate refused when offered by a man whose property is rated at three hundred thousand dollars, and that after the District Attorney had considered and, in fact, promised to accept the property for one of the defendants, Alexander Berkman, thus breaking every right guaranteed even to the most heinous criminal.

Finally the third act, played by the Government in this court during the last week. The pity of it is that the prosecution knows so little of dramatic construction, else it would have equipped itself with better dramatic material to sustain the continuity of the play. As it was, the third act fell flat, utterly, and presents the question, Why such a tempest in a teapot? Gentlemen of the jury, my comrade and co-defendant having carefully and thoroughly gone into the evidence presented by the prosecution, and having demonstrated its entire failure to prove the charge of conspiracy or any overt acts to carry out that conspiracy, I shall not impose upon your patience by going over the same ground, except to emphasize a few points. To charge people with having conspired to do something which they have been engaged in doing most of their lives, namely their campaign against war, militarism and conscription as contrary to the best interests of humanity, is an insult to human intelligence.

And how was that charge proven? By the fact that *Mother Earth* and *The Blast* were printed by the same printer and bound in the same bindery. By the further evidence that the same expressman had delivered the two publications! And by the still more illuminating fact that on June 2nd *Mother Earth* and *The Blast* were given to a reporter at his request, if you please, and gratis.

Gentlemen of the jury, you saw the reporter who testified to this overt act. Did any one of you receive the impression that the man was of conscriptable age, and if not, in what possible way is the giving of *Mother Earth* to a reporter for news purposes proof demonstrating the overt act?

It was brought out by our witnesses that the *Mother Earth* magazine has been published for twelve years; that it was never held up, and that it has always gone through the U.S. mail as second-class mail matter. It was further proven that the magazine appeared each month about the first or second, and that it was sold or given away at the office to whoever wanted a copy. Where, then, is the overt act?

Just as the prosecution has utterly failed to prove the charge of conspiracy, so has it also failed to prove the overt act by the flimsy testimony that *Mother Earth* was given to a reporter. The same holds good regarding *The Blast*.

Gentlemen of the jury, the District Attorney must have learned from the reporters the gist of the numerous interviews which they had with us. Why did he not examine them as to whether or not we had counseled young men not to register? That would have been a more direct way of getting at the facts. In the case of the reporter from the *New York Times*, there can be no doubt that the man would have been only too happy to accommodate the District Attorney with the required information. A man who disregards every principle of decency and ethics of his profession as a newspaper man, by turning material given him as news over to the District Attorney, would have been glad to oblige a friend. Why did Mr. Content neglect such a golden opportunity? Was it not because the reporter of the *Times*, like all the other reporters, must have told the District Attorney that the two defendants stated, on each and every occasion, they would not tell people not to register?

Perhaps the *Times* reporter refused to go to the extent of perjuring himself. Patrolmen and detectives are not so timid in such matters. Hence Mr. Randolph and Mr. Cadell, to rescue the situation. Imagine employing tenth-rate stenographers to report the very important speeches of dangerous trouble-makers! What lack of forethought and efficiency on the part of the District Attorney! But even these two members of the police department failed to prove by their notes that we advised people not to register. But since they had to produce something incriminating against Anarchists, they conveniently resorted to the old standby, always credited to us, "We believe in violence and we will use violence."

Assuming, gentlemen of the jury, that this sentence was really used at the meeting of May 18th, it would still fail to prove the indictment which charges conspiracy and overt acts to carry out the conspiracy. And that is all we are charged with. Not violence, not Anarchism. I will go further and say that had the indictment been for the advocacy of violence, you gentlemen of the jury, would still have to render a verdict of "Not Guilty," since the mere belief in a thing or even the announcement that you would carry out that belief, can not possibly constitute a crime.

However, I wish to say emphatically that no such expression as "We believe in violence and we will use violence" was uttered at the meeting of May 18th, or at any other meeting. I could not have employed such a phrase, as there was no occasion for it. If for no other reason, it is because I want my lectures and speeches to be coherent and logical. The sentence credited to me is neither.

I have read to you my position toward political violence from a lengthy essay called "The Psychology of Political Violence."

But to make that position clearer and simpler, I wish to say that I am a social student. It is my mission in life to ascertain the cause of our social evils and of our social difficulties. As a student of social wrongs it is my aim to diagnose a wrong. To simply condemn the man who has committed an act of political violence, in order to save my skin, would be as unpardonable as it would be on the part of the physician who is called to diagnose a case, to condemn the patient because the patient has tuberculosis, cancer, or some other disease. The honest, earnest, sincere physician does not only prescribe medicine, he tries to find out the cause of the disease. And if the patient is at all capable as to means, the doctor will say to him, "Get out of this putrid air, get out of the factory, get out of the place where your lungs are being infected." He will not merely give him medicine. He will tell him the cause of the disease. And that is precisely my position in regard to acts of violence. That is what I have said on every platform. I have attempted to explain the cause and the reason for acts of political violence.

It is organized violence on top which creates individual violence at the bottom. It is the accumulated indignation against organized wrong, organized crime, organized injustice, which drives the political offender to his act. To condemn him means to be blind to the causes which make him. I can no more do it, nor have I the right to, than the physician who were to condemn the patient for his disease. You and I and all of us who remain indifferent to the crimes of poverty, of war, of human degradation, are equally responsible for the act committed by the political offender. May I therefore be permitted to say, in the words of a great teacher: "He who is without sin among you, let him cast the first stone." Does that mean advocating violence? You might as well accuse Jesus of advocating prostitution, because He took the part of the prostitute, Mary Magdalene.

Gentlemen of the jury, the meeting of the 18th of May was called primarily for the purpose of voicing the position of the conscientious objector and to point out the evils of conscription. Now, who and what is the conscientious objector? Is he really a shirker, a slacker, or a coward? To call him that is to be guilty of dense ignorance of the forces which impel men and women to stand out against the whole world like a glittering lone star upon a dark horizon. The conscientious objector is impelled by what President Wilson in his speech of Feb. 3, 1917, called "the righteous passion for justice upon which all war, all structure of family, State and of mankind must rest as the ultimate base of our existence and our liberty." The righteous passion for justice which can never express itself in human slaughter—that is the force which makes the conscientious objector. Poor indeed is the country which fails to recognize the importance of that new type of humanity as the "ultimate base of our existence and liberty." It will find itself barren of that which makes for character and quality in its people.

The meeting of May 18th was held before the Draft Bill had actually gone into effect. The President signed it late in the evening of the 18th. Whatever was said at that meeting, even if I had counseled young men not to register, that meeting cannot serve as proof of an overt act. Why, then, has the Prosecuting

Attorney dwelt so much, at such length, and with such pains on that meeting, and so little on the other meetings held on the eve of registration and after? Is it not because the District Attorney knew that we had no stenographic notes of that meeting? He knew it because he was approached by Mr. Weinberger and other friends for a copy of the transcript, which request he refused. Evidently, the District Attorney felt safe to use the notes of a patrolman and a detective, knowing that they would swear to anything their superiors wanted. I never like to accuse anyone—I wouldn't go so far as my co-defendant, Mr. Berkman, in saying that the District Attorney doctored the document; I don't know whether he did or not. But I do know that Patrolman Randolph and Detective Cadell doctored the notes, for the simple reason that I didn't say those things. But though we could not produce our own stenographic notes, we have been able to prove by men and women of unimpeachable character and high intelligence that the notes of Randolph are utterly false. We have also proven beyond a reasonable doubt, and Mr. Content did not dare question our proof, that at the Hunts' Point Palace, held on the eve of registration, I expressly stated that I cannot and will not tell people not to register. We have further proven that this was my definite stand, which was explained in my statement sent from Springfield and read at the meeting of May 23rd.

When we go through the entire testimony given on behalf of the prosecution, I insist that there is not one single point to sustain the indictment for conspiracy or to prove the overt acts we are supposed to have committed. But we were even compelled to bring a man eighty years of age to the witness stand in order to stop, if possible, any intention to drag in the question of German money. It is true, and I appreciate it, that Mr. Content said he had no knowledge of it. But, gentlemen of the jury, somebody from the District Attorney's office or someone from the Marshal's office must have given out the statement that a bank receipt for $2,400 was found in my office and must have told the newspapers the fake story of German money. As if we would ever touch German money, or Russian money, or American money coming from the ruling class, to advance our ideas! But in order to forestall any suspicion, any insinuation, in order to stand clear before you, we were compelled to bring an old man here to inform you that he has been a radical all his life, that he is interested in our ideas, and that he is the man who contributed the money for radical purposes and for the work of Miss Goldman.

Gentlemen of the jury, you will be told by the Court, I am sure, that when you render a verdict you must be convinced beyond a reasonable doubt; that you must not assume that we are guilty before we are proven guilty; and that it is your duty to assume that we are innocent. And yet, as a matter of fact, the burden of proof has been laid upon us. We had to bring witnesses. If we had had time we could have brought fifty more witnesses, each corroborating the others. Some of those people have no relation with us. Some are writers, poets, contributors to the most conventional magazines. Is it likely that they would swear to something in our favor if it were not the truth? Therefore I insist, as did my co-defendant Alexander Berkman, that the prosecution has made a very poor showing in proving the conspiracy or any overt act.

Gentlemen of the jury, we have been in public life for twenty-seven years. We have been hauled into court, in and out of season—we have never denied our position. Even the police know that Emma Goldman and Alexander Berkman are not shirkers. You have had occasion during this trial to convince yourselves that we do not deny. We have gladly and proudly claimed responsibility, not only for what we ourselves have said and written, but even for things written by others and with which we did not agree. Is it plausible, then, that we would go through the ordeal, trouble and expense of a lengthy trial to escape responsibility in this instance? A thousand times no! But we refuse to be tried on a trumped-up charge, or to be convicted by perjured testimony, merely because we are Anarchists and hated by the class whom we have openly fought for many years.

Gentlemen, during our examination of talesmen, when we asked whether you would be prejudiced against us if it were proven that we propagated ideas and opinions contrary to those held by the majority, you were instructed by the Court to say, "If they are within the law." But what the Court did not tell you is that no new faith—not even the most humane and peaceable—has ever been considered "within the law" by those who were in power. The history of human growth is at the same time the history of every new idea heralding the approach of a brighter dawn, and the brighter dawn has always been considered illegal, outside of the law.

Gentlemen of the jury, most of you, I take it, are believers in the teachings of Jesus. Bear in mind that he was put to death by those who considered his views as being against the law. I also take it that you are proud of your Americanism. Remember that those who fought and bled for your liberties were in their time considered as being against the law, as dangerous disturbers and trouble-makers. They not only preached violence, but they carried out their ideas by throwing tea into the Boston harbor. They said that "Resistance to tyranny is obedience to God." They wrote a dangerous document called the Declaration of Independence. A document which continues to be dangerous to this day, and for the circulation of which a young man was sentenced to ninety days prison in a New York Court, only the other day. They were the Anarchists of their time—they were never within the law.

Your Government is allied with the French Republic. Need I call your attention to the historic fact that the great upheaval in France was brought about by extra-legal means? The Dantons, the Robespierres, the Marats, the Herberts, aye even the man who is responsible for the most stirring revolutionary music, the *Marseillaise* (which unfortunately has deteriorated into a war tune), even Camille Desmoulins, were never within the law. But for those great pioneers and rebels, France would have continued under the yoke of the idle Louis XVI, to whom the sport of shooting jack rabbits was more important than the destiny of the people of France.

Ah, gentlemen, on the very day when we were being tried for conspiracy and overt acts, your city officials and representatives welcomed with music and festivities the Russian Commission. Are you aware of the fact that nearly all of the members of that Commission have only recently been released from exile? The ideas they propagated were never within the law. For nearly a hundred years, from 1825 to 1917, the Tree of Liberty in Russia was watered by the blood of her martyrs. No greater heroism, no nobler lives had ever been dedicated to humanity. Not one of them worked within the law. I could continue to enumerate almost endlessly the hosts of men and women in every land and in every period whose ideas and ideals redeemed the world because they were not within the law.

Never can a new idea move within the law. It matters not whether that idea pertains to political and social changes or to any other domain of human thought and expression—to science, literature, music; in fact, everything that makes for freedom and joy and beauty must refuse to move within the law. How can it be otherwise? The law is stationary, fixed, mechanical, "a chariot wheel" which grinds all alike without regard to time, place and condition, without ever taking into account cause and effect, without ever going into the complexity of the human soul.

Progress knows nothing of fixity. It cannot be pressed into a definite mould. It cannot bow to the dictum, "I have ruled," "I am the regulating finger of God." Progress is ever renewing, ever becoming, ever changing—never is it within the law.

If that be crime, we are criminals even like Jesus, Socrates, Galileo, Bruno, John Brown and scores of others. We are in good company, among those whom Havelock Ellis, the greatest living psychologist, describes as the political criminals recognized by the whole civilized world, except America, as men and women who out of deep love for humanity, out of a passionate reverence for liberty and an all-absorbing devotion to an ideal are ready to pay for their faith even with their blood. We cannot do otherwise if we are to be true to ourselves—we know that the political criminal is the precursor of human progress—the political criminal of today must needs be the hero, the martyr and the saint of the new age.

But, says the Prosecuting Attorney, the press and the unthinking rabble, in high and low station, "that is a dangerous doctrine and unpatriotic at this time." No doubt it is. But are we to be held responsible for something which is as unchangeable and unalienable as the very stars hanging in the heavens unto time and all eternity?

Gentlemen of the jury, we respect your patriotism. We would not, if we could, have you change its meaning for yourself. But may there not be different kinds of patriotism as there are different kinds of liberty? I for one cannot believe that love of one's country must needs consist in blindness to its social faults, to deafness to its social discords, of inarticulation to its social wrongs. Neither can I believe that the mere accident of birth in a certain country or the mere scrap of a citizen's paper constitutes the love of country.

I know many people—I am one of them—who were not born here, nor have they applied for citizenship, and who yet love America with deeper passion and greater intensity than many natives whose patriotism manifests itself by pulling, kicking, and insulting those who do not rise when the national anthem is played. Our patriotism is that of the man who loves a woman with open eyes. He is enchanted by her beauty, yet he sees her faults. So we, too, who know America, love her beauty, her richness, her great possibilities; we love her mountains, her canyons, her forests, her Niagara, and her deserts—above all do we love the people that have produced her wealth, her artists who have created beauty, her great apostles who dream and work for liberty—but with the same passionate emotion we hate her superficiality, her cant, her corruption, her mad, unscrupulous worship at the altar of the Golden Calf.

We say that if America has entered the war to make the world safe for democracy, she must first make democracy safe in America. How else is the world to take America seriously, when democracy at home is daily being outraged, free speech suppressed, peaceable assemblies broken up by overbearing and brutal gangsters in uniform; when free press is curtailed and every independent opinion gagged. Verily, poor as we are in democracy, how can we give of it to the world? We further say that a democracy conceived in the military servitude of the masses, in their economic enslavement, and nurtured in their tears and blood, is not democracy at all. It is despotism—the cumulative result of a chain of abuses which, according to that dangerous document, the Declaration of Independence, the people have the right to overthrow.

The District Attorney has dragged in our Manifesto, and he has emphasized the passage, "Resist conscription." Gentlemen of the jury, please remember that that is not the charge against us. But admitting that the Manifesto contains the expression, "Resist conscription," may I ask you, is there only one kind of resistance? Is there only the resistance which means the gun, the bayonet, the bomb or flying machine? Is there not another kind of resistance? May not the people simply fold their hands and declare, "We will not fight when we do not believe in the necessity of war"? May not the people who believe in the repeal of the Conscription Law, because it is unconstitutional, express their opposition in word and by pen, in meetings and in other ways? What right has the District Attorney to interpret that particular passage to suit himself? Moreover, gentlemen of the jury, I insist that the indictment against us does not refer to conscription. We are charged with a conspiracy against registration. And in no way or manner has the prosecution proven that we are guilty of conspiracy or that we have committed an overt act.

Gentlemen of the jury, you are not called upon to accept our views, to approve of them or to justify them. You are not even called upon to decide whether our views are within or against the law. You are called upon to decide whether the prosecution has proven that the defendants Emma Goldman and Alexander Berkman have conspired to urge people not to register. And whether their speeches and writings represent overt acts.

Whatever your verdict, gentlemen, it cannot possibly affect the rising tide of discontent in this country against war which, despite all boasts, is a war for conquest and military power. Neither can it affect the ever-increasing opposition to conscription which is a military and industrial yoke placed upon the necks of the American people. Least of all will your verdict affect those to whom human life is sacred, and who will not become a party to the world slaughter. Your verdict can only add to the opinion of the world as to whether or not justice and liberty are a living force in this country or a mere shadow of the past. Your verdict may, of course, affect us temporarily, in a physical sense—it can have no effect whatever upon our spirit. For even if we were convicted and found guilty and the penalty were that we be placed against a wall and shot dead, I should nevertheless cry out with the great Luther: "Here I am and here I stand and I cannot do otherwise." And gentlemen, in conclusion let me tell you that my co-defendant, Mr. Berkman, was right when he said the eyes of America are upon you. They are upon you not because of sympathy for us or agreement with Anarchism. They are upon you because it must be decided sooner or later whether we are justified in telling people that we will give them democracy in Europe, when we have no democracy here? Shall free speech and free assemblage, shall criticism and opinion—which even the espionage bill did not include—be destroyed? Shall it be a shadow of the past, the great historic American past? Shall it be trampled underfoot by any detective, or policeman, anyone who decides upon it? Or shall free speech and free press and free assemblage continue to be the heritage of the American people?

Gentlemen of the jury, whatever your verdict will be, as far as we are concerned, nothing will be changed. I have held ideas all my life. I have publicly held my ideas for twenty-seven years. Nothing on earth would ever make me change my ideas except one thing; and that is, if you will prove to me that our position is wrong, untenable, or lacking in historic fact. But never would I change my ideas because I am found guilty. I may remind you of two great Americans, undoubtedly not unknown to you, gentlemen of the jury; Ralph Waldo Emerson and Henry David Thoreau. When Thoreau was placed in prison for refusing to pay taxes, he was visited by Ralph Waldo Emerson and Emerson said: "David, what are you doing in jail?" and Thoreau replied: "Ralph, what are you doing outside, when honest people are in jail for their ideals?" Gentlemen of the jury, I do not wish to influence you. I do not wish to appeal to your passions. I do not wish to influence you by the fact that I am a woman. I have no such desires and no such designs. I take it that you are sincere enough and honest enough and brave enough to render a verdict according to your convictions, beyond the shadow of a reasonable doubt.

Please forget that we are Anarchists. Forget that it is claimed that we propagated violence. Forget that something appeared in *Mother Earth* when I was thousands of miles away, three years ago. The bomb exploded in the apartment of anarchist Louise Berger, half sister of Charles Berg, at 1626 Lexington Avenue between 103rd and 104th Streets, a large tenement area populated mainly by recently arrived immigrants. Forget all that, and merely consider the evidence. Have we been engaged in a conspiracy? Has that conspiracy been proven? Have we committed overt acts? Have those overt acts been proven? We for the defense say they have not been proven. And therefore your verdict must be not guilty.

But whatever your decision, the struggle must go on. We are but the atoms in the incessant human struggle towards the light that shines in the darkness — the Ideal of economic, political and spiritual liberation of mankind!

The Truth About The Bolsheviki

1918

The attitude of dense ignorance and stupidity toward the most gigantic event since the French Revolution, the Bolsheviki movement in Russia, is not typically American. All great movements have met with the same fate in every land, since stupidity and ignorance have never been the monopoly of any particular country.

The Bolsheviki, like all revolutionary movements, have faced three characteristic stages. First, calumny, misrepresentation, hatred, opposition, and persecution. After that came ridicule, scoffing, and cheap derision of the movement. Finally, in the third stage, recognition—though stinted and grudging.

It took the great movements of the past more than a century to pass these varying stages, and that at the expense of untold suffering and sacrifice. The Bolsheviki have swept on and all but reached the third stage in just a few months.

It is indeed unfortunate that we in America depend upon the press for information on all urgent questions. Yet everybody knows that there is no other medium so hopelessly inaccurate, so much of a falsifier of facts, as the press. Not only because it is inspired entirely by material interests, and therefore opposed to every movement which is likely to hurt those interests, but because the profession of journalism is in the hands of the most undeveloped, uninformed, provincial type of men and women. People who know almost nothing of the social currents in their own country cannot be expected to even remotely grasp the character and purpose of a movement which promises the salvation of the world. Therefore the utterly stupid, conscious and unconscious misrepresentation of the Bolsheviki.

And yet it is of the utmost importance that the people in America should understand the true meaning of the Bolsheviki, their origin, and the historic background which makes their position and their challenge to the world so significant to the masses.

Bolsheviki is the plural term for those revolutionists in Russia who represent the interests of the largest social groups, and who insist upon the maximum social and economic demands for those groups.

At a Social Democratic Congress, held in 1903, the extreme revolutionists, impatient of the ever-growing tendency of compromise and reform in the party, organized the Bolsheviki wing as opposed to those known as the Mensheviki, or the group content to move slowly, gaining reform step by step. Nikolai Lenin, and later Trotsky, were the prime factors in the separation, and have since worked incessantly to build up the Bolsheviki party along straight revolutionary lines, but nevertheless in keeping with Marxian theoretical reasoning.

Then came the miracle of miracles, the Russian Revolution of 1917, which to the politicians in and out of the different Socialist groups meant the overthrow of the Tsar and the establishment of a liberal or quasi-Socialist government. Lenin and Trotsky, with their followers, saw deeper into the nature of the Revolution, and, seeing, they had the wisdom to respond—not so much to their own theoretical predilections but to the compelling needs of the awakened Russian people themselves.

Thus the Russian Revolution is a miracle in more than one respect. Among other extraordinary paradoxes it presents the phenomenon of the Marxian Social Democrats, Lenin and

Trotsky, adopting Anarchist Revolutionary tactics, while the Anarchists Kropotkin, Tcherkessov, Tchaikovsky are denying these tactics and falling into Marxian reasoning, which they had during all their lives repudiated as "German metaphysics."

The Russian Revolution is indeed a miracle. It demonstrates every day how insignificant all theories are in comparison with the actuality of the revolutionary awakening of the people.

The Bolsheviki of 1903, though revolutionists, adhered to the Marxian doctrine concerning the industrialization of Russia and the historic mission of the bourgeoisie as a necessary evolutionary process before the Russian masses could come into their own. The Bolsheviki of 1918 no longer believe in the predestined function of the bourgeoisie. They have been swept forward upon the waves of the Revolution to the point of view held by the Anarchists since Bakunin; namely, that once the masses become conscious of their economic power, they make their own history and need not be bound by the traditions and processes of a dead past, which—like secret treaties—are made at the round table and are not dictated by life itself.

In other words, the Bolsheviki now represent not only a limited group of theorists but a Russia reborn and virile. Never would Lenin and Trotsky have attained their present importance had they merely voiced cut-and-dried theoretical formulae. They have their ears close to the heart-beat of the Russian people, who, while yet inarticulate, know how to register their demands much more powerfully through action. That, however, does not lessen the importance of Lenin, Trotsky and the other heroic figures who hold the world in awe by their personality, their prophetic vision and their intense revolutionary spirit.

It is not so long ago that Trotsky and Lenin were denounced as German agents, working for the Kaiser. Only those who are still influenced by newspaper lies, who know nothing about the two men, believe such accusations. Incidentally it is well to bear in mind that there is nothing quite so contemptible or cheap as to call a man a "German agent" because he refuses to believe in the high-sounding phrase "to make the world safe for

Democracy," with Democracy whipped in Tulsa, lynched in Butte, shut up in prison, and otherwise outraged and banished from our shores.

Lenin and Trotsky need no defense. Yet it is well to call the attention of the credulous ones, whose daily papers "cannot tell a lie," that when Trotsky was in America he lived in a cheap apartment house, and was so poor that he had hardly enough to live on. To be sure, he was offered a comfortable position on one of the successful Jewish Socialist dailies, on condition that he learn to compromise and curb his revolutionary zeal. Trotsky preferred poverty and the right to retain his self-respect. When he decided to return to Russia, at the very beginning of the Revolution, a private subscription had to be taken up by his friends to cover his fare—so much did Trotsky earn as a "German agent."

As to Lenin, his whole life has been one long, endless struggle for Russia. In fact, he comes to his revolutionary ideals through heritage. His own brother was executed by order of the Tsar. Thus Lenin has a personal as well as a universal reason to hate autocracy and to dedicate his life to the liberation of Russia. What absurdity it is to accuse a man like that of sympathy with German imperialism! But even the loud-mouthed accusers of Lenin and Trotsky have been shamed into silence by the powerful personalities and the incorruptible integrity of these great figures of the Revolution.

In one respect it is not at all surprising that there should be so little understanding in America for the Bolsheviki. The Russian Revolution still remains an enigma to the American mind. Without a trace of feeling for his own revolutionary traditions, and ever prostrate before the majesty of the State, the average American has been trained to believe that Revolution has no justification in his own country and that in "darkest Russia" it was only for the purpose of getting rid of the Tsar, provided it was done in a gentlemanly manner and with respectful apologies to the autocrat. And, further, that the moment a stable government like ours is established, the Russian people ought to "get behind the President."

Imagine, then, the surprise when the Russian people, after driving out the Tsar, destroyed the throne itself, and sent the "liberal" Miliukovs and Lvovs, and even the Socialist Kerensky, in the direction the Tsar had gone. And then, to cap the climax, come the Bolsheviki, who declare against both king and master. That is too much for the democratic mind of the American.

Fortunately for Russia, her people have never enjoyed the blessings of Democracy, with its institutionalized, legalized, classified values of education and culture; all of which are "machine made and ravel out the moment one begins at the first knot." The Russians are a literal people with an unspoiled, uncorrupted mind. Revolution to them has never meant mere political scene shifting, the overthrow of one autocrat for another. The Russian people have been taught for nearly a hundred years—not in stuffy schools by sterile teachers and stale text books, but by their great revolutionary martyrs, the noblest spirits the world has ever known—that Revolution means a fundamental social and economic change, something which has its roots in the needs and hopes of the people and which must not end until the disinherited of the earth come into their own. In a word, the Russian people saw in the overthrow of the autocracy the beginning and not the finale of the Revolution.

More than the tyranny of the Tsar, the *muzhik* hated the tyranny of the tax collector sent by the landed proprietor to rob him of his last cow or horse, and finally of the land itself, or to flog him and drag him off to prison when he could not pay his taxes. What was it to the *muzhik* that the Tsar had been driven from his throne, if his direct enemy, the *Barin* (master) still continued in possession of the key to life-the land? *Mrztzezka Zemlya* (Mother Earth) is the pet name which the Russian language alone has for the soil. To the Russian the soil is everything, life and joy giver, the nourisher, the beloved *Matwhka* (Little Mother).

The Russian Revolution can mean nothing to him unless it sets the land free and joins to the dethroned Tsar his partner, the dethroned land-owner, the capitalist. That explains the historic background of the Bolsheviki, their social and economic justification. They are powerful only because they represent the people. The moment they cease to do that they will go, as the Provisional Government and Kerensky had to go. For never will the Russian people be content, or Bolshevism cease, until the land and the means of life become the heritage of the children of Russia. They have for the first time in centuries determined that they shall be heard, and that their voices shall reach the heart, not of the governing classes—they know these have no heart—but the hearts of the peoples of the world, including the people of the United States. Therein lies the deep import and significance of the Russian Revolution as symbolized by the Bolsheviki.

Starting from the historic premise that all wars are capitalist wars, and that the masses can have no interest whatever in strengthening the imperialistic designs of their exploiters, it is perfectly consistent for the Bolsheviki to insist upon peace and to demand that there shall be neither indemnities nor annexations involved in that peace.

To begin with, Russia has been bled in a war ordered by the bloody Tsar. Why should they continue to sacrifice their strong manhood, which could be employed to better purpose for the reconstruction of Russia? To make the world safe for Democracy? What a farce! Did not the so-called Democracies forfeit the sympathy of the Russian people when they tied their Goddess to the knout of the Russian autocracy? How dare they complain of Russia that she is longing for peace now that she has successfully thrown off her back the weight of centuries of oppression!

Are the Allies really sincere in their boast of Democracy? Why, then, did they fail to recognize the Russian Revolution even before the "terrible Bolsheviki" had taken charge of its direction? England, the famous liberator of small nations, with India and Ireland in her clutches, would have none of the Revolution. France, the would-be cradle of liberty, repudiated the Russian Delegate to her Conference. To be sure, America recognized Revolutionary Russia, but only because she fondly hoped that Miliukov or Kerensky would remain in power. Under such circumstances why should Russia help to continue the war?

Yet it is not for this reason that the Bolsheviki insist upon peace. It is because nothing vital or constructive can be built up during war, and the Russian people are eager to build up, to create, to found a new, a free, a rich Russia. For that they need peace; and, above all other considerations, the Bolsheviki want to help the other peoples of the earth toward peace—the peoples who, like themselves, never wanted war.

Already the Bolsheviki have taught the world the lesson that peace negotiations must be initiated by the peoples themselves. Peace cannot be declared in the name of those who make wars and gain by them. That is one of the most significant contributions to world progress that the Bolsheviki have made. Furthermore, they maintain that negotiations for peace must be made openly, frankly and with the full consent of the peoples represented. They will have none of the secret diplomatic intrigue that betrays the peoples, leading them to irretrievable disaster.

On this basis the Bolsheviki invited the other powers to participate in the General Peace Conference held at Brest-Litovsk. Their suggestion was met with scorn. The democratic boast of the Allies, when put to the test, was found sadly wanting. The treachery of the Allies in forsaking the Russian people itself warrants the Bolsheviki in making a separate peace. They stand guiltless when they declare for a separate peace after their repudiation by the Allies.

Abandoned, the Bolsheviki are no less strong. It was Trotsky who expressed the moral influence of the Bolsheviki in the seeming paradox, "Our weakness will be our strength." Weak in the instruments of an autocracy, the Bolsheviki are strengthened by a common Revolutionary purpose. The moral opinion of the world will be more deeply influenced by a simple-hearted Russian's desire to act honestly at the peace table, than by all the connivance, evasion and hypocrisy of highly cultured diplomats.

The Bolsheviki demand that the obligations and indemnities incurred by the other governing classes should be repudiated. Why should they live up to the obligations of the Tsar? The people have not incurred those obligations; they have not pledged themselves to the other warring countries; they were no more consulted whether they should be slaughtered than the people of America were consulted. Why should they bear the brunt of punishment for an autocrat's crimes? Why should they saddle their children and their children's children with war loans and indemnities? They say that arrangements or contracts made by the enemies of the people must be lived up to by the enemies of the people, but not by the people themselves. If the Tsar pledged himself to other countries, the other countries should import him and make him responsible for what he pledged. But the people who were not consulted in the first place, who fought and bled and sacrificed their lives for three and a half years—they say that they will only pay the debts incurred by themselves, with their knowledge, with their understanding, and for a purpose of which they have approved. These are the only war debts, war loans and war indemnities they intend to pay.

The Bolsheviki have no imperialistic designs. They have libertarian plans, and those that understand the principles of liberty do not want to annex other peoples and other countries. Indeed, the true libertarian does not want even to annex other individuals, for he knows that so long as a single nation, people or individual is enslaved, he too is in danger.

That is why the Bolsheviki demand a peace without annexations and without indemnities. They do not feel ethically called upon to live up to the obligations incurred by the Tsar, the Kaiser or other imperialistic gentlemen.

The Bolsheviki are accused of betraying the Allies. Were the Russian people asked whether they wanted to join the Allies? The Bolsheviki, as Communists, as men who adhere with all the passion and intensity of their beings to the principle of Internationalism, declare: "Our allies are not the governments of England, France, Italy or America; our allies are the English,

French, Italian, American and German peoples. They are our only allies, and these allies we will never betray; these allies we will never deceive. We want to serve our allies, but our allies are the peoples of the world, not the governing classes, not the diplomats, not the prime ministers, not the gentlemen who make war." That is the position of the Bolsheviki to this present moment. They have demonstrated this within the last few weeks, when they saw that the German peace terms implied the enslavement and dependency of other peoples. They said, "We want peace, but in asking for peace for ourselves we do so because we feel certain that our peace will induce all the other peoples of the world to demand and make peace, whether the governing classes want it or not."

Trotsky, in a letter to the "Citizen Ambassador" of Persia, said: "The Anglo-Russian agreement of 1907 was directed against the liberty and independence of the Persian people, and is, therefore, null and void for all time. Moreover, we denounce all agreements preceding and following the said agreement which may restrict the rights of the Persian people to a free and independent existence."

The Bolsheviki are accused of taking possession of the land. This is a terrible charge, of course, if you believe in private property. It is considered the greatest crime of all to offend against private possessions. Human slaughter may be justified, but the sanctity of private property is inviolate. Fortunately, the Bolsheviki have learned from the past. They know that past revolutions failed because the masses did not take possession of the means of life.

The Bolsheviki have done another terrible thing — they have taken possession of the banks. The Bolsheviki remembered that during the Paris Commune, when women and children were starving on the streets, the Communards foolishly sent their comrades to protect the Bank of France, and that afterwards the French Government used the bank's funds to pay Bismark in return for the 500,000 German war prisoners who marched into Paris and drowned the Commune in the blood of 30,000 French workers.

At that time, in 1871, the French bourgeoisie had not the slightest objection to the use of German guns to slaughter the French people. The "end justifies the means," which the bourgeoisie would not hesitate—now as then—to use for the maintenance of its own supremacy.

The Bolsheviki are ardent students of history. They know that the ruling classes would prefer even the Tsar or the Kaiser to the Revolution. They know that if the bourgeoisie could retain the wealth stolen from the people, in the form of land and money, they would bribe the devil himself to save them from the Revolution, and the people, starved and destitute, might succumb to the cruel bargain.

That is why the Bolsheviki took possession of the banks and are urging the peasants to confiscate the land. They have no desire to turn the banks and land, the raw material and the products of Labor's toil over to the state. They want to place all the natural resources and the wealth of the country in the hands of the people for common holding and common use, because the Russian people are by instinct and tradition communists, and have neither need nor desire for the competitive system.

The Bolsheviki are translating into reality the very things many people have been dreaming about, hoping for, planning and discussing in private and public. They are building a new social order which is to come out of the chaos and conflicts now confronting them.

Why is it that many Russian revolutionists are opposed to the Bolsheviki? Some of the finest types of men and women in Russia, such as our beloved Babushka Breshkovskaia, Peter Kropotkin, and others, are antagonistic to the Bolsheviki. It is because these good people have been lured by the glamor of political liberalism as represented by Republican France, Constitutional England and Democratic America. Alas, they have yet to realize that the line of demarcation between liberalism and autocracy is purely imaginary, the sole difference being that the people under autocracy know that they are enslaved, and love liberty to such an extent that they would fight and die for it, while the people in a democracy imagine they are free and are content with their bondage.

The Russian revolutionists who are opposed to the Bolsheviki will soon come to appreciate that the Bolsheviki represent the most fundamental, far-reaching and all-embracing principles of human freedom and of economic well-being.

It might be asked, what would the Bolsheviki do if they were opposed by all the other governments? It is not at all unlikely that if the Bolsheviki attain to complete economic and social power in Russia, the combined governments might make common cause with German Imperialism in order to crush the Bolsheviki. It can be safely predicted that the imperialistic elements will join the bourgeoisie to defeat the Russian Revolution.

The Bolsheviki are alive to these dangers and are using the most effective measures to combat them. Their influence on the proletariat of Germany and Austria has been immeasurable. Returning German prisoners of war are carrying the message of Bolshevism into trench and barracks, into the fields and factories, awakening the people to the only power that can crush autocracy. The educational work of the Bolsheviki among the German people is beginning to have its effect. Certainly it has already accomplished a hundred-fold more than all the prattlings of the Allies about the necessity of spreading revolt in the Central Empires.

Even though the Bolsheviki should fail in actually carrying out their wonderful dream, their conception of universal peace, their attempt to ally themselves with all the oppressed peoples of the world, their demand that the land be given to the peasants and that the workers who produce the wealth of the world should enjoy the things they produce the very fact of their being and demanding must exert such influence upon the rest of the world that human beings can never again be quite so commonplace, so contented and ordinary as they were before the Bolsheviki made their appearance upon the horizon of human life.

That is the part the Bolsheviki are playing in our lives, in the lives of the German, the French and all the other peoples of the earth. We can never be the same, because at all times, in moments of despair, in moments of pessimism, in moments when we believe everything crushed, we shall turn toward Russia and there behold the Great Hope risen, incarnate, breaking up the blackness that has filled our hearts with the hatred of our brothers, paralyzed our minds and chained our limbs, bent our backs and emasculated our wills.

The Bolsheviki have come to challenge the world. It can nevermore rest in its old sordid indolence. It must accept the challenge. It has already accepted it in Germany, in Austria and Romania, in France and Italy, aye, even in America. Like sudden sunlight Bolshevism is spreading over the entire world, illuminating the great Vision and warming it into being—the New Life of human brotherhood and social well-being.

From:

My Two Years in Russia

1923.

The strongest of us are loath to give up a long-cherished dream. I had come to Russia possessed by the hope that I should find a new-born country, with its people wholly consecrated to the great, though very difficult, task of revolutionary reconstruction. And I had fervently hoped that I might become an active part of the inspiring work.

I found reality in Russia grotesque, totally unlike the great ideal that had borne me upon the crest of high hope to the land of promise. It required fifteen long months before I could get my bearings. Each day, each week, each month added new links to the fatal chain that pulled down my cherished edifice. I fought desperately against the disillusionment. For a long time I strove against the still voice within me which urged me to face the overpowering facts. I would not and could not give up.

Then came Kronstadt. It was the final wrench. It completed the terrible realization that the Russian Revolution was no more.

I saw before me the Bolshevik State, formidable, crushing every constructive revolutionary effort, suppressing, debasing, and disintegrating everything. Unable and unwilling to become a cog in that sinister machine, and aware that I could be of no practical use to Russia and her people, I decided to leave the country. Once out of it, I would relate honestly, frankly, and as objectively as humanly possible to me the story of my two years' stay in Russia. . . .

Superstitions die hard. In the case of this modern superstition the process is doubly hard because various factors have combined to administer artificial respiration. International intervention, the blockade, and the very efficient world propaganda of the Communist Party have kept the Bolshevik myth alive. Even the terrible famine is being exploited to that end.

How powerful a hold that superstition wields I realize from my own experience. I had always known that the Bolsheviki are Marxists. For thirty years I fought the Marxian theory as a cold, mechanistic, enslaving formula. In pamphlets, lectures and debates I argued against it. I was therefore not unaware of what might be expected from the Bolsheviki. But the Allied attack upon them made them the symbol of the Russian Revolution, and brought me to their defence.

From November, 1917, until February, 1918, while out on bail for my attitude against the war, I toured America in defence of the Bolsheviki. I published a pamphlet in elucidation of the Russian Revolution and in justification of the Bolsheviki. I defended them as embodying in practice the spirit of the revolution, in spite of their theoretic Marxism. . . .

Observation and study, extensive travel through various parts of the country, meeting with every shade of political opinion and every variety of friend and enemy of the Bolsheviki—all convinced me of the ghastly delusion which had been foisted upon the world. . . .

Anarchism to me never was a mechanistic arrangement of social relationships to be imposed upon man by political scene-shifting or by a transfer of power from one social class to another. Anarchism to me was and is the child, not of destruction, but of construction—the result of growth and development of the conscious creative social efforts of a regenerated people. I do not therefore expect Anarchism to follow in the immediate footsteps of centuries of despotism and submission. And I certainly did not expect to see it ushered in by the Marxian theory.

I did, however, hope to find in Russia at least the beginnings of the social changes for which the Revolution had been fought. Not the fate of the individual was my main concern as a revolutionist. I should have been content if the Russian workers and peasants as a whole had derived essential social betterment as a result of the Bolshevik régime.

Two years of earnest study, investigation, and research convinced me that the great benefits brought to the Russian people by Bolshevism exist only on paper, painted in glowing colours to the masses of Europe and America by efficient Bolshevik propaganda. As advertising wizards the Bolsheviki excel anything the world had ever known before. But in reality the Russian people have gained nothing from the Bolshevik experiment. To be sure, the peasants have the land; not by the grace of the Bolsheviki, but through their own direct efforts, set in motion long before the October change. That the peasants were able to retain the land is due mostly to the static Slav tenacity; owing to the circumstance that they form by far the largest part of the population and are deeply rooted in the soil, they could not as easily be torn away from it as the workers from their means of production.

The Russian workers, like the peasants, also employed direct action. They possessed themselves of the factories, organized their own shop committees, and were virtually in control of the economic life of Russia. But soon they were stripped of their power and placed under the industrial yoke of the Bolshevik State. Chattel slavery became the lot of the Russian proletariat. It was suppressed and exploited in the name of something which was later to bring it comfort, light, and warmth. Try as I might I could find nowhere any evidence of benefits received either by the workers or the peasants from the Bolshevik régime.

On the other hand, I did find the revolutionary faith of the people broken, the spirit of solidarity crushed, the meaning of comradeship and mutual helpfulness distorted. One must have lived in Russia, close to the everyday affairs of the people; one must have seen and felt their utter disillusionment and despair to appreciate fully the disintegrating effect of the Bolshevik principle and methods— disintegrating all that was once the pride and the glory of revolutionary Russia. . . .

True Communism was never attempted in Russia, unless one considers thirty-three categories of pay, different food rations, privileges to some and indifference to the great mass as Communism.

In the early period of the Revolution it was comparatively easy for the Communist Party to possess itself of power. All the revolutionary elements, carried away by the ultra-revolutionary promises of the Bolsheviki, helped the latter to power. Once in possession of the State the Communists began their process of elimination. All the political parties and groups which refused to submit to the new dictatorship had to go. First the Anarchists and Left Social Revolutionists, then the Mensheviki and other opponents from the Right, and finally everybody who dared aspire to an opinion of his own. Similar was the fate of all independent organizations. They were either subordinated to the needs of the new State or destroyed altogether, as were the Soviets, the trade unions and the coöperatives—three great factors for the realization of the hopes of the Revolution.

The Soviets first manifested themselves in the revolution of 1905 They played an important part during that brief but significant period. Though the revolution was crushed, the Soviet idea remained rooted in the minds and hearts of the Russian masses. At the first dawn which illuminated Russia in February, 1917, the Soviets revived again and came into bloom in a very short time. To the people the Soviets by no means represented a curtailment of the spirit of the Revolution. On the contrary, the Revolution was to find its highest, freest practical expression through the Soviets. That was why the Soviets so spontaneously and rapidly spread throughout Russia. The

Bolsheviki realized the significance of the popular trend and joined the cry. But once in control of the Government the Communists saw that the Soviets threatened the supremacy of the State. At the same time they could not destroy them arbitrarily without undermining their own prestige at home and abroad as the sponsors of the Soviet system. They began to shear them gradually of their powers and finally to subordinate them to their own needs.

The Russian trade unions were much more amenable to emasculation. Numerically and in point of revolutionary fibre they were still in their childhood. By declaring adherence to the trade unions obligatory the Russian labour organizations gained in physical stature, but mentally they remained in the infant stage. The Communist State became the wet nurse of the trade unions. In return, the organizations served as the flunkeys of the State. "A school for Communism," said Lenin in the famous controversy on the functions of the trade unions. Quite right. But an antiquated school where the spirit of the child is fettered and crushed. Nowhere in the world are labour organizations as subservient to the will and the dictates of the State as they are in Bolshevik Russia.

The fate of the coöperatives is too well known to require elucidation. The coöperatives were the most essential link between the city and the country. Their value to the Revolution as a popular and successful medium of exchange and distribution and to the reconstruction of Russia was incalculable. The Bolsheviki transformed them into cogs of the Government machine and thereby destroyed their usefulness and efficiency.

III

It is now clear why the Russian Revolution, as conducted by the Communist Party, was a failure. The political power of the Party, organized and centralized in the State, sought to maintain itself by all means at hand. The central authorities attempted to force the activities of the people into forms corresponding with the purposes of the Party. The sole aim of the latter was to strengthen the State and monopolize all economical, political, and social activities—even all cultural manifestations. The Revolution had an entirely different object, and in its very character it was the negation of authority and centralization. It strove to open ever-larger fields for proletarian expression and to multiply the phases of individual and collective effort. The aims and tendencies of the Revolution were diametrically opposed to those of the ruling political party.

Just as diametrically opposed were the methods of the Revolution and of the State. Those of the former were inspired by the spirit of the Revolution itself: that is to say, by emancipation from all oppressive and limiting forces; in short; by libertarian principles. The methods of the State, on the contrary—of the Bolshevik State as of every government—were based on coercion, which in the course of things necessarily developed into systematic violence, oppression, and terrorism. Thus two opposing tendencies struggled for supremacy: the Bolshevik State against the Revolution. That struggle was a life-and-death struggle. The two tendencies, contradictory in aims and methods, could not work harmoniously: the triumph of the State meant the defeat of the Revolution. . . .

It remains true, as it has through all progress, that only the libertarian spirit and method can bring man a step further in his eternal striving for the better, finer, and freer life. Applied to the great social upheavals known as revolutions, this tendency is as potent as in the ordinary evolutionary process. The authoritarian method has been a failure all through history and now it has again failed in the Russian Revolution. So far human ingenuity has discovered no other principle except the libertarian, for man has indeed uttered the highest wisdom when he said that liberty is the mother of order, not its daughter. All political tenets and parties notwithstanding, no revolution can be truly and permanently successful unless it puts its emphatic veto upon all tyranny and centralization, and determinedly strives to make the revolution a real revaluation of all economic, social, and cultural values. Not mere substitution of one political party for another in the control of the Government, not the masking of autocracy by proletarian slogans, not the dictatorship of a new class over an old one, not political scene shifting of any kind, but the complete reversal of all these authoritarian principles will alone serve the revolution.

In the economic field this transformation must be in the hands of the industrial masses: the latter have the choice between an industrial State and anarcho-syndicalism. In the case of the former the menace to the constructive development of the new social structure would be as great as from the political State. It would become a dead weight upon the growth of the new forms of life. For that very reason syndicalism (or industrialism) alone is not, as its exponents claim, sufficient unto itself. It is only when the libertarian spirit permeates the economic organizations of the workers that the manifold creative energies of the people can manifest themselves. and the revolution be safeguarded and defended. Only free initiative and popular participation in the affairs of the revolution can prevent the terrible blunders committed in Russia. For instance, with fuel only a hundred *versts* [about sixty-six miles] from Petrograd there would have been no necessity for that city to suffer from cold had the workers' economic organizations of Petrograd been free to exercise their initiative for the common good. The peasants of the Ukraina would not have been hampered in the cultivation of their land had they had access to the farm implements stacked up in the warehouses of Kharkov and other industrial centres awaiting orders from Moscow for their distribution. These are characteristic examples of Bolshevik governmentalism and centralization, which should serve as a warning to the workers of Europe and America of the destructive effects of Statism.

The industrial power of the masses, expressed through their libertarian associations — Anarcho-syndicalism — is alone able to organize successfully the economic life and carry on production. On the other hand, the coöperatives, working in harmony with the industrial bodies, serve as the distributing and exchange media between city and country, and at the same time link in fraternal bond the industrial and agrarian masses. A common tie of mutual service and aid is created which is the strongest bulwark of the revolution—far more effective then compulsory labour, the Red Army, or terrorism. In that way alone can revolution act as a leaven to quicken the development of new social forms and inspire the masses to greater achievements. . .

If I were to sum up my whole argument in one sentence I should say: The inherent tendency of the State is to concentrate, to narrow, and monopolize all social activities; the nature of revolution is, on the contrary, to grow, to broaden, and disseminate itself in ever-wider circles. In other words, the State is institutional and static; revolution is fluent, dynamic. These two tendencies are incompatible and mutually destructive. The State idea killed the Russian Revolution and it must have the same result in all other revolutions, unless the libertarian ideas prevail.

Samuel Gompers

The Road to Freedom, March 1925

The numerous tributes paid to the late President of the American Federation of Labor emphasized his great leadership. "Gompers was a leader of men," they said. One would have expected that the disaster brought upon the world by leadership would have proven that to be a leader of men is far from a virtue. Rather is it a vice for which those who are being led are usually made to pay very heavily.

The last fifteen years are replete with examples of what the leaders of men have done to the peoples of the world. The Lenins, Clemenceaus, the Lloyd Georges and Wilsons, have all posed as great leaders. Yet they have brought misery, destruction and death. They have led the masses away from the promised goal.

Pious Communists will no doubt consider it heresy to speak of Lenin in the same breath with the other statesmen, diplomats and generals who have led the people to slaughter and half of the world to ruin. To be sure, Lenin was the greatest of them all. He at least had a new vision, he had daring, he faced fire and death, which is more than can be said for the others. Yet it remains a tragic fact that even Lenin brought havoc to Russia. It was his leadership which emasculated the Russian revolution and stifled the aspirations of the Russian people.

Gompers was far from being a Lenin, but in his small way his leadership has done a great harm to the American workers. One has but to examine into the nature of the American Federation of Labor, over which Mr. Gompers lorded for so many years, to see the evil results of leadership. It cannot be denied that the late President raised the organization to some power and material improvement, but at the same time, he prevented the growth and development of the membership towards a higher aim or purpose. In all these years of its existence the A.F. of L. has not gone beyond its craft interests. Neither has it grasped the social abyss which separates labor from its masters, an abyss which can never be bridged by the struggle for mere immediate material gains. That does not mean, however, that I am opposed to the fight labor is waging for a higher standard of living and saner conditions of work. But I do mean to stress that without an ultimate goal of complete industrial and social emancipation, labor will achieve only as much as is in keeping with the interests of the privileged class, hence remain dependent always upon that class.

Samuel Gompers was no fool, he knew the causes underlying the social struggle, yet he set his face sternly against them. He was content to create an aristocracy of labor, a trade union trust, as it were, indifferent to the needs of the rest of the workers outside of the organization. Above all, Gompers would have none of a liberating social idea. The result is that after forty years of Gompers' leadership the A.F. of L. has really remained stationary, without feeling for, or understanding of, the changing factors surrounding it.

The workers who have developed a proletarian consciousness and fighting spirit are not in the A.F. of L. They are in the organization of the Industrial Workers of the World. The bitterest opponent of this heroic band of American proletarians was Samuel Gompers. But then, Mr. Gompers was inherently reactionary. This tendency asserted itself on more than one occasion in his career. Most flagrantly did his reactionary leanings come to the fore in the MacNamara case, the War, and the Russian Revolution.

The story of the MacNamara case is very little known in Europe. Yet their story has played a significant part in the industrial warfare of the United States, the warfare between the Steel Trust, the Merchants' Manufacturers' Association, and the infamous Labor baiter, the *Los Angeles Times*, arrayed against the Iron Structural Union. The savage methods of the unholy trinity expressed themselves in a system of espionage, the employment of thugs for the purpose of slugging strikers with violence of every form, besides the use of the entire machinery of the American Government, which is always at the beck and call of American capitalism. This formidable conspiracy against labor, the Iron Structural Union, in defence of its existence fought desperately for a period of years.

J.J. and Jim MacNamara, being among the most ardent and unflinching members of the Union, consecrated their lives and took the most active part in the war against the forces of American industrialism and high finance until they were trapped by the despicable spies employed in the organization of William J. Burns, the infamous man hunter. With the MacNamaras were two other victims, Matthew A. Schmidt, one of the finest types of American proletarians, and David Caplan.

Samuel Gompers, as the President of the A.F. of L. could not have been unaware of the things these poor men were charged with. He stood by them as long as they were considered innocent. But when the two brothers, led by their desire to shield "the higher ups" admitted their acts, it was Gompers who turned from them and left them to their doom. The whitewash of the organization was more to him than his comrades, who had carried out the work in constant danger to their own lives, while Mr. Samuel Gompers enjoyed the safety and the glory as President of the A.F. of L. The four men were sacrificed. Jim MacNamara and Matthew A. Schmidt were sent to life imprisonment, while J.J. MacNamara and David Caplan received fifteen and ten years respectively. The latter two have since been released, while the former are continuing a living death in St. Quentin Prison, California. And Samuel Gompers was buried with the highest honors by the class which hounded his comrades to their doom.

In the War, the late President of the A.F. of L. turned the entire organization over to those he had ostensibly fought all his life. Some of his friends insist that Gompers became obsessed by the War mania because the German Social Democrats had betrayed the spirit of Internationalism. As if two wrongs ever made a right! The fact is that Gompers was never able to swim against the tide. Hence he made common cause with the war lords and delivered the membership of the A.F. of L. to be slaughtered in the War, which is now being recognized by many erstwhile ardent patriots to have been a war not for democracy, but for conquest and power.

The attitude of Samuel Gompers to the Russian Revolution, more than anything else, showed his dominant reactionary leanings. It is claimed for him that he had the "goods" on the Bolsheviki. Therefore he supported the blockade and intervention. That is absurd for two reasons: First, when Gompers began his campaign against Russia, he could not possibly have had any knowledge of the evil doings of Bolshevism. Russia was then cut off from the rest of the world. And no one knew exactly what was happening there. Secondly, the blockade and intervention struck down the Russian people, at the same time strengthening the power of the Communist State.

No, it was not his knowledge of the Bolsheviki which made Gompers go with the slayers of Russian women and children. It was his fear for and his hatred of the Revolution itself. He was too steeped in the old ideas to grasp the gigantic events that had swept over Russia, the burning idealism of the people who had made the Revolution. He never took the slightest pains to differentiate between the Revolution and the machine set up to sidetrack its course. Most of us who now must stand out against the present rulers of Russia do so because we have learned to see the abyss between the Russian Revolution, the ideals of the people, and the crushing dictatorship now in power. Gompers never realized that.

Well, Samuel Gompers is dead. It is to be hoped that his soul will not be marching on in the ranks of the A.F. of L. More and more the conditions in the United States are drawing the line rigidly between the classes. More and more it is becoming imperative for the workers to prepare themselves for the fundamental changes that are before them. They will have to acquire the knowledge and the will as well as the ability to reconstruct society along such economic and social lines that will prevent the repetition of the tragic debacle of the Russian Revolution. The masses everywhere will have to realize that leadership, whether by one man or a political group, must inevitably lead to disaster.

Not leadership, but the combined efforts of the workers and the cultural elements in society can successfully pave the way for new forms of life which shall guarantee freedom and well-being for all.

Socialism: Caught in the Political Trap

July, 1929

Legend tells us that healthy newborn infants aroused the envy and hatred of evil spirits. In the absence of the proud mothers, the evil ones stole into the houses, kidnapped the babies, and left behind them deformed, hideous-looking monsters.

Socialism has met with such a fate. Young and lusty, crying out defiance to the world, it aroused the envy of the evil ones. They stole near when Socialism least expected and made off with it, leaving behind a deformity which is now stalking about under the name of Socialism.

At its birth, Socialism declared war on all constituted institutions. Its aim was to fell every injustice to the ground and replace it with economic and social well-being and harmony.

Two fundamental principles gave Socialism its life and strength: the wage system and its master, private property. The cruelty, criminality, and injustice of these principles were the enemies against which Socialism hurled its bitterest attacks and criticisms. Private property and the wage system being the staunchest pillars of society, everyone who dared expose their cruelty was denounced as an enemy of society, a dangerous character, a revolutionist. Time was when Socialism carried these epithets with head erect, feeling that the hatred and persecution of its enemies were its greatest attributes.

Not so the Socialism that has been caught in the trap of the evil ones, of the political monsters. This sort of Socialism has either given up altogether the unflinching attacks against the bulwarks of the present system, or has weakened and changed its form to an unrecognizable extent.

The aim of Socialism today is the crooked path of politics as a means of capturing the State. Yet it is the State which represents the mightiest weapon sustaining private property and our system of wrong and inequality. It is the power which protects the system against every rebellious, determined revolutionary attack.

The State is organized exploitation, organized force, and crime. And to the hypnotic manipulation of this very monster, Socialism has become a willing prey. Indeed, the representatives or Socialism are more devout in their religious faith in the State than the most conservative statists.

The Socialist contention is that the State is not half centralized enough. The State, they say, should not only control the political phase of society, it should become the arch manager, the very fountain-head, of the industrial life of the people as well, since that alone would do away with special privileges, with trusts and monopolies. Never does it occur to these abortionists of a great idea that the State is the coldest, most inhuman monopolist, and if once economic dictatorship were added to the already supreme political power of the State, its iron heel would cut deeper into the flesh of labor than that of capitalism today.

Of course, I will be told that Socialism does not aim for such a State, that it wants a true, just, democratic, real State. Alas, the true, real, and just State is like the true, real, just God, who has never yet been discovered. The real God, according to our good Christians, is kind and loving, just and fair. But what has he proven to be in reality? A God of tyranny, of war and bloodshed, of crime and injustice. The same is the case with the State, whether of Republican, Democratic, or Socialist color.

Always and everywhere it has and must stand for supremacy, hence for slavery, submission, and dependency.

How the political scene-shifters must grin when they see the rush of the people to the newest attraction in the political moving-picture show. The poor, deluded, childish people, who are forever fed on the political patent medicine, either of the Republican elephant, the Democratic cow, or the Socialist mule, the grunting of each merely representing a new ragtime from the political music box.

The muddy waters of the political life run high for a time, while underneath moves the giant beast of greed and strife, of corruption and decay, mercilessly devouring its victims. All politicians, no matter how sincere (if such an anomaly is at all thinkable), are but petty reformers, hence the perpetuators of the present system.

Socialism in its inception was absolutely and irrevocably opposed to this system. It was anti-authoritarian, anti-capitalistic, anti-religious; in short, it could not and would not make peace with a single institution of today. But since it was led astray by the evil spirit of politics, it landed in the trap and has now but one desire—to adjust itself to the narrow confines of its cage, to become part of the authority, part of the very power that has slain the beautiful child Socialism and left behind a hideous monster.

Since the days of the old Internationale, since the strife between Bakunin, Marx and Engels, Socialism has slowly but surely been losing its fighting plumes—its rebellious spirit and its strong revolutionary tendencies—as more and more it has allowed itself to be deceived by political gains and government offices. And more and more, Socialism has grown powerless to arouse itself from the political hypnosis, thereby spreading apathy and passivity in proportion to its political successes.

The masses are being drilled and canned for the political cold storage of Socialist campaigns. Every direct, independent, and courageous attack on capitalism and the State is being discouraged or tabooed. The stupid voters wait patiently from one political performance to another for the comrade actors in the theater of representation to give a show, and perhaps perform a new stunt. Meanwhile, the Socialist congressman introduces yard upon yard of resolutions for the waste basket, proposing the perpetuation of the very things Socialism once set out to overthrow. And the Socialist mayors are busy assuring the business interests of their towns that they may rest in peace, no harm will ever come to them from a Socialist mayor. And if such Punch-and-Judy shows are criticised, the good Socialist adherents grow indignant and say that we must wait until the Socialists have the majority.

The political trap has transferred Socialism from the proud, uncompromising position of a revolutionary minority, fighting fundamentals and undermining the strongholds of wealth and power, to the camp of the scheming, compromising, inert political majority, busying itself with non-essentials, with things that barely touch the surface, measures that have been used as political bait by the most lukewarm reformers: old age pensions, initiative and referendum, the recall of judges, and other such very startling and terrible things.

In order to achieve these "revolutionary" measures, the elite in the Socialist ranks go down on their knees to the majority, holding out the palm leaf of compromise, catering to every superstition, every prejudice, every silly tradition. Even the Socialist politicians know that the voting majority is intellectually steeped in ignorance, that it does not know as much as the ABC of Socialism. One would therefore assume that the aim of these "scientific" Socialists would be to lift the mass up to its intellectual heights. But no such thing. That would hurt the feelings of the majority too much. Therefore the leaders must sink to the low level of their constituency, therefore they must cater to the ignorance and prejudice of the voters. And that is precisely what Socialism has been doing since it was caught in the political trap.

One of the commonplaces of Socialism today is the notion of evolution. For heaven's sake, let's have nothing of revolution, we are peace-loving people, we want evolution. I shall not now attempt to prove that evolution must mean growth from a lower to a higher state of mind, and that thus Socialists, from their own evolutionary standpoint, have failed miserably, since they have gone back on every one of their original principles. I only wish to examine into this wonderful thing, Socialist evolution.

Thanks to Karl Marx and Engels, we are assured that Socialism has developed from a Utopia to a science. Softly, gentlemen, Utopian Socialism is not the kind that would allow itself to be caught in the political trap, it is the kind that will never make peace with our murderous system, it is the kind that has inspired and still inspires enthusiasm, zeal, courage, and idealism. It is the kind of Socialism that will have none of the disgustingly cringing compromise of a Berger, a Hillquit, a Ghent, and other-such "scientific" gentlemen.

Every daring attempt to make a great change in existing conditions, every lofty vision of new possibilities for the human race, has been labeled Utopian. If "scientific" Socialism is to substitute stagnation for activity, cowardice for courage, acquiescence for daring, submission for defiance, then Marx and Engels might never have lived, for all the service they have done to Socialism.

But I deny that so-called scientific Socialism has proven its superiority to Utopian Socialism. Certainly, if we examine into the failure of some of the predictions the great prophets have made, we will see how arrogant and overbearing the scientific contentions are. Marx was determined that the middle class would get off the scene of action, leaving but two fighting forces, the capitalistic and proletarian classes. But the middle class has had the impudence not to oblige comrade Marx.

The middle class is growing everywhere, and is indeed the strongest ally of capitalism. In fact, the middle class was never more powerful than it is today, as can be adduced by a thousand facts, but mainly by the very gentlemen in the Socialist ranks—the lawyers, ministers, and small businessmen—who infest the movement. They are making of Socialism a respectable, middle-class, law-abiding issue because they themselves represent that very tendency. It is inevitable that they should espouse methods of propaganda to fit everybody's taste and strengthen the system of robbery and exploitation.

Marx prophesied that the workers would grow poorer in proportion to the increase of wealth. That did not come to pass, either, in the way Marx hoped. The masses of workers are really getting poorer, but that has not prevented the rise of an aristocracy of labor in the very ranks of labor. A class of snobs who—because of superior wages and more respected positions, but mainly because they have saved a little or acquired some property—have lost sympathy with their own kind, and are now the loudest proclaimers against revolutionary means. Truth is, the entire Socialist Party of today is recruited from these very aristocrats of labor; that's why they will have nothing to do with those who stand for revolutionary, anti-political methods. The possibility of becoming mayor, congressman, or some other high official is too alluring to allow these upstarts to do anything that would jeopardize such a glorious chance.

But what about the much-extolled class consciousness of the workers which is to act as such leaven? Where and how does it assert itself? Surely, if it were an innate quality the workers would long since have demonstrated this fact, and their first act would have been to sweep clean from the Socialist ranks lawyers, ministers, and real-estate sharks, the most parasitic types in society.

Class consciousness can never be demonstrated in the political arena, for the interests of the politician and the voter are not identical. The one aims for office while the other must stand the cost. How then can there be a fellow-feeling between them?

Solidarity of interests develops class consciousness, as is demonstrated in the Syndicalist and every other revolutionary movement, in the determined effort to overthrow the present system, in the great war that is being waged against every institution of today in behalf of a new edifice.

The political Socialists care nothing at all for such a class consciousness. On the contrary, they fight it tooth and nail. In Mexico, class consciousness is being demonstrated as it has not been since the great French Revolution. The real and true proletarians, the robbed and enslaved peons, are fighting for land and liberty. It is true they know nothing of the theory of scientific Socialism, nor yet of the materialistic interpretation of history, as laid down in Marx's *Das Kapital*, but they know with mathematical accuracy that they have been sold into slavery. They also know that their interests are inimical to the interests of the land robbers, and they have risen in revolt against that class, against those interests.

How do the class-conscious monopolists of scientific Socialism meet this wonderful uprising? With the cries of "bandits, filibusters, anarchists, ignoramuses" — unfit to understand or interpret economic necessity. And predictably, the paralysing effect of the political trap does not permit of sympathy with the sublime wrath of the oppressed. It must move in straight-laced legal bounds, while the Indian Yaquis, the Mexican peons, have broken all laws, all propriety, they have even had the impudence to expropriate the land from the expropriators, they have driven back their tyrants and tormentors. How then can peaceful aspirants for political jobs approve such conduct? Trying hard for the fleshpots of the State, which is the staunchest protector of property, the Socialist cannot possibly affiliate with any movement that so brazenly attacks property. On the other hand, it is quite consistent with the political aims of the party to oblige those who might add to the voting strength of class-conscious Socialism. Witness how tenderly religion is treated, how prohibition is patted on the back, how the anti-Asiatic and Negro question is met with, in short how every spook prejudice is treated with kid gloves so as not to hurt its sensitive souls.

Sacco and Vanzetti

with Alexander Berkman

The Road to Freedom, Aug. 1929.

The names of the "good shoe-maker and poor fish-peddler" have ceased to represent merely two Italian workingmen. Throughout the civilised world Sacco and Vanzetti have become a symbol, the shibboleth of Justice crushed by Might. That is the great historic significance of this twentieth century crucifixion, and truly prophetic, were the words of Vanzetti when he declared, "The last moment belongs to us—that agony is our triumph."

We hear a great deal of progress and by that people usually mean improvements of various kinds, mostly life-saving discoveries and labor-saving inventions, or reforms in the social and political life. These may or may not represent a real advance because reform is not necessarily progress.

It is an entirely false and vicious conception that civilisation consists of mechanical or political changes. Even the greatest improvements do not, in themselves, indicate real progress: they merely symbolise its results. True civilization, real progress, consists in humanising mankind, in making the world a decent place to live in. From this viewpoint we are very far from being civilised, in spite of all the reforms and improvements.

True progress is a struggle against the inhumanity of our social existence, against the barbarity of dominant conceptions. In other words, progress is a spiritual struggle, a struggle to free man from his brutish inheritance, from the fear and cruelty of his primitive condition. Breaking the shackles of ignorance and superstition; liberating man from the grip of enslaving ideas and practices; driving darkness out of his mind and terror out of his heart; raising him from his abject posture to man's full stature — that is the mission of progress. Only thus does man, individually and collectively, become truly civilised and our social life more human and worthwhile.

This struggle marks the real history of progress. Its heroes are not the Napoleons and the Bismarcks, not the generals and politicians. Its path is lined with the unmarked graves of the Saccos and Vanzettis of humanity, dotted with the *auto-da-fé*, the torture chambers, the gallows and the electric chair. To those martyrs of justice and liberty we owe what little of real progress and civilization we have today.

The anniversary of our comrades' death is therefore by no means an occasion for mourning. On the contrary, we should rejoice that in this time of debasement and degradation, in the hysteria of conquest and gain, there are still men that dare defy the dominant spirit and raise their voices against inhumanity and reaction: That there are still men who keep the spark of reason and liberty alive and have the courage to die, and die triumphantly, for their daring.

For Sacco and Vanzetti died, as the entire world knows today, because they were Anarchists. That is to say, because they believed and preached human brotherhood and freedom. As such, they could expect neither justice nor humanity. For the Masters of Life can forgive any offense or crime but never an attempt to undermine their security on the backs of the masses. Therefore Sacco and Vanzetti had to die, notwithstanding the protests of the entire world.

Yet Vanzetti was right when he declared that his execution was his greatest triumph, for all through history it has been the martyrs of progress that have ultimately triumphed. Where are the Caesars and Torquemadas of yesterday? Who remembers the names of the judges who condemned Giordano Bruno and John Brown? The Parsons and the Ferrers, the Saccos and Vanzettis, live eternal and their spirits still march on.

Let no despair enter our hearts over the graves of Sacco and Vanzetti. The duty we owe them for the crime we have committed in permitting their death is to keep their memory green and the banner of their Anarchist ideal high. And let no near-sighted pessimist confuse and confound the true facts of man's history, of his rise to greater manhood and liberty. In the long struggle from darkness to light, in the age-old fight for greater freedom and welfare, it is the rebel, the martyr, who has won. Slavery has given way, absolutism is crushed, feudalism and serfdom had to go, thrones have been broken and republics established in their stead. Inevitably, the martyrs and their ideas have triumphed, in spite of gallows and electric chairs. Inevitably, the people, the masses, have been gaining on their masters, till now the very citadels of Might, Capital and the State, are being endangered. Russia has shown the direction of the further progress by its attempt to eliminate both the economic and political master. That initial experiment has failed, as all first great social revaluations require repeated efforts for their realisation. But that magnificent historic failure is like unto the martyrdom of Sacco and Vanzetti—the symbol and guarantee of ultimate triumph.

Let it be clearly remembered, however, that the failure of *first* attempts at fundamental social change is always due to the false method of trying to establish the *new* by *old* means and practices. The *new* can conquer only by means of its own new spirit. Tyranny lives by suppression; Liberty thrives on freedom. The fatal mistake of the great Russian Revolution was that it tried to establish new forms of social and economic life on the old foundation of coercion and force. The entire development of human society has been *away* from coercion and government, away from authority towards greater freedom and independence. In that struggle the spirit of liberty has ultimately won out. In the same direction lies further achievement. All history proves it and Russia is the most convincing recent demonstration of it. Let us then learn that lesson and be inspired to greater efforts in behalf of a new world of humanity and freedom, and may the triumphant martyrdom of Sacco and Vanzetti give us greater strength and endurance in this superb struggle.

"An Anarchist Looks at Life"

March 1, 1933.

Mr. Henry W. Nevinson, introducing Miss Emma Goldman, said:

Before introducing our distinguished guest, I want to read two short letters which we have received. The first is from Miss Ethel Mannin, who was chairman once, I think, about two months ago:

"I am very sorry indeed not to be able to come to the Emma Goldman and Paul Robeson luncheon, as they are both people for whom I have a profound admiration. Will you please send me her book. A friend has recommended it to me, and I have been meaning to read it for some time."

I hope she will carry out that intention.

The second letter is from one of the greatest men now living in England, Mr. Havelock Ellis:

"I have appreciated the invitation to attend the luncheon for Miss Emma Goldman, for whom I have a high regard and admiration, but I regret I am unable to accept as I have never taken any part in such functions, and at my age I feel it is too late to begin. I wish all success to the gathering, and I shall be pleased if you would give to those present my hearty good wishes."

That is a good send-off from a very distinguished man, and one of the most distinguished writers and men of science in this country.

The very name of Miss Emma Goldman recalls to me the times, some years ago now, when I was very intimate with those great Russians, the most distinguished of whom was Kropotkin. I am glad to say they were all friends of mine, and I lament it very deeply that after all they have suffered and sacrificed for the cause of freedom, it had been, in their opinion, quite futile.

Freedom is almost disappearing from the world. You all know it. If you want further proof, read this morning's papers and the description of the conditions in Germany. Hardly any freedom, political freedom, or even social freedom, is now left in Europe, and it is not much better in Japan.

We have with us now a real champion of freedom, a woman who has devoted all her life, amidst terrible sufferings, indignities and loss to the cause of freedom and freedom alone. You ought to read her book, as Miss Mannin I believe intends to do, and read that book called "Living My Life." It is one of the most remarkable documents ever written by man or woman, of a courageous, devoted life.

I do not expect everyone here to adopt at once her idea of society or government—well, she has no idea of government. It is true that our greatest thinker—I need not mention his name— as an Irishman has said, "Every Englishman is an anarchist at heart." Well, I wish it were so, and then we might get something like a free and noble form of existence. We have had in this country many fine anarchists, not only Russian anarchists, but real Englishmen, like Edward Carpenter, and I do hope that Englishmen, anarchists at heart, as they are called, will give a generous and fine welcome to a woman who has suffered all her life for the cause of freedom. May I now call upon Miss Emma Goldman. (Applause)

MISS EMMA GOLDMAN, speaking on "An Anarchist Looks at Life," said:

Mr. Chairman, Ladies and Gentlemen, the subject this noon is, "An Anarchist Looks at Life." I cannot speak for all my fellow anarchists, but for myself I wish to say that I have been so furiously busy living my life that I had not a moment left to look at it. I am aware that a period comes to everybody when we are obliged, perforce, to sit back and look at life. That period is a wise old age, but never having grown wise I do not expect to ever reach that point. Most people who look at life never live it. What they see is not life but a mere shadow of it. Have they not been taught that life is a curse visited upon them by a bungling God who has made man in his own image? Therefore most people look at life and upon life as a sort of stepping-stone to a heaven in the hereafter. They dare not live life, or get the living spirit out of life as it presents itself to them. It means a risk; it means the giving up their little material achievements. It means going against "public opinion" and the laws and rules of one's country. There are few people who have the daring and the courage to give up what they hug at their hearts. They fear that their possible gain will not be the equivalent for what they give up. As for myself, I can say that I was like Topsy. I was not born and raised—I "grewed." I grew with life, life in all its aspects, in its heights and in its depths. The price to pay was high, of course, but if I had to pay it all over again, I should gladly do it, for unless you are willing to pay the price, unless you are willing to plunge into the very depths, you will never be able to remount to the heights of life.

Naturally, life presents itself in different forms to different ages. Between the age of eight and twelve I dreamed of becoming a Judith. I longed to avenge the sufferings of my people, the Jews, to cut off the head of their Holofernos. When I was fourteen I wanted to study medicine, so as to be able to help my fellow-beings. When I was fifteen I suffered from unrequited love, and I wanted to commit suicide in a romantic way by drinking a lot of vinegar. I thought that would make me look ethereal and interesting, very pale and poetic when in my grave, but at sixteen I decided on a more exalted death. I wanted to dance myself to death.

Then came America, America with its huge factories, the pedaling of a machine for ten hours a day at two dollars fifty a week. It was followed by the greatest event in my life, which made me what I am. It was the tragedy of Chicago, in 1887, when five of the noblest men were judicially murdered by the State of Illinois. They were the famous anarchists of America—Albert Parsons, Spies, Fischer, Engels, and Lingg, who were legally assassinated on the 11th of November, 1887. Brave young Lingg cheated his executioners, preferring to die by his own hand, while three other comrades of the executed—Neebe, Fielden and Schwab—were doomed to prison. The death of those Chicago martyrs was my spiritual birth: their ideal became the motive of my entire life.

I realise that most of you have but a very inadequate, very strange and usually false conception of Anarchism. I do not blame you. You get your information from the daily press. Yet that is the very last place on earth to seek for truth in any state of form. Anarchism, to the great teachers and leaders in the spiritual aspect of life, was not a dogma, not a thing that drains the blood from the heart and makes people zealots, dictators or impossible bores. Anarchism is a releasing and liberating force because it teaches people to rely on their own possibilities, teaches them faith in liberty, and inspires men and women to strive for a state of social life where every one shall be free and secure. There is neither freedom nor security in the world today: whether one be rich or poor, whether his station high or low, no one is secure as long as there is a single slave in the world. No one is safe or secure as long as he must submit to the orders, whim or will of another who has the power to punish him, to send him to prison or to take his life, to dictate the terms of his existence, even from the cradle to the grave.

It is not only because of love of one's fellow-men—it is for their own sake that people must learn to understand the meaning and significance of Anarchism, and it will not be long before they will appreciate the great importance and the beauty of its philosophy.

Anarchism repudiates any attempt of a group of men or of any individual to arrange life for others. Anarchism rests on faith in humanity and its potentialities, while all other social philosophies have no faith in humanity whatever. The other philosophies insist that man cannot govern himself and that he must be ruled over. Nowadays most people believe that the stronger the Government the greater the success of society will be. It is the old belief in the rod. The more used on the child the finer will it be when grown to manhood or womanhood. We have emancipated ourselves from that stupidity. We have come to understand that education does not mean knocking in, does not mean crippling, warping and dwarfing the young growth. We have learned that freedom in the development of the child secures better results, both so far as the child and society are concerned.

That, ladies and gentlemen, is Anarchism. The greater the freedom and the opportunities for every unit in society, the finer will be the individual and the better for society; and the more creative and constructive the life of the collectivity. That, in brief, has been the ideal to which I have devoted my life.

Anarchism is not a cut-and-dried theory. It is a vital spirit embracing all of life. Therefore I do not address myself only to some particular elements in society: I do not address myself only to the workers. I address myself to the upper classes as well, for indeed they need enlightenment even more than the workers. Life itself teaches the masses, and it is a strict, effective teacher. Unfortunately life does not teach those who consider themselves the socially select, the better educated, the superior. I have always held that every form of information and instruction that helps to widen the mental horizon of men and women is most useful and should be employed. For in the last analysis, the grand adventure—which is liberty, the true inspiration of all idealists, poets and artists—is the only human adventure worth striving and living for.

I do not know how many of you have read Gorki's marvelous prose-poem called "The Snake and the Falcon." The snake cannot understand the falcon. "Why don't you rest here in the dark, in the good slimy moisture?" the snake demands. "Why soar to the heavens? Don't you know the dangers lurking there, the stress and storm awaiting you there, and the hunter's gun which will bring you down and destroy your life?" But the falcon paid no heed. It spread its wings and soared through space, its triumphant song resounding through the heavens. One day the falcon was brought down, blood streaming from its heart, and the snake said: "You fool, I warned you, I told you to stay where I am, in the dark, in the good warm moisture, where no one could find you and harm you." But with its last breath the falcon replied: "I have soared through space, I have scaled dazzling heights, I have beheld the light, I have lived, I have lived!"

Was My Life Worth Living?

Harper's, December 1934

It is strange what time does to political causes. A generation ago it seemed to many American conservatives as if the opinions which Emma Goldman was expressing might sweep the world. Now she fights almost alone for what seems to be a lost cause; contemporary radicals are overwhelmingly opposed to her; more than that, her devotion to liberty and her detestation of government interference might be regarded as placing her anomalously in the same part of the political spectrum as the gentlemen of the Liberty League, only in a more extreme position at its edge. Yet in this article, which might be regarded as her last will and testament, she sticks to her guns. Needless to say, her opinions are not ours. We offer them as an exhibit of valiant consistency, of really rugged individualism unaltered by opposition or by advancing age. — The Editors.

How much a personal philosophy is a matter of temperament and how much it results from experience is a moot question. Naturally we arrive at conclusions in the light of our experience, through the application of a process we call reasoning to the facts observed in the events of our lives. The child is susceptible to fantasy. At the same time he sees life more truly in some respects than his elders do as he becomes conscious of his surroundings. He has not yet become absorbed by the customs and prejudices which make up the largest part of what passes for thinking. Each child responds differently to his environment. Some become rebels, refusing to be dazzled by social superstitions. They are outraged by every injustice perpetrated upon them or upon others. They grow ever more sensitive to the suffering round them and the restriction registering every convention and taboo imposed upon them.

I evidently belong to the first category. Since my earliest recollection of my youth in Russia I have rebelled against orthodoxy in every form. I could never bear to witness harshness whether I was outraged over the official brutality practiced on the peasants in our neighborhood. I wept bitter tears when the young men were conscripted into the army and torn from homes and hearths. I resented the treatment of our servants, who did the hardest work and yet had to put up with wretched sleeping quarters and the leavings of our table. I was indignant when I discovered that love between young people of Jewish and Gentile origin was considered the crime of crimes, and the birth of an illegitimate child the most depraved immorality.

On coming to America I had the same hopes as have most European immigrants and the same disillusionment, though the latter affected me more keenly and more deeply. The immigrant without money and without connections is not permitted to cherish the comforting illusion that America is a benevolent uncle who assumes a tender and impartial guardianship of nephews and nieces. I soon learned that in a republic there are myriad ways by which the strong, the cunning, the rich can seize power and hold it. I saw the many work for small wages which kept them always on the borderline of want for the few who made huge profits. I saw the courts, the halls of legislation, the press, and the schools—in fact every avenue of education and protection—effectively used as an instrument for the safeguarding of a minority, while the masses were denied every right. I found that the politicians knew how to befog every issue, how to control public opinion and manipulate votes to their own advantage and to that of their financial and industrial allies. This was the picture of democracy I soon discovered on my arrival in the United States. Fundamentally there have been few changes since that time.

This situation, which was a matter of daily experience, was brought home to me with a force that tore away shams and made reality stand out vividly and clearly by an event which occurred shortly after my coming to America. It was the so-called Haymarket riot, which resulted in the trial and conviction of eight men, among them five Anarchists. Their crime was an all-embracing love for the fellow-men and their determination to emancipate the oppressed and disinherited masses. In no way had the State of Illinois succeeded in proving their connection with the bomb that had been thrown at an open-air meeting in Haymarket Square in Chicago. It was their Anarchism which resulted in their conviction and execution on the 11th of November, 1887. This judicial crime left an indelible mark on my mind and heart and sent me forth to acquaint myself with the ideal for which these men had died so heroically. I dedicated myself to their cause.

It requires something more than personal experience to gain a philosophy or point of view from any specific event. It is the quality of our response to the event and our capacity to enter into the lives of others that help us to make their lives and experiences our own. In my own case my convictions have derived and developed from events in the lives of others as well as from my own experience. What I have seen meted out to others by authority and repression, economic and political, transcends anything I myself may have endured.

I have often been asked why I maintained such a non-compromising antagonism to government and in what way I have found myself oppressed by it. In my opinion every individual is hampered by it. It exacts taxes from production. It creates tariffs, which prevent free exchange. It stands ever for the status quo and traditional conduct and belief. It comes into private lives and into most intimate personal relations, enabling the superstitious, puritanical, and distorted ones to impose their ignorant prejudice and moral servitudes upon the sensitive, the imaginative, and the free spirits. Government does this by its divorce laws, its moral censorships, and by a thousand petty persecutions of those who are too honest to wear the moral mask of respectability. In addition, government protects the strong at the expense of the weak, provides courts and laws which the rich may scorn and the poor must obey. It enables the predatory rich to make wars to provide foreign markets for the favored ones, with prosperity for the rulers and wholesale death for the ruled. However, it is not only government in the sense of the state which is destructive of every individual value and quality. It is the whole complex of authority and institutional domination which strangles life. It is the superstition, myth, pretense, evasions, and subservience which support authority and institutional domination. It is the reverence for these institutions instilled in the school, the church and the home in order that man may believe and obey without protest. Such a process of devitalizing and distorting personalities of the individual and of whole communities may have been a part of historical evolution; but it should be strenuously combated by every honest and independent mind in an age which has any pretense to enlightenment.

It has often been suggested to me that the Constitution of the United States is a sufficient safeguard for the freedom of its citizens. It is obvious that even the freedom it pretends to guarantee is very limited. I have not been impressed with the adequacy of the safeguard. The nations of the world, with centuries of international law behind them, have never hesitated to engage in mass destruction when solemnly pledged to keep the peace; and the legal documents in America have not prevented the United States from doing the same. Those in authority have and always will abuse their power. And the instances when they do not do so are as rare as roses growing on icebergs. Far from the Constitution playing any liberating part in the lives of the American people, it has robbed them of the capacity to rely on their own resources or do their own thinking. Americans are so easily hoodwinked by the sanctity of law and authority. In fact, the pattern of life has become standardized, routinized, and mechanized like canned food and Sunday sermons. The hundred-percenter easily swallows syndicated information and factory-made ideas and beliefs. He thrives on the wisdom given him over the radio and cheap magazines by corporations whose philanthropic aim is selling America out. He accepts the standards of conduct and art in the same breath with the advertising of chewing gum, toothpaste, and shoe polish. Even songs are turned out like buttons or automobile tires—all cast from the same mold.

II

Yet I do not despair of American life. On the contrary, I feel that the freshness of the American approach and the untapped stores of intellectual and emotional energy resident in the country offer much promise for the future. The War has left in its wake a confused generation. The madness and brutality they had seen, the needless cruelty and waste which had almost wrecked the world made them doubt the values their elders had given them. Some, knowing nothing of the world's past, attempted to create new forms of life and art from the air. Others experimented with decadence and despair. Many of them, even in revolt, were pathetic. They were thrust back into submission and futility because they were lacking in an ideal and were further hampered by a sense of sin and the burden of dead ideas in which they could no longer believe.

Of late there has been a new spirit manifested in the youth which is growing up with the depression. This spirit is more purposeful though still confused. It wants to create a new world, but is not clear as to how it wants to go about it. For that reason the young generation asks for saviors. It tends to believe in dictators and to hail each new aspirant for that honor as a messiah. It wants cut and dried systems of salvation with a wise minority to direct society on some one-way road to utopia. It has not yet realized that it must save itself. The young generation has not yet learned that the problems confronting them can be solved only by themselves and will have to be settled on the basis of social and economic freedom in co-operation with the struggling masses for the right to the table and joy of life.

As I have already stated, my objection to authority in whatever form has been derived from a much larger social view, rather than from anything I myself may have suffered from it. Government has, of course, interfered with my full expression, as it has with others. Certainly the powers have not spared me. Raids on my lectures during my thirty-five years' activity in the United States were a common occurrence, followed by innumerable arrests and three convictions to terms of imprisonment. This was followed by the annulment of my citizenship and my deportation. The hand of authority was forever interfering with my life. If I have none the less expressed myself, it was in spite of every curtailment and difficulty put in my path and not because of them. In that I was by no means alone. The whole world has given heroic figures to humanity, who in the face of persecution and obloquy have lived and fought for their right and the right of mankind to free and unstinted expression. America has the distinction of having contributed a large quota of native-born children who have most assuredly not lagged behind. Walt Whitman, Henry David Thoreau, Voltairine de Cleyre, one of America's great Anarchists, Moses Harman, the pioneer of woman's emancipation from sexual bondage, Horace Traubel, sweet singer of liberty, and quite an array of other brave souls have expressed themselves in keeping with their vision of a new social order based on freedom from every form of coercion. True, the price they had to pay was high. They were deprived of most of the comforts society offers to ability and talent, but denies when they will not be subservient. But whatever the price, their lives were enriched beyond the common lot. I, too, feel enriched beyond measure. But that is due to the discovery of Anarchism, which more than anything else has strengthened my conviction that authority stultifies human development, while full freedom assures it.

I consider Anarchism the most beautiful and practical philosophy that has yet been thought of in its application to individual expression and the relation it establishes between the individual and society. Moreover, I am certain that Anarchism is too vital and too close to human nature ever to die. It is my conviction that dictatorship, whether to the right or to the left, can never work—that it never has worked, and that time will prove this again, as it has been proved before. When the failure of modern dictatorship and authoritarian philosophies becomes more apparent and the realization of failure more general, Anarchism will be vindicated. Considered from this point, a recrudescence of Anarchist ideas in the near future is very probable. When this occurs and takes effect, I believe that humanity will at last leave the maze in which it is now lost and will start on the path to sane living and regeneration through freedom.

There are many who deny the possibility of such regeneration on the ground that human nature cannot change. Those who insist that human nature remains the same at all times have learned nothing and forgotten nothing. They certainly have not the faintest idea of the tremendous strides that have been made in sociology and psychology, proving beyond a shadow of a doubt that human nature is plastic and can be changed. Human nature is by no means a fixed quantity. Rather, it is fluid and responsive to new conditions. If, for instance, the so-called instinct of self-preservation were as fundamental as it is supposed to be, wars would have been eliminated long ago, as would all dangerous and hazardous occupations.

Right here I want to point out that there would not be such great changes required as is commonly supposed to insure the success of a new social order, as conceived by Anarchists. I feel that our present equipment would be adequate if the artificial oppressions and inequalities and the organized force and violence supporting them were removed.

Again it is argued that if human nature can be changed, would not the love of liberty be trained out of the human heart? Love of freedom is a universal trait, and no tyranny has thus far succeeded in eradicating it. Some of the modern dictators might try it, and in fact are trying it with every means of cruelty at their command. Even if they should last long enough to carry on such a project — which is hardly conceivable — there are other difficulties. For one thing, the people whom the dictators are attempting to train would have to be cut off from every tradition in their history that might suggest to them the benefits of freedom. They would also have to isolate them from contact with any other people from whom they could get libertarian ideas. The very fact, however, that a person has a consciousness of self, of being different from others, creates a desire to act freely. The craving for liberty and self-expression is a very fundamental and dominant trait.

As is usual when people are trying to get rid of uncomfortable facts, I have often encountered the statement that the average man does not want liberty; that the love for it exists in very few; that the American people, for instance, simply do not care for it. That the American people are not wholly lacking in the desire for freedom was proved by their resistance to the late Prohibition Law, which was so effective that even the politicians finally responded to popular demand and repealed the amendment. If the American masses had been as determined in dealing with more important issues, much more might have been accomplished. It is true, however, that the American people are just beginning to be ready for advanced ideas. This is due to the historical evolution of the country. The rise of capitalism and a very powerful state are, after all, recent in the United States. Many still foolishly believe themselves back in the pioneer tradition when success was easy, opportunities more plentiful than now, and the economic position of the individual was not likely to become static and hopeless.

It is true, none the less, that the average American is still steeped in these traditions, convinced that prosperity will yet return. But because a number of people lack individuality and the capacity for independent thinking I cannot admit that for this reason society must have a special nursery to regenerate them. I would insist that liberty, real liberty, a freer and more flexible society, is the only medium for the development of the best potentialities of the individual.

I will grant that some individuals grow to great stature in revolt against existing conditions. I am only too aware of the fact that my own development was largely in revolt. But I consider it absurd to argue from this fact that social evils should be perpetrated to make revolt against them necessary. Such an argument would be a repetition of the old religious idea of purification. For one thing it is lacking in imagination to suppose that one who shows qualities above the ordinary could have developed only in one way. The person who under this system has developed along the lines of revolt might readily in a different social situation have developed as an artist, scientist, or in any other creative and intellectual capacity.

III

Now I do not claim that the triumph of my ideas would eliminate all possible problems from the life of man for all time. What I do believe is that the removal of the present artificial obstacles to progress would clear the ground for new conquests and joy of life. Nature and our own complexes are apt to continue to provide us with enough pain and struggle. Why then maintain the needless suffering imposed by our present social structure, on the mythical grounds that our characters are thus strengthened, when broken hearts and crushed lives about us every day give the lie to such a notion?

Most of the worry about the softening of human character under freedom comes from prosperous people. It would be difficult to convince the starving man that plenty to eat would ruin his character. As for individual development in the society to which I look forward, I feel that with freedom and abundance unguessed springs of individual initiative would be released.

Human curiosity and interest in the world could be trusted to develop individuals in every conceivable line of effort.

Of course those steeped in the present find it impossible to realize that gain as an incentive could be replaced by another force that would motivate people to give the best that is in them. To be sure, profit and gain are strong factors in our present system. They have to be. Even the rich feel a sense of insecurity. That is, they want to protect what they have and to strengthen themselves. The gain and profit motives, however, are tied up with more fundamental motives. When a man provides himself with clothes and shelter, if he is the money-maker type, he continues to work to establish his status — to give himself prestige of the sort admired in the eyes of his fellow-men. Under different and more just conditions of life these more fundamental motives could be put to special uses, and the profit motive, which is only their manifestation, will pass away. Even today the scientist, inventor, poet, and artist are not primarily moved by the consideration of gain or profit. The urge to create is the first and most impelling force in their lives. If this urge is lacking in the mass of workers it is not at all surprising, for their occupation is deadly routine. Without any relation to their lives or needs, their work is done in the most appalling surroundings, at the behest of those who have the power of life and death over the masses. Why then should they be impelled to give of themselves more than is absolutely necessary to eke out their miserable existence?

In art, science, literature, and in departments of life which we believe to be somewhat removed from our daily living we are hospitable to research, experiment, and innovation. Yet, so great is our traditional reverence for authority that an irrational fear arises in most people when experiment is suggested to them. Surely there is even greater reason for experiment in the social field than in the scientific. It is to be hoped, therefore, that humanity or some portion of it will be given the opportunity in the not too distant future to try its fortune living and developing under an application of freedom corresponding to the early stages of an anarchistic society. The belief in freedom assumes that human beings can co-operate. They do it even now to a surprising extent, or organized society would be impossible. If the devices by which men can harm one another, such as private property, are removed and if the worship of authority can be discarded, co-operation will be spontaneous and inevitable, and the individual will find it his highest calling to contribute to the enrichment of social well-being.

Anarchism alone stresses the importance of the individual, his possibilities and needs in a free society. Instead of telling him that he must fall down and worship before institutions, live and die for abstractions, break his heart and stunt his life for taboos, Anarchism insists that the center of gravity in society is the individual—that he must think for himself, act freely, and live fully. The aim of Anarchism is that every individual in the world shall be able to do so. If he is to develop freely and fully, he must be relieved from the interference and oppression of others. Freedom is, therefore, the cornerstone of the Anarchist philosophy. Of course, this has nothing in common with a much boasted "rugged individualism." Such predatory individualism is really flabby, not rugged. At the least danger to its safety it runs to cover of the state and wails for protection of armies, navies, or whatever devices for strangulation it has at its command. Their "rugged individualism" is simply one of the many pretenses the ruling class makes to unbridled business and political extortion.

Regardless of the present trend toward the strong-armed man, the totalitarian states, or the dictatorship from the left, my ideas have remained unshaken. In fact, they have been strengthened by my personal experience and the world events through the years. I see no reason to change, as I do not believe that the tendency of dictatorship can ever successfully solve our social problems. As in the past, so I do now insist that freedom is the soul of progress and essential to every phase of life. I consider this as near a law of social evolution as anything we can postulate. My faith is in the individual and in the capacity of free individuals for united endeavor.

The fact that the Anarchist movement for which I have striven so long is to a certain extent in abeyance and overshadowed by philosophies of authority and coercion affects me with concern, but not with despair. It seems to me a point of special significance that many countries decline to admit Anarchists. All governments hold the view that while parties of the right and left may advocate social changes, still they cling to the idea of government and authority. Anarchism alone breaks with both and propagates uncompromising rebellion. In the long run, therefore, it is Anarchism which is considered deadlier to the present regime than all other social theories that are now clamoring for power.

Considered from this angle, I think my life and my work have been successful. What is generally regarded as success—acquisition of wealth, the capture of power or social prestige—I consider the most dismal failures. I hold when it is said of a man that he has arrived, it means that he is finished—his development has stopped at that point. I have always striven to remain in a state of flux and continued growth, and not to petrify in a niche of self-satisfaction. If I had my life to live over again, like anyone else, I should wish to alter minor details. But in any of my more important actions and attitudes I would repeat my life as I have lived it. Certainly I should work for Anarchism with the same devotion and confidence in its ultimate triumph.

There Is No Communism in Russia

American Mercury, April 1935

Communism is now on everybody's lips. Some talk of it with the exaggerated enthusiasm of a new convert, others fear and condemn it as a social menace. But I venture to say that neither its admirers—the great majority of them—nor those who denounce it have a very clear idea of what Bolshevik Communism really is.

Speaking generally, Communism is the ideal of human equality and brotherhood. It considers the exploitation of man by man as the source of all slavery and oppression. It holds that economic inequality leads to social injustice and is the enemy of moral and intellectual progress. Communism aims at a society where classes have been abolished as a result of common ownership of the means of production and distribution. It teaches that only in a classless, solidaric commonwealth can man enjoy liberty, peace and well-being.

My purpose is to compare Communism with its application in Soviet Russia, but on closer examination I find it an impossible task. As a matter of fact, there is no Communism in the U.S.S.R. Not a single Communist principle, not a single item of its teaching is being applied by the Communist party there.

To some this statement may appear as entirely false; others may think it vastly exaggerated. Yet I feel sure that an objective examination of conditions in present-day Russia will convince the unprejudiced reader that I speak with entire truth.

It is necessary to consider here, first of all, the fundamental idea underlying the alleged Communism of the Bolsheviki. It is admittedly of a centralized, authoritarian kind. That is, it is based almost exclusively on governmental coercion, on violence. It is not the Communism of voluntary association. It is compulsory State Communism. This must be kept in mind in order to understand the method applied by the Soviet state to carry out such of its plans as may seem to be Communistic.

The first requirement of Communism is the socialization of the land and of the machinery of production and distribution. Socialized land and machinery belong to the people, to be settled upon and used by individuals or groups according to their needs. In Russia land and machinery are not socialized but *nationalized*. The term is a misnomer, of course. In fact, it is entirely devoid of content. In reality there is no such thing as national wealth. A nation is too abstract a term to "own" anything. Ownership may be by an individual, or by a group of individuals; in any case by some quantitatively defined reality. When a certain thing does not belong to an individual or group, it is either nationalized or socialized. If it is nationalized, it belongs to the state; that is, the government has control of it and may dispose of it according to its wishes and views. But when a thing is socialized, every individual has free access to it and use it without interference from anyone.

In Russia there is no socialization either of land or of production and distribution. Everything is nationalized; it belongs to the government, exactly as does the post-office in America or the railroad in Germany and other European countries. There is nothing of Communism about it.

No more Communistic than the land and means of production is any other phase of the Soviet economic structure. All sources of existence are owned by the central government; foreign trade is its absolute monopoly; the printing presses belong to the state, and every book and paper issued is a government publication. In short, the entire country and everything in it is the property of the state, as in ancient days it used to be the property of the crown. The few things not yet nationalized, as some old ramshackle houses in Moscow, for instance, or some dingy little stores with a pitiful stock of cosmetics, exist on sufferance only, with the government having the undisputed right to confiscate them at any moment by simple decree.

Such a condition of affairs may be called state capitalism, but it would be fantastic to consider it in any sense Communistic.

II.

Let us now turn to production and consumption, the levers of all existence. Maybe in them we shall find a degree of Communism that will justify us in calling life in Russia Communistic, to some extent at least.

I have already pointed out that the land and the machinery of production are owned by the state. The methods of production and the amounts to be manufactured by every industry in each and every mill, shop and factory are determined by the state, by the central government—by Moscow—through its various organs.

Now, Russia is a country of vast extent, covering about one sixth of the earth's surface. It is peopled by a mixed population of 165,000,000. It consists of a number of large republics, of various races and nationalities, each region having its own particular interests and needs. No doubt, industrial and economic planning is vitally necessary for the well-being of a community. True Communism—economic equality as between man and man and between communities—requires the best and most efficient planning by each community, based upon its local requirements and possibilities. The basis of such planning must be the complete freedom of each community to produce according to its needs and to dispose of its products according to its judgment: to change its surplus with other similarly independent communities without let or hindrance by any external authority.

That is the essential politico-economic nature of Communism. It is neither workable nor possible on any other basis. It is necessarily libertarian, Anarchistic.

There is no trace of such Communism—that is to say, of any Communism—in Soviet Russia. In fact, the mere suggestion of such a system is considered criminal there, and any attempt to carry it out is punished by death.

Industrial planning and all the processes of production and distribution are in the hands of the central government. Supreme Economic Council is subject only to the authority of the Communist Party. It is entirely independent of the will or wishes of the people comprising the Union of Socialist Soviet Republics. Its work is directed by the policies and decisions of the Kremlin. This explains why Soviet Russia exported vast amounts of wheat and other grain while wide regions in the south and southeast of Russia were stricken with famine, so that more than two million of its people died of starvation (1932-1933).

There were "reasons of state" for it. The euphonious has from time immemorial masked tyranny, exploitation and the determination of every ruler to prolong and perpetuate his rule. Incidentally, I may mention that—in spite of country-wide hunger and lack of the most elemental necessities of life in Russia—the entire First Five-Year Plan aimed at developing that branch of heavy industry which serves, or can be made to serve, *military* purposes.

As with production, so with distribution and every other form of activity. Not only individual cities and towns, but the constituent parts of the Soviet Union are entirely deprived of independent existence. Politically mere vassals of Moscow, their whole economic, social and cultural activity is planned, cut out for them and ruthlessly controlled by the "proletarian dictatorship" in Moscow. More: the life of every locality, of every individual even, in the so-called "Socialist" republics, is managed in the very last detail by the "general line" laid down by the "center." In other words, by the Central Committee and Politbureau of the Party, both of them controlled absolutely by one man, Stalin. To call such a dictatorship, this personal autocracy more powerful and absolute than any Czar's, by the name of Communism seems to me the acme of imbecility.

III.

Let us see now how Bolshevik "Communism" affects the lives of the masses and of the individual.

There are naive people who believe that at least some features of Communism have been introduced into the lives of the Russian people. I wish it were true, for that would be a hopeful sign, a promise of potential development along that line. But the truth is that in no phase of Soviet life, no more in the social than in individual relations, has there ever been any attempt to apply Communist principles in any shape or form. As I have pointed out before, the very suggestion of free, voluntary Communism is taboo in Russia and is regarded as counter-revolutionary and high treason against the infallible Stalin and the holy "Communist" Party.

And here I do not speak of the libertarian, Anarchist Communism. What I assert is that there is not the least sign in Soviet Russia even of authoritarian, State Communism. Let us glance at the actual facts of everyday life there.

The essence of Communism, even of the coercive kind, is the absence of social classes. The introduction of economic equality is its first step. This has been the basis of all Communist philosophies, however they may have differed in other respects. The purpose common to all of them was to secure social justice; and all of them agreed that it was not possible without establishing economic equality. Even Plato, in spite of the intellectual and moral strata in his Republic, provided for absolute economic equality, since the ruling classes were not to enjoy greater rights or privileges than the lowest social unit.

Even at the risk of condemnation for telling the whole truth, I must state unequivocally and unconditionally that the very opposite is the case in Soviet Russia. Bolshevism has not abolished the classes in Russia: it has merely reversed their former relationship. As a matter of fact, it has multiplied the social divisions which existed before the Revolution.

When I arrived in Soviet Russia in January 1920, I found innumerable economic categories, based on the food rations received from the government. The sailor was getting the best ration, superior in quality, quantity and variety to the food issued to the rest of the population. He was the aristocrat of the Revolution: economically and socially he was universally considered to belong to the new privileged classes. After him came the soldier, the Red Army man, who received a much smaller ration, even less bread. Below the soldier in the scale was the worker in the military industries; then came other workers, subdivided into the skilled, the artisan, the laborer, etc. Each category received a little less bread, fats, sugar, tobacco, and other products (whenever they were to be had at all). Members of the former bourgeoisie, officially abolished as a class and expropriated, were in the last economic category and received practically nothing. Most of them could secure neither work nor lodgings, and it was no one's business how they were to exist, to keep from stealing or from joining the counter-revolutionary armies and robber bands.

The possession of a red card, proving membership in the Communist Party, placed one above all these categories. It entitled its owner to a special ration, enabled him to eat in the Party *stolovaya* (mess-room) and produced, particularly if supported by recommendations from party members higher up, warm underwear, leather boots, a fur coat, or other valuable articles. Prominent party men had their own dining-rooms, to which the ordinary members had no access. In the Smolny, for instance, then the headquarters of the Petrograd government, there were two different dining-rooms, one for Communists in high position, the other for the lesser lights. Zinoviev, then chairman of the Petrograd Soviet and virtual autocrat of the Northern District, and other government heads took their meals at home in the Astoria, formerly the best hotel in the city, turned into the first Soviet House, where they lived with their families.

Later on I found the same situation in Moscow, Kharkov, Kiev, Odessa—everywhere in Soviet Russia.

It was the Bolshevik system of "Communism." What dire effects it had in causing dissatisfaction, resentment and antagonism throughout the country, resulting in industrial and agrarian sabotage, in strikes and revolts—of this further on. It is said that man does not live by bread alone. True, but he cannot live at all without it. To the average man, to the masses in Russia, the different rations established in the country for the liberation of which they had bled, was the symbol of the new regime. It signified to them the great lie of Bolshevism, the broken promises of freedom, for freedom meant to them social justice, economic equality. The instinct of the masses seldom goes wrong; in this case it proved prophetic. What wonder, then, that the universal enthusiasm over the Revolution soon turned into disillusionment and bitterness, to opposition and hatred. How often Russian workers complained to me: "We don't mind working hard and going hungry. It's the injustice which we mind. If the country is poor, if there is little bread, then let us all share that little, but let us share equally. As things are now, it's the same as it used to be; some get more, others less, and some get nothing at all."

The Bolshevik system of privilege and inequality was not long in producing its inevitable results. It created and fostered social antagonisms; it alienated the masses from the Revolution, paralysed their interest in it and their energies, and thus defeated all the purposes of the Revolution.

The same system of privilege and inequality, strengthened and perfected, is in force today.

The Russian Revolution was in the deepest sense a social upheaval: its fundamental tendency was libertarian, its essential aim economic and social equality. Long before the October-November days (1917) the city proletariat began taking possession of the mills, shops and factories, while the peasants expropriated the big estates and turned the land to communal use. The continued development of the Revolution in its Communist direction depended on the unity of the revolutionary forces and the direct, creative initiative of the laboring masses. The people were enthusiastic in the great object before them; they eagerly applied their energies to the work of social reconstruction. Only they who had for centuries borne the heaviest burdens could, through free and systematic effort, find the road to a new, regenerated society.

But Bolshevik dogmas and "Communist" statism proved a fatal handicap to the creative activities of the people. The fundamental characteristic of Bolshevik psychology is distrust of the masses. Their Marxist theories, centering all power in the exclusive hands of their party, quickly resulted in the destruction of revolutionary cooperation, in the arbitrary and ruthless suppression of all other political parties and movements. Bolshevik tactics encompassed the systematic eradication of every sign of dissatisfaction, stifled all criticism and crushed independent opinion, popular initiative and effort. Communist dictatorship, with its extreme mechanical centralization, frustrated the economic and industrial activities of the country. The great masses were deprived of the opportunity to shape the policies of the Revolution or to take part in the administration of their own affairs. The labor unions were governmentalized and turned into mere transmitters of the orders of the state. The people's cooperatives—that vital nerve of active solidarity and mutual help between city and country—were liquidated. The Soviets of peasants and workers were castrated and transformed into obedient committees. The government monopolized every phase of life. A bureaucratic machine was created, appalling in its inefficiency, corruption, brutality. The Revolution was divorced from the people and thus doomed to perish; and over all hung the dreaded sword of Bolshevik terrorism.

That was the "Communism" of the Bolsheviki in the first stages of the Revolution. Everyone knows that it brought the complete paralysis of industry, agriculture and transport. It was the period of "military Communism," of agrarian and industrial conscription, of the razing of peasant villages by Bolshevik artillery—those "constructive" social and economic policies of

Bolshevik Communism which resulted in the fearful famine in 1921.

IV.

And today? Has that "Communism" changed its nature? Is it actually different from the "Communism" of 1921? To my regret I must state that, in spite of all widely advertised changes and new economic policies, Bolshevik "Communism" is essentially the same as it was in 1921. Today the peasantry in Soviet Russia is entirely dispossessed of the land. The *sovkhozi* are government farms on which the peasant works as a hired man, just as the man in the factory. This is known as "industrialization" of agriculture, "transforming the peasant into a proletarian." In the *kolkhoz* the land only nominally belongs to the village. Actually it is owned by the government. The latter can at any moment — and often does — commandeer the *kolkhoz* members for work in other parts of the country or exile whole villages for disobedience. The *kolkhozi* are worked collectively, but the government control of them amounts to expropriation. It taxes them at its own will; it sets whatever price it chooses to pay for grain and other products, and neither the individual peasant nor the village Soviet has any say in the matter. Under the mask of numerous levies and compulsory government loans, it appropriates the products of the *kolkhozi*, and for some actual or pretended offenses punishes them by taking away all their grain.

The fearful famine of 1921 was admittedly due chiefly to the *razverstka*, the ruthless expropriation practiced at the time. It was because of it, and of the rebellion that resulted, that Lenin decided to introduce the NEP — the New Economic Policy — which limited state expropriation and enabled the peasant to dispose of some of his surplus for his own benefit. The NEP immediately improved economic conditions throughout the land. The famine of 1932-1933 was due to similar "Communist" methods of the Bolsheviki: to enforced collectivization.

The same result as in 1921 followed. It compelled Stalin to revise his policy somewhat. He realised that the welfare of a country, particularly of one predominantly agricultural as Russia is, depends primarily on the peasantry. The motto was proclaimed: the peasant must be given opportunity to greater "well-being." This "new" policy is admittedly only a breathing spell for the peasant. It has no more of Communism in it than the previous agrarian policies. From the beginning of Bolshevik rule to this day, it has been nothing but expropriation in one form or another, now and then differing in degree but always the same in kind—a continuous process of state robbery of the peasantry, of prohibitions, violence, chicanery and reprisals, exactly as in the worst days of Czarism and the World War. The present policy is but a variation of the "military Communism" of 1920-1921, with more of the military and less of the Communist element in it. Its "equality" is that of a penitentiary; its "freedom" that of a chain gang. No wonder the Bolsheviki declare that liberty is a bourgeois prejudice.

Soviet apologists insist that the old "military Communism" was justified in the initial period of the Revolution, in the days of the blockade and military fronts. But more than sixteen years have passed since. There are no more blockades, no more fighting fronts, no more counter-revolution. Soviet Russia has secured the recognition of all the great governments of the world. It emphasizes its good will toward the bourgeois states, solicits their cooperation, and is doing a large business with them. In fact, the Soviet government is on terms of friendship even with Mussolini and Hitler, those famous champions of liberty. It is helping capitalism to weather its economic storms by buying millions of dollars' worth of products and opening new markets to it.

This is, in the main, what Soviet Russia has accomplished during seventeen years since the Revolution. But as to Communism—that is another matter. In this regard, the Bolshevik government has followed exactly the same course as before, and worse. It has made some superficial changes politically and economically, but fundamentally it has remained exactly the same state, based on the same principle of violence and coercion and using the same methods of tenor and compulsion as in the period of 1920-1921.

There are more classes in Soviet Russia today than in 1917, more than in most other countries in the world. The Bolsheviki have created a vast Soviet bureaucracy, enjoying special privileges and almost unlimited authority over the masses, industrial and agricultural. Above that bureaucracy is the still more privileged class of "responsible comrades," the new Soviet aristocracy. The industrial class is divided and subdivided into numerous gradations. There are the *udarniki,* the shock troops of labor, entitled to various privileges; the "specialists," the artisans, the ordinary workers and laborers. There are the factory "cells," the shop committees, the pioneers, the *komsomoltsi,* the party members, all enjoying material advantages and authority. There is the large class of *lishentsi,* persons deprived of civil rights, the greater number of them also of the chance to work, of the right to live in certain places, practically cut off from all means of existence. The notorious "pale" of the Czarist times, which forbade Jews to live in certain parts of the country, has been revived for the entire population by the introduction of the new Soviet passport system. Over and above all these classes is the dreaded G.P.U., secret, powerful and arbitrary, a government within the government. The G.P.U., in its turn, has its own class divisions. It has its own armed forces, its own commercial and industrial establishments, its own laws and regulations, and a vast slave army of convict labor. Aye, even in the Soviet prisons and concentration camps there are various classes with special privileges.

In the field of industry the same kind of "Communism" prevails as in agriculture. A sovietized Taylor system is in vogue throughout Russia, combining a minimum standard of production and piece work—the highest degree of exploitation and human degradation, involving also endless differences in wages and salaries. Payment is made in money, in rations, in reduced charges for rent, lighting, etc., not to speak of the special rewards and premiums for *udarniki.* In short, it is the *wage system* which is in operation in Russia.

Need I emphasize that an economic arrangement based on the wage system cannot be considered as in any way related to Communism? It is its antithesis.

V.

All these features are to be found in the present Soviet system. It is unpardonable naivete, or still more unpardonable hypocrisy, to pretend — as the Bolshevik apologists do — that the compulsory labor service in Russia is "the self-organization of the masses for purposes of production."

Strange to say, I have met seemingly intelligent persons who claim that by such methods the Bolsheviki "are building Communism." Apparently they believe that building consists in ruthless destruction, physically and morally, of the best values of mankind. There are others who pretend to think that the road to freedom and cooperation leads through labor slavery and intellectual suppression. According to them, to instill the poison of hatred and envy, of universal espionage and terror, is the best preparation for manhood and the fraternal spirit of Communism.

I do not think so. I think that there is nothing more pernicious than to degrade a human being into a cog of a soulless machine, turn him into a serf, into a spy or the victim of a spy. There is nothing more corrupting than slavery and despotism.

There is a psychology of political absolutism and dictatorship, common to all forms: the means and methods used to achieve a certain end in the course of time themselves become the end. The ideal of Communism, of Socialism, has long ago ceased to inspire the Bolshevik leaders as a class. Power and the strengthening of power has become their sole object. But abject subjection, exploitation and degradation are developing a new psychology in the great mass of the people also.

The young generation in Russia is the product of Bolshevik principles and methods. It is the result of sixteen years of official opinions, the only opinions permitted in the land. Having grown up under the deadly monopoly of ideas and values, the youth in the U.S.S.R. knows hardly anything about Russia itself. Much less does it know of the world outside. It consists of blind fanatics, narrow and intolerant, it lacks all ethical perception, it is devoid of the sense of justice and fairness. To this element is added a class of climbers and careerists, of self-seekers reared on the Bolshevik dogma: "The end justifies the means." Yet it were wrong to deny the exceptions in the ranks of Russia's youth. There are a goodly number who are deeply sincere, heroic, idealistic. They see and feel the force of the loudly professed party ideals. They realize the betrayal of the masses. They suffer deeply under the cynicism and callousness towards every human emotion. The presence of *komsomolszi* in the Soviet political prisons, concentration camps and exile, and the escapes under most harrowing difficulties, prove that the young generation does not consist entirely of cringing adherents. No, not all of Russia's youth has been turned into puppets, obsessed bigots, or worshippers at Stalin's shrine and Lenin's tomb.

Already the dictatorship has become an absolute necessity for the continuation of the regime. For where there are classes and social inequality, there the state must resort to force and suppression. The ruthlessness of such a situation is always in proportion to the bitterness and resentment imbuing the masses. That is why there is more governmental terrorism in Soviet Russia than anywhere else in the civilized world today, for Stalin has to conquer and enslave a stubborn peasantry of a hundred million. It is popular hatred of the regime which explains the stupendous industrial sabotage in Russia, the disorganization of the transport after sixteen years of virtual military management; the terrific famine in the South and Southeast, notwithstanding favorable natural conditions and in spite of the severest measures to compel the peasants to sow and reap, in spite even of wholesale extermination and of the deportation of more than a million peasants to forced labor camps.

Bolshevik dictatorship is an absolutism which must constantly be made more relentless in order to survive, calling for the complete suppression of independent opinion and criticism within the party, within even its highest and most exclusive circles. It is a significant feature of this situation that official Bolshevism and its paid and unpaid agents are constantly assuring the world that "all is well in Soviet Russia and getting better." It is of the same quality as Hitler's constant emphasis of how greatly he loves peace while he is feverishly increasing his military strength.

Far from getting better, the dictatorship is daily growing more relentless. The latest decree against so-called counter-revolutionists, or traitors to the Soviet State, should convince even some of the most ardent apologists of the wonders performed in Russia. The decree adds strength to the already existing laws against everyone who cannot or will not reverence the infallibility of the holy trinity, Marx, Lenin and Stalin. And it is more drastic and cruel in its effect upon everyone deemed a culprit. To be sure, hostages are nothing new in the U.S.S.R. They were already part of the terror when I came to Russia. Peter Kropotkin and Vera Figner had protested in vain against this black spot on the escutcheon of the Russian Revolution. Now, after seventeen years of Bolshevik rule, a new decree was thought necessary. It not only revives the taking of hostages; it even aims at cruel punishment for every adult member of the real or imaginary offender's family. The new decree defines treason to the state as "any acts committed by citizens of the U.S.S.R. detrimental to the military forces of the U.S.S.R., its independence or the inviolability of its territory, such as espionage, betrayal of military or state secrets, going over to the side of the enemy, fleeing to a foreign country or flight [this time the word used means airplane flight] to a foreign country."

Traitors have, of course, always been shot. What makes the new decree more terrifying is the remorseless punishment it demands for everyone living with or supporting the hapless victim, whether he knows of the crime or not. He may be imprisoned, or exiled, or even shot. He may lose his civil rights, and he may forfeit everything he owns. In other words, the new decree sets a premium on informers who, to save their own skins, will ingratiate themselves with the G.P.U., will readily turn over the unfortunate kin of the offenders to the Soviet henchmen.

This new decree must forever put to rest any remaining doubts as to the existence of true Communism in Russia. It departs from even the pretense of internationalism and proletarian class interest. The old tune is now changed to a paean song of the Fatherland, with the ever servile Soviet press loudest in the chorus:

"Defense of the Fatherland is the supreme law of life, and he who raises his hand against the Fatherland, who betrays it, must be destroyed."

Soviet Russia, it must now be obvious, is an absolute despotism politically and the crassest form of state capitalism economically.

Durruti Is Dead, Yet Living

1936

Durruti, whom I saw but a month ago, lost his life in the street-battles of Madrid.

My previous knowledge of this stormy petrel of the Anarchist and revolutionary movement in Spain was merely from reading about him. On my arrival in Barcelona I learned many fascinating stories of Durruti and his column. They made me eager to go to the Aragon front, where he was the leading spirit of the brave and valiant militias, fighting against fascism.

I arrived at Durruti's headquarters towards evening, completely exhausted from the long drive over a rough road. A few moments with Durruti was like a strong tonic, refreshing and invigorating. Powerful of body as if hewn from the rocks of Montserrat, Durruti easily represented the most dominating figure among the Anarchists I had met since my arrival in Spain. His terrific energy electrified me as it seemed to effect everyone who came within its radius.

I found Durruti in a veritable beehive of activity. Men came and went, the telephone was constantly calling for Durruti. In addition was the deafening hammering of workers who were constructing a wooden shed for Durruti's staff. Through all the din and constant call on his time Durruti remained serene and patient. He received me as if he had known me all his life. The graciousness and warmth from a man engaged in a life and death struggle against fascism was something I had hardly expected.

I had heard much about Durruti's mastery over the column that went by his name. I was curious to learn by what means other than military drive he had succeeded in welding together 10,000 volunteers without previous military training and experience of any sort. Durruti seemed surprised that I, an old Anarchist, should even ask such a question.

"I have been an Anarchist all my life," he replied, "I hope I have remained one. I should consider it very sad indeed, had I to turn into a general and rule the men with a military rod. They have come to me voluntarily, they are ready to stake their lives in our antifascist fight. I believe, as I always have, in freedom. The freedom which rests on the sense of responsibility. I consider discipline indispensable, but it must be inner discipline, motivated by a common purpose and a strong feeling of comradeship." He had gained the confidence of the men and their affection because he had never played the part of a superior. He was one of them. He ate and slept as simply as they did. Often even denying himself his own portion for one weak or sick, and needing more than he. And he shared their danger in every battle. That was no doubt the secret of Durruti's success with his column. The men adored him. They not only carried out all his instructions, they were ready to follow him in the most perilous venture to repulse the fascist position.

I had arrived on the eve of an attack Durruti had prepared for the following morning. At daybreak Durruti, like the rest of the militia with his rifle over his shoulder, led the way. Together with them he drove the enemy back four kilometers, and he also succeeded in capturing a considerable amount of arms the enemies had left behind in their flight.

The moral example of simple equality was by no means the only explanation of Durruti's influence. There was another, his capacity to make the militiamen realize the deeper meaning of the antifascist war—the meaning that had dominated his own life and that he had learned to articulate to the poorest and most undeveloped of the poor.

Durruti told me of his approach to the difficult problems of the men who come for leave of absence at moments when they were most needed at the front. The men evidently knew their leader—they knew his decisiveness—his iron will. But also they knew the sympathy and gentleness hidden behind his austere exterior. How could he resist when the men told him of illness at home—parents, wife or child?

Durruti hounded before the glorious days of July 1936, like a wild beast from country to country. Imprisoned time on end as a criminal. Even condemned to death. He, the hated Anarchist, hated by the sinister trinity, the bourgeoisie, the state and the church. This homeless vagabond incapable of feeling as the whole capitalistic puck proclaimed. How little they knew Durruti. How little they understood his loving heart. He had never remained indifferent to the needs of his fellows. Now however, he was engaged in a desperate struggle with fascism in the defense of the Revolution, and every man was needed at his place. Verily a difficult situation to meet. But Durruti's ingeniousness conquered all difficulties. He listened patiently to the story of woe and then held forth on the cause of illness among the poor. Overwork, malnutrition, lack of air, lack of joy in life.

"Don't you see comrade, the war you and I are waging is to safeguard our Revolution and the Revolution is to do away with the misery and suffering of the poor. We must conquer our fascist enemy. We must win the war. You are an essential part of it. Don't you see, comrade?" Durruti's comrades did see, they usually remained.

Sometimes one would prove abdurate, and insist on leaving the front. "All right," Durruti tells him, "but you will go on foot, and by the time you reach your village, everybody will know that your courage had failed you, that you have run away, that you have shirked your self-imposed task." That worked like magic. The man pleads to remain. No military brow-beating, no coercion, no disciplinary punishment to hold the Durruti column at the front. Only the vulcanic energy of the man carries everyone along and makes them feel as one with him.

A great man this Anarchist Durruti, a born leader and teacher of men, thoughtful and tender comrade all in one. And now Durruti is dead. His great heart beats no more. His powerful body felled down like a giant tree. And yet, and yet— Durruti is not dead. The hundreds of thousands that turned out Sunday, November 22nd, 1936, to pay Durruti their last tribute have testified to that.

No, Durruti is not dead. The fires of his flaming spirit lighted in all who knew and loved him, can never be extinguished. Already the masses have lifted high the torch that fell from Durruti's hand. Triumphantly they are carrying it before them on the path Durruti had blazoned for many years. The path that leads to the highest summit of Durruti's ideal. This ideal was Anarchism—the grand passion of Durruti's life. He had served it utterly. He remained faithful to it until his last breath.

If proof were needed of Durruti's tenderness, his concern in my safety gave it to me. There was no place to house me for the night at the General-Staff quarters. And the nearest village was Pina. But it had been repeatedly bombarded by the fascists. Durruti was loathe to send me there. I insisted it was alright. One dies but once. I could see the pride in his face that his old comrade had no fear. He let me go under strong guard.

I was grateful to him because it gave me a rare chance to meet many of the comrades in arms of Durruti and also to speak with the people of the village. The spirit of these much-tried victims of fascism was most impressive.

The enemy was only a short distance from Pina on the other side of a creek. But there was no fear or weakness among the people. Heroically they fought on. "Rather dead, than fascist rule," they told me. "We stand and fall with Durruti in the antifascist fight to the last man."

In Pina I discovered a child of eight years old, an orphan who had already been harnessed to daily toil with a fascist family. Her tiny hands were red and swollen. Her eyes, full of horror from the dreadful shocks she had already suffered at the hands of Franco's hirelings. The people of Pina are pitifully poor. Yet everyone gave this ill-treated child care and love she had never known before.

The European Press has from the very beginning of the antifascist war competed with each other in calumny and vilification of the Spanish defenders of liberty. Not a day during the last four months but what these satraps of European fascism did not write the most sensational reports of atrocities committed by the revolutionary forces. Every day the readers of these yellow sheets were fed on the riots and disorders in Barcelona and other towns and villages, free from the fascist invasion.

Having traveled over the whole of Catalonia, Aragon, and the Levante, having visited every city and village on the way, I can testify that there is not one word of truth in any of the bloodcurdling accounts I had read in some of the British and Continental press.

A recent example of the utter unscrupulous news-fabrication was furnished by some of the papers in regard to the death of the Anarchist and heroic leader of the antifascist struggle, Buenaventura Durruti.

According to this perfectly absurd account, Durruti's death is supposed to have called forth violent dissension and outbreaks in Barcelona among the comrades of the dead revolutionary hero Durruti.

Whoever it was who wrote this preposterous invention he could not have been in Barcelona. Much less know the place of Buenaventura Durruti in the hearts of the members of the CNT and FAI. Indeed, in the hearts and estimation of all regardless of their divergence with Durruti's political and social ideas.

In point of truth, there never was such complete oneness in the ranks of the popular front in Catalonia, as from the moment when the news of Durruti's death became known until the last when he was laid to rest.

Every party of every political tendency fighting Spanish fascism turned out en masse to pay loving tribute to Buenaventura Durruti. But not only the direct comrades of Durruti, numbering hundreds of thousands and all the allies in the antifascist struggle, the largest part of the population of Barcelona represented an incessant stream of humanity. All had come to participate in the long and exhausting funeral procession. Never before had Barcelona witnessed such a human sea whose silent grief rose and fell in complete unison.

As to the comrades of Durruti—comrades closely knit by their ideal and the comrades of the gallant column he had created. Their admiration, their love, their devotion and respect left no place for discord and dissension. They were as one in their grief and in their determination to continue the battle against fascism and for the realization of the Revolution for which Durruti had lived, fought and had staked his all until his last breath.

No, Durruti is not dead! He is more alive than living. His glorious example will now be emulated by all the Catalan workers and peasants, by all the oppressed and disinherited. The memory of Durruti's courage and fortitude will spur them on to great deeds until fascism has been slain. Then the real work will begin—the work on the new social structure of human value, justice and freedom.

No, no! Durruti is not dead! He lives in us for ever and ever.

Address to the International Working Men's Association Congress
1937

Life imposes strange situations on all of us. For forty-eight years I was considered an extremist in our ranks. One who refused to compromise our ideas or tactics for any purpose whatsoever — one who always insisted that the Anarchist aim and methods must harmonize, or the aim would never be achieved. Yet here I am trying to explain the action of our Spanish comrades to the European opponents, and the criticism of the latter to the comrades of the CNT-FAI. In other words, after a lifetime of an extreme left position I find myself in the center, as it were.

I have seen from the moment of my first arrival in Spain in September 1936 that our comrades in Spain are plunging head foremost into the abyss of compromise that will lead them far away from their revolutionary aim. Subsequent events have proven that those of us who saw the danger ahead were right. The participation of the CNT-FAI in the government, and concessions to the insatiable monster in Moscow, have certainly not benefited the Spanish Revolution, or even the anti-Fascist struggle. Yet closer contact with reality in Spain, with the almost insurmountable odds against the aspirations of the CNT-FAI, made me understand their tactics better, and helped me to guard against any dogmatic judgment of our comrades.

I am inclined to believe that the critics in our ranks outside of Spain would be less rigid in their appraisal if they too had come closer to the life-and-death struggle of the CNT-FAI—not that I do not agree with their criticism. I think them 95 percent right. However, I insist that independent thinking and the right of criticism have ever been our proudest Anarchist boast, indeed, the very bulwark of Anarchism. The trouble with our Spanish comrades is their marked sensitivity to criticism, or even to advice from any comrade outside of Spain. But for that, they would understand that their critics are moved not by villainy, but by their deepest concern for the fate of the CNT-FAI.

The Spanish Anarcho-Syndicalist and Anarchist movements until very recently have held out the most glaring fulfillment of all our dreams and aspirations. I cannot therefore blame those of our comrades who see in the compromises of the Spanish Anarchists a reversal of all they had held high for well nigh seventy years. Naturally some comrades have grown apprehensive and have begun to cry out against the slippery road which the CNT-FAI entered on. I have known these comrades for years. They are among my dearest friends. I know it is their revolutionary integrity which makes them so critical, and not any ulterior motive. If our Spanish comrades could only understand this, they would be less indignant, nor consider their critics their enemies.

Also, I fear that the critics too are very much at fault. They are no less dogmatic than the Spanish comrades. They condemn every step made in Spain unreservedly. In their sectarian attitude they have overlooked the motive element recognised in our time even in capitalist courts. Yet it is a fact that one can never judge human action unless one has discovered the motive back of the action.

When I have pointed this out to our critical comrades they have insisted that Lenin and his group were also moved by the best intentions, "and see what they have made of the Revolution." I fail to see even the remotest similarity. Lenin aimed at a formidable State machine, a deadly dictatorship. From the very beginning, this spelled the death of the Russian Revolution—whereas the CNT-FAI not only aimed at, but actually gave life to, libertarian economic reconstructions. From the very moment they had driven the Fascists and militarists out of Catalonia, this herculean task was never lost sight of. The work achieved, considering the insurmountable obstacles, was extraordinary. Already on my first visit I was amazed to find so many collectives in the large cities and the villages.

I returned to Spain with apprehension because of all the rumours that had reached me after the May events of the destruction of the collectives. It is true that the Lister and Karl Marx Brigades went through Aragon and places in Catalonia like a cyclone, devastating everything in their way; but it is nevertheless the fact that most of the collectives were keeping up as if no harm had come to them. In fact I found the collectives in September and October 1937 in better-organised condition and in better working order—and that, after all, is the most important achievement that must be kept in mind in any appraisal of the mistakes made by our comrades in Spain. Unfortunately, our critical comrades do not seem to see this all-important side of the CNT-FAI. Yet it is this which differentiates them from Lenin and his crowd who, far from even attempting to articulate the Russian Revolution in terms of constructive effort, destroyed everything during the civil war and even many years after.

Strangely enough, the very comrades of the civil war in Russia who had explained every step of the dictatorship as "revolutionary necessity" are now the most unyielding opponents of the CNT-FAI. "We have learned our lesson from the Russian Revolution," they say. But as no one learns anything from the experience of others, we must, whether we like it or not, give our Spanish comrades a chance to find their bearings through their own experience. Surely our own flesh and blood are entitled to the same patient help and solidarity some of us have given generously to our archenemies the Communists.

The CNT-FAI are not so wrong when they insist that the conditioning in Spain is quite different from that which actuated the struggle in Russia. In point of fact the two social upheavals are separate and distinct from each other.

The Russian Revolution came on top of a war-exhausted people, with all the social fabric in Russia disintegrated, the country far removed from outside influences. Whatever dangers it encountered during the civil war came entirely from within the country itself. Even the help given to the interventionists by England, Poland, and France were contributed sparingly. Not that these countries were not ready to crush the Revolution by means of well-equipped armies; but Europe was too sapped. There were neither men nor arms enough to enable the Russian counter-revolutionists to destroy the Revolution and its people.

The revolution in Spain was the result of a military and Fascist conspiracy. The first imperative need that presented itself to the CNT-FAI was to drive out the conspiratorial gang. The Fascist danger had to be met with almost bare hands. In this process the Spanish workers and peasants soon came to see that their enemies were not only Franco and his Moorish hordes. They soon found themselves beseiged by formidable armies and an array of modern arms furnished to Franco by Hitler and Mussolini, with all the imperialist pack playing their sinister underhanded game. In other words, while the Russian Revolution and the civil war were being fought out on Russian soil and by Russians, the Spanish revolution and anti-Fascist war involves all the powers of Europe. It is no exaggeration to say that the Spanish Civil War has spread out far beyond its own confines.

As if that were not enough to force the CNT-FAI to hold themselves up by any means, rather than to see the revolution and the masses drowned in the bloodbath prepared for them by Franco and his allies—our comrades had also to contend with the inertia of the international proletariat. Herein lies another tragic difference between the Russian and Spanish revolutions.

The Russian Revolution had met with almost instantaneous response and unstinted support from the workers in every land. This was soon followed by the revolution in Germany, Austria, and Hungary; and the general strike of the British workers who refused to load arms intended for the counter-revolutionists and interventionists. It brought about the mutiny in the Black Sea, and raised the workers everywhere to the highest pitch of enthusiasm and sacrifice.

The Spanish revolution, on the other hand, just because its leaders are Anarchists, immediately became a sore in the eyes not only of the bourgeoisie and the democratic governments, but also of the entire school of Marxists and liberals. In point of truth the Spanish revolution was betrayed by the whole world.

It has been suggested that our comrades in every country have contributed handsomely in men and money to the Spanish struggle, and that they alone should have been appealed to.

Well, comrades, we are members of the same family and we are among ourselves. We therefore need not beat around the bush. The deplorable fact is that there is no Anarchist or Anarcho-Syndicalist movement of any great consequence outside of Spain, and in a smaller degree France, with the exception of Sweden. Whatever Anarchist movements there are in other countries consist of small groups. In all England, for instance, there is no organised movement—only a few groups.

With the most fervent desire to aid the revolution in Spain, our comrades outside of it were neither numerically nor materially strong enough to turn the tide. Thus finding themselves up against a stone wall, the CNT-FAI was forced to descend from its lofty traditional heights to compromise right and left: participation in the government, all sorts of humiliating overtures to Stalin, superhuman tolerance for his henchmen who were openly plotting and conniving against the Spanish revolution.

Of all the unfortunate concessions our people have made, their entry into ministries seemed to me the least offensive. No, I have not changed my attitude toward government as an evil. As all through my life, I still hold that the State is a cold monster, and that it devours everyone within its reach. Did I not know that the Spanish people see in government a mere makeshift, to be kicked overboard at will, that they had never been deluded and corrupted by the parliamentary myth, I should perhaps be more alarmed for the future of the CNTFAI. But with Franco at the gate of Madrid, I could hardly blame the CNT-FAI for choosing a lesser evil—participation in the government rather than dictatorship, the most deadly evil.

Russia has more than proven the nature of this beast. After twenty years it still thrives on the blood of its makers. Nor is its crushing weight felt in Russia alone. Since Stalin began his invasion of Spain, the march of his henchmen has been leaving death and ruin behind them. Destruction of numerous collectives, the introduction of the Tcheka with its "gentle" methods of treating political opponents, the arrest of thousands of revolutionaries, and the murder in broad daylight of others. All this and more has Stalin's dictatorship given Spain, when he sold arms to the Spanish people in return for good gold. Innocent of the jesuitical trick of "our beloved comrade" Stalin, the CNT-FAI could not imagine in their wildest dreams the unscrupulous designs hidden behind the seeming solidarity in the offer of arms from Russia.

Their need to meet Franco's military equipment was a matter of life and death. The Spanish people had not a moment to lose if they were not to be crushed. What wonder if they saw in Stalin the saviour of the anti-Fascist war? They have since learned that Stalin helped to make Spain safe against the Fascists so as to make it safer for his own ends.

The critical comrades are not at all wrong when they say that it does not seem worthwhile to sacrifice one ideal in the struggle against Fascism, if it only means to make room for Soviet Communism. I am entirely of their view—that there is no difference between them. My own consolation is that with all their concentrated criminal efforts, Soviet Communism has not taken root in Spain. I know whereof I speak. On my recent visit to Spain I had ample opportunity to convince myself that the Communists have failed utterly to win the sympathies of the masses; quite the contrary. They have never been so hated by the workers and peasants as now.

It is true that the Communists are in the government and have political power—that they use their power to the detriment of the revolution, the anti-Fascist struggle, and the prestige of the CNT-FAI. But strange as it may seem, it is nevertheless no exaggeration when I say that in a moral sense the CNT has gained immeasurably. I give a few proofs.

Since the May events the Madrid circulation of the CNT [paper] has almost doubled, while the two Communist papers in that city have only 26,000. The CNT alone has 100,000 throughout Castile. The same has happened with our paper, *Castilla Libre*. In addition, there is the *Frente Libertario*, with a circulation of 100,000 copies.

A more significant fact is that when the Communists call a meeting it is poorly attended. When the CNT-FAI hold meetings the halls are packed to overflowing. I had one occasion to convince myself of this truth. I went to Allecante with comrade Federica Montseney and although the meeting was held in the forenoon, and rain came down in a downpour. the hall was nevertheless packed to capacity. It is the more surprising that the Communists can lord it over everybody; but it is one of the many contradictions of the situation in Spain.

If our comrades have erred in permitting the Communist invasion it was only because the CNT-FAI are the implacable enemies of Fascism. They were the first, not only in Spain but in the whole world, to repulse Fascism, and they are determined to remain the last on the battlefield, until the beast is slain. This supreme determination sets the CNT-FAI apart in the history of indomitable champions and fighters for freedom the world has ever known. Compared with this, their compromises appear in a less glaring light.

True, the tacit consent to militarization on the part of our Spanish comrades was a violent break with their Anarchist past. But grave as this was, it must also be considered in the light of their utter military inexperience. Not only theirs but ours as well. All of us have talked rather glibly about antimilitarism. In our zeal and loathing of war we have lost sight of modern warfare, of the utter helplessness of untrained and unequipped men face to face with mechanized armies, and armed to their teeth for the battle on land, sea, and air. I still feel the same abhorrence of militarism, its dehumanization, its brutality and its power to turn men into automatons. But my contact with our comrades at the various fronts during my first visit in 1936 convinced me that some training was certainly needed if our militias were not to be sacrificed like newborn children on the altar of war.

While it is true that after July 19 tens of thousands of old and young men volunteered to go to the front—they went with flying colours and the determination to conquer Franco in a short time—they had no previous military training or experience. I saw a great many of the militia when I visited the Durruti and Huesca fronts. They were all inspired by their ideal—by the hatred of Fascism and passionate love of freedom. No doubt that would have carried them a long way if they had had only the Spanish Fascists to face; but when Germany and Italy began pouring in hundreds of thousands of men and masses of war materiel, our militias proved very inadequate indeed. If it was inconsistent on the part of the CNT-FAI to consent to militarisation, it was also inconsistent for us to change our attitude toward war, which some of us had held all our lives. We had always condemned war as serving capitalism and no other purpose; but when we realised that our heroic comrades in Barcelona had to continue the anti-Fascist struggle, we immediately rallied to their support, which was undoubtedly a departure from our previous stand on war. Once we realised that it would be impossible to meet hordes of Fascists armed to the very teeth, we could not escape the next step, which was militarisation. Like so many actions of the CNT-FAI undoubtedly contrary to our philosophy, they were not of their making or choosing. They were imposed upon them by the development of the struggle, which if not brought to a successful end, would exterminate the CNT-FAI, destroy their constructive achievements, and set back Anarchist thought and ideas not only in Spain but in the rest of the world.

Dear comrades, it is not a question of justification of everything the CNT-FAI have been doing. It is merely trying to understand the forces that drove and drive them on. Whether to triumph or defeat will depend a great deal on how much we can awaken the international proletariat to come to the rescue of the struggle in Spain; and unless we can create unity among ourselves, I do not see how we can call upon the workers of the world to unite in their efforts to conquer Fascism and to rescue the Spanish revolution.

Our comrades have a sublime ideal to inspire them; they have great courage and the iron will to conquer Fascism. All that goes a long way to hold up their morale. Airplanes bombarding towns and villages and all the other monster mechanisms cannot be stopped by spiritual values. The greater the pity that our side was not prepared, nor had the physical means to match the inexhaustible supplies streaming into Franco's side.

It is a miracle of miracles that our people are still on deck, more than ever determined to win. I cannot but think that the training our comrades are getting in the military schools will make them fitter to strike, and with greater force. I have been strengthened in this belief by my talks with young comrades in the military schools—with some of them at the Madrid front and with CNT-FAI members occupying high military positions. They all assured me that they had gained much through the military training, and that they feel more competent and surer of themselves to meet the enemy forces. I am not forgetting the danger of militarisation in a prolonged war. If such a calamity should happen, there will not be many of our gallant militias left to return as military ultimatums. I fervently hope that Fascism will be conquered quickly, and that our comrades can return from the front in triumph to where they came from—the collectives, land and industries. For the present there is no danger that they will become cogs in the military wheel.

All these factors directing the course of the CNT-FAI should be taken into consideration by the comrade critics, who after all are far removed from the struggle, hence really not in a position to see the whole tragic drama through the eyes of those who are in the actual struggle.

I do not mean to say that I may not also reach the painful point of disagreement with the CNT-FAI. But until Fascism is conquered, I would not raise my hand against them. For the present my place is at the side of the Spanish comrades and their great struggle against a whole world.

Comrades, the CNT-FAI are in a burning house; the flames are shooting up through every crevice, coming nearer and nearer to scorch our comrades. At this crucial moment, and with but few people trying to help save our people from the consuming flame, it seems to me a breach of solidarity to pour the acid of your criticism on their burned flesh. As for myself, I cannot join you in this. I know the CNT-FAI have gone far afield from their and our ideology. But that cannot make me forget their glorious revolutionary traditions of seventy years. Their gallant struggle—always haunted, always driven at bay, always in prison and exile. This makes me think that the CNT-FAI have remained fundamentally the same, and that the time is not far off when they will again prove themselves the symbol, the inspirational force, that the Spanish Anarcho-Syndicalists and Anarchists have always been to the rest of the Anarchists in the world.

Since I have been privileged to be in Spain twice—near the comrades, near their splendid constructive labour—since I was able to see their selflessness and determination to build a new life on their soil, my faith in our comrades has deepened into a firm conviction that, whatever their inconsistencies, they will return to first principles. Tested by the fires of the anti-Fascist war and the revolution, the CNT-FAI will emerge unscathed. Therefore I am with them, regardless of everything. A thousand times would I have rather remained in Spain to risk my life in their struggle than returned to the so-called safety in England. But since that could not be, I mean to strain every muscle and every nerve to make known, in as far as my pen and voice can reach, the great moral and organisational force of the CNT-FAI and the valour and heroism of our Spanish comrades.

Trotsky Protests Too Much

1938

Introduction.

This pamphlet grew out of an article for *Vanguard*, the Anarchist monthly published in New York City. It appeared in the July issue, 1938, but as the space of the magazine is limited, only part of the manuscript could be used. It is here given in a revised and enlarged form.

Leon Trotsky will have it that criticism of his part in the Kronstadt tragedy is only to aid and abet his mortal enemy, Stalin. It does not occur to him that one might detest the savage in the Kremlin and his cruel regime and yet not exonerate Leon Trotsky from the crime against the sailors of Kronstadt.

In point of truth I see no marked difference between the two protagonists of the benevolent system of the dictatorship except that Leon Trotsky is no longer in power to enforce its blessings, and Josef Stalin is. No, I hold no brief for the present ruler of Russia. I must, however, point out that Stalin did not come down as a gift from heaven to the hapless Russian people. He is merely continuing the Bolshevik traditions, even if in a more relentless manner.

The process of alienating the Russian masses from the Revolution had begun almost immediately after Lenin and his party had ascended to power. Crass discrimination in rations and housing, suppression of every political right, continued persecution and arrests, early became the order of the day. True, the purges undertaken at that time did not include party members, although Communists also helped to fill the prisons and concentration camps. A case in point is the first Labour Opposition whose rank and file were quickly eliminated and their leaders Shlapnikov sent to the Caucasus for "a rest," and Alexandra Kollontay placed under house arrest. But all the other political opponents, among them Mensheviki, Social Revolutionists, Anarchists, many of the Liberal intelligentsia and workers as well as peasants, were given short shrift in the cellars of the Cheka, or exiled to slow death in distant parts of Russia and Siberia. In other words, Stalin has not originated the theory or methods that have crushed the Russian Revolution and have forged new chains for the Russian people.

I admit, the dictatorship under Stalin's rule has become monstrous. That does not, however, lessen the guilt of Leon Trotsky as one of the actors in the revolutionary drama of which Kronstadt was one of the bloodiest scenes.

I have before me two numbers, February and April 1938, of the *New International*, Trotsky's official magazine. They contain articles by John G. Wright, a hundred percent Trotskyist, and the Grand Mogul himself, purporting to be a refutation of the charges against him in re Kronstadt. Mr. Wright is merely echoing the voice of his master, and his material is in no way first hand, or from personal contact with the events of 1921. I prefer to pay my respects to Leon Trotsky. He has at least the doubtful merit of having been a party to the "liquidation" of Kronstadt.

There are, however, several very rash mis-statements in Wright's article that need to be knocked on the head. I shall, therefore, proceed to do so at once and deal with his master afterwards.

John G. Wright claims that *The Kronstadt Rebellion*, by Alexander Berkman, "is merely a restatement of the alleged facts and interpretations of the Right Social Revolutionists with a few insignificant alterations" — (culled from "The Truth About Russia in Volya, Russia, Prague, 1921").

The writer further accuses Alexander Berkman of "brazenness, plagiarism, and making, as is his custom, a few insignificant alterations, and hiding the real source of what appears as his own appraisal." Alexander Berkman's life and work have placed him among the greatest revolutionary thinkers and fighters, utterly dedicated to his ideal. Those who knew him will testify to his sterling quality in all his actions, as well as his integrity as a serious writer. They will certainly be amused to learn from Mr. Wright that Alexander Berkman was a "plagiarist" and "brazen," and that "his custom is making a few insignificant alterations. . . . ."

The average Communist, whether of the Trotsky or Stalin brand, knows about as much of Anarchist literature and its authors as, let us say, the average Catholic knows about Voltaire or Thomas Paine. The very suggestion that one should know what one's opponents stand for before calling them names would be put down as heresy by the Communist hierarchy. I do not think, therefore, that John G. Wright deliberately lies about Alexander Berkman. Rather do I think that he is densely ignorant.

It was Alexander Berkman's life-long habit to keep diaries. Even during the fourteen years' purgatory he had endured in the Western Penitentiary in the United States, Alexander Berkman had managed to keep up his diary which he succeeded in sending out sub rosa to me. On the S.S. *Buford* which took us on our long perilous cruise of 28 days, my comrade continued his diary and he kept up this old habit through the 23 months of our stay in Russia.

Prison Memoirs of an Anarchist, conceded by conservative critics even to be comparable with Feodor Dostoyevsky's *Dead House*, was fashioned from his diary. *The Kronstadt Rebellion* and his *Bolshevik Myth* are also the offspring of his day-by-day record in Russia. It is stupid, therefore, to charge that Berkman's brochure about Kronstadt "is merely a restatement of the alleged facts. . . . ." from the S.R. work that appeared in Prague.

On a par in accuracy with this charge against Alexander Berkman by Wright is his accusation that my old pal had denied the existence of General Kozlovsky in Kronstadt.

The Kronstadt Rebellion, page 15, states: "There was indeed a former General Kozlovsky in Kronstadt. It was Trotsky who had placed him there as an artillery specialist. He played no role whatever in the Kronstadt events." This was borne out by none other than Zinoviev who was then still at the zenith of his glory. At the Extraordinary Session of the Petrograd Soviet, 4th March, 1921, called to decide the fate of Kronstadt, Zinoviev said: "Of course Kozlovsky is old and can do nothing, but the White Officers are back of him and are misleading the sailors." Alexander Berkman, however, stressed the fact that the sailors would have none of Trotsky's former pet General, nor would they accept the offer of provisions and other help of Victor Tchernov, leader of the Right S.R.'s in Paris (Socialist Revolutionists).

Trotskyists no doubt consider it bourgeois sentimentality to permit the maligned sailors the right to speak for themselves. I insist that this approach to one's opponent is damnable Jesuitism and has done more to disintegrate the whole labour movement than anything else of the "sacred" tactics of Bolshevism.

That the reader may be in a position to decide between the criminal charge against Kronstadt and what the sailors had to say for themselves, I here reproduce the radio message to the workers of the world, 6th March, 1921:

"Our cause is just: we stand for the power of soviets, not parties. We stand for freely elected representatives of the labouring masses. The substitute Soviets manipulated by the Communist Party have always been deaf to our needs and demands; the only reply we have ever received was shooting. . . . . Comrades! They not only deceive you; they deliberately pervert the truth and resort to most despicable defamation. . . .

In Kronstadt the whole power is exclusively in the hands of the revolutionary sailors, soldiers and workers—not with counter revolutionists led by some Kozlovsky, as the lying Moscow radio tries to make you believe. . . . Do not delay, comrades! Join us, get in touch with us; demand admission to Kronstadt for your delegates. Only they will tell you the whole truth and will expose the fiendish calumny about Finnish bread and Entente offers.

"Long live the revolutionary proletariat and the peasantry!"

"Long live the power of freely elected Soviets!"

The sailors "led" by Kozlovsky, yet pleading with the workers of the world to send delegates that they might see whether there was any truth in the black calumny spread against them by the Soviet Press!

Leon Trotsky is surprised and indignant that anyone should dare to raise such a hue and cry over Kronstadt. After all, it happened so long ago, in fact seventeen years have passed, and it was a mere "episode in the history of the relation between the proletarian city and the petty bourgeois village." Why should anyone want to make so much ado at this late day unless it is to "compromise the only genuine revolutionary current which has never repudiated its banner, has not compromised with its enemies, and which alone represents the future." Leon Trotsky's egotism, known far and wide by his friends and his foes, has never been his weakest spot. Since his mortal enemy has endowed him with nothing short of a magic wand, his self-importance has reached alarming proportions.

Leon Trotsky is outraged that people should have revived the Kronstadt "episode" and ask questions about his part. It does not occur to him that those who have come to his defence against his detractor have a right to ask what methods he had employed when he was in power, and how he had dealt with those who did not subscribe to his dictum as gospel truth. Of course it was ridiculous to expect that he would beat his chest and say, "I, too, was but human and made mistakes. I, too, have sinned and have killed my brothers or ordered them to be killed." Only sublime prophets and seers have risen to such heights of courage. Leon Trotsky is certainly not one of them. On the contrary, he continues to claim omnipotence in all his acts and judgments and to call anathema on the heads of anyone who foolishly suggests that the great god Leon Trotsky also has feet of clay.

He jeers at the documentary evidence left by the Kronstadt sailors and the evidence of those who had been within sight and hearing of the dreadful siege of Kronstadt. He calls them "false labels." That does not, however, prevent him from assuring his readers that his explanation of the Kronstadt rebellion could be "substantiated and illustrated by many facts and documents." Intelligent people may well ask why Leon Trotsky did not have the decency to present these "false labels" so that the people might be in a position to form a correct opinion of them.

Now, it is a fact that even capitalist courts grant the defendant the right to present evidence on his own behalf. Not so Leon Trotsky, the spokesman of the one and only truth, he who has "never repudiated his banner and has never compromised with its enemies."

One can understand such lack of common decency in John G. Wright. He is, as I have already stated, merely quoting holy Bolshevik scripture. But for a world figure like Leon Trotsky to silence the evidence of the sailors seems to me indicative of a very small character. The old saying of the leopard changing his spots but not his nature forcibly applies to Leon Trotsky. The Calvary he has endured during his years of exile, the tragic loss of those near and dear to him, and, more poignantly still, the betrayal by his former comrades in arms, have taught him nothing. Not a glimmer of human kindness or mellowness has affected Trotsky's rancorous spirit.

What a pity that the silence of the dead sometimes speaks louder than the living voice. In point of truth the voices strangled in Kronstadt have grown in volume these seventeen years. Is it for this reason, I wonder, that Leon Trotsky resents its sound?

Leon Trotsky quotes Marx as saying, "that it is impossible to judge either parties or people by what they say about themselves." How pathetic that he does not realise how much this applies to him! No man among the able Bolshevik writers has managed to keep himself so much in the foreground or boasted so incessantly of his share in the Russian Revolution and after as Leon Trotsky. By this criterion of his great teacher, one would have to declare all Leon Trotsky's writing to be worthless, which would be nonsense of course.

In discrediting the motives which conditioned the Kronstadt uprising, Leon Trotsky records the following: "From different fronts I sent dozens of telegrams about the mobilisation of new 'reliable' detachments from among the Petersburg workers and Baltic fleet sailors, but already in 1918, and in any case not later than 1919, the fronts began to complain that a new contingent of 'Kronstadters' were unsatisfactory, exacting, undisciplined, unreliable in battle and doing more harm than good." Further on, on the same page, Trotsky charges that, "when conditions became very critical in hungry Petrograd the Political Bureau more than once discussed the possibility of securing an 'internal loan' from Kronstadt where a quantity of old provisions still remained, but the delegates of the Petrograd workers answered, 'You will never get anything from them by kindness; they speculate in cloth, coal and bread. At present in Kronstadt every kind of riff-raff has raised its head.'" How very Bolshevik that is, not only to slay one's opponents but also to besmirch their characters. From Marx and Engels, Lenin, Trotsky to Stalin, this method has ever been the same.

Now, I do not presume to argue what the Kronstadt sailors were in 1918 or 1919. I did not reach Russia until January 1920. From that time on until Kronstadt was "liquidated", the sailors of the Baltic fleet were held up as the glorious example of valour and unflinching courage. Time on end I was told not only by Anarchists, Mensheviks and social revolutionists, but by many Communists, that the sailors were the very backbone of the Revolution. On the 1st of May, 1920, during the celebration and the other festivities organised for the first British Labour Mission, the Kronstadt sailors presented a large clear-cut contingent, and were then pointed out as among the great heroes who had saved the Revolution from Kerensky, and Petrograd from Yudenich. During the anniversary of October the sailors were again in the front ranks, and their re-enactment of the taking of the Winter Palace was wildly acclaimed by a packed mass.

Is it possible that the leading members of the party, save Leon Trotsky, were unaware of the corruption and the demoralisation of Kronstadt, claimed by him? I do not think so. Moreover, I doubt whether Trotsky himself held this view of the Kronstadt sailors until March 1921. His story must, therefore, be an afterthought, or is it a rationalisation to justify the senseless "liquidation" of Kronstadt?

Granted that the personnel had undergone a change, it is yet a fact that the Kronstadters in 1921 were nevertheless far from the picture Leon Trotsky and his echo have painted. In point of actual fact, the sailors met their doom only because of their deep kinship and solidarity with the Petrograd workers whose power of endurance of cold and hunger had reached the breaking point in a series of strikes in February 1921. Why have Leon Trotsky and his followers failed to mention this? Leon Trotsky knows perfectly well, if Wright does not, that the first scene of the Kronstadt drama was staged in Petrograd on 24th February, and played not by the sailors but by the strikers. For it was on this date that the strikers had given vent to their accumulated wrath over the callous indifference of the men who had prated about the dictatorship of the proletariat which had long ago deteriorated into the merciless dictatorship of the Communist Party.

Alexander Berkman's entry in his diary of this historic day reads:

"The Trubotchny mill workers have gone on strike. In the distribution of winter clothing, they complain, the Communists received undue advantage over the non-partisans. The Government refuses to consider the grievances till the men return to work.

"Crowds of strikers gathered in the street near the mills, and soldiers were sent to disperse them. They were Kursanti,

Communist youths of the military academy. There was no violence.

"Now the strikers have been joined by the men from the Admiralty shops and Calernaya docks. There is much resentment against the arrogant attitude of the Government. A street demonstration was attempted, but mounted troops suppressed it."

It was after the report of their Committee of the real state of affairs among the workers in Petrograd that the Kronstadt sailors did in 1921 what they had done in 1917. They immediately made common cause with the workers. The part of the sailors in 1917 was hailed as the red pride and glory of the Revolution. Their identical part in 1921 was denounced to the whole world as counter-revolutionary treason. Naturally, in 1917 Kronstadt helped the Bolsheviks into the saddle. In 1921 they demanded a reckoning for the false hopes raised in the masses, and the great promise broken almost immediately the Bolsheviks had felt entrenched in their power. A heinous crime indeed. The important phase of this crime, however, is that Kronstadt did not "mutiny" out of a clear sky. The cause for it was deeply rooted in the suffering of the Russian workers; the city proletariat, as well as the peasantry.

To be sure, the former commissar assures us that "the peasants reconciled themselves to the requisition as a temporary evil," and that "the peasants approved of the Bolsheviki, but became increasingly hostile to the 'Communists'." But these contentions are mere fiction, as can be demonstrated by numerous proofs—not the least of them the liquidation of the peasant soviet, headed by Maria Spiridonova, and iron and fire used to force the peasants to yield up all their produce, including their grain for their spring sowing.

In point of historic truth, the peasants hated the régime almost from the start, certainly from the moment when Lenin's slogan, "Rob the robbers," was turned into "Rob the peasants for the glory of the Communist Dictatorship." That is why they were in constant ferment against the Bolshevik Dictatorship. A case in point was the uprising of the Karelian Peasants drowned in blood by the Tsarist General Slastchev-Krimsky. If the peasants were so enamoured with the Soviet régime, as Leon Trotsky would have us believe, why was it necessary to rush this terrible man to Karelia.

He had fought against the Revolution from its very beginning and had led some of the Wrangel forces in the Crimea. He was guilty of fiendish barbarities to war prisoners and infamous as a maker of pogroms. Now Slastchev-Krimsky recanted and he returned to "his Fatherland." This arch counter-revolutionist and Jew-baiter, together with several Tsarist generals and White Guardists, was received by the Bolsheviki with military honours. No doubt it was just retribution that the anti-Semite had to salute the Jew, Trotsky, his military superior. But to the Revolution and the Russian people the triumphal return of the imperialist was an outrage.

As a reward for his newly-fledged love of the Socialist Fatherland, Slastchev-Krimsky was commissioned to quell the Karelian peasants who demanded self-determination and better conditions.

Leon Trotsky tells us that the Kronstadt sailors in 1919 would not have given up provisions by "kindness" — not that kindness had been tried at any time. In fact, this word does not exist in Bolshevik lingo. Yet here are these demoralised sailors, the riff-raff speculators, etc., siding with the city proletariat in 1921, and their first demand is for equalisation of rations. What villains these Kronstadters were, really!

Much is being made by both writers against Kronstadt of the fact that the sailors who, as we insist, did not premeditate the rebellion, but met on the 1st of March to discuss ways and means of aiding their Petrograd comrades, quickly formed themselves into a Provisional Revolutionary Committee. The answer to this is actually given by John G. Wright himself. He writes: "It is by no means excluded that the local authorities in Kronstadt bungled in their handling of the situation. . . . . It is no secret that Kalinin and Commissar Kusmin, were none too highly esteemed by Lenin and his colleagues. . . . . In so far as the local authorities were blind to the full extent of the danger or failed to take proper and effective measures to cope with the crisis, to that extent their blunders played a part in the unfolding events. . . . ."

The statement that Lenin did not esteem Kalinin or Kusmin highly is unfortunately an old trick of Bolshevism to lay all blame on some bungler so that the heads may remain lily pure.

Indeed, the local authorities in Kronstadt did "bungle." Kuzmin attacked the sailors viciously and threatened them with dire results. The sailors evidently knew what to expect from such threats. They could not but guess that if Kuzmin and Vassiliev were permitted to be at large their first step would be to remove arms and provisions from Kronstadt. This was the reason why the sailors formed their Provisional Revolutionary Committee. An additional factor, too, was the news that a committee of 30 sailors sent to Petrograd to confer with the workers had been denied the right to return to Kronstadt, that they had been arrested and placed in the Cheka.

Both writers make a mountain of a molehill of the rumours announced at the meeting of 1st March to the effect that a truckload of soldiers heavily armed were on their way to Kronstadt. Wright has evidently never lived under an air-tight dictatorship. I have. When every channel of human contact is closed, when every thought is thrown back on itself and expression stifled, then rumours rise like mushrooms from the ground and grow into terrifying dimensions. Besides, truckloads of soldiers and Chekists armed to their very teeth tearing along the streets in the day, throwing out their nets at night and dragging their human haul to the Cheka, was a frequent sight in Petrograd and Moscow during the time when I was there. In the tension of the meeting after Kuzmin's threatening speech, it was perfectly natural for rumours to be given credence.

The news in the Paris Press about the Kronstadt uprising two weeks before it happened had been stressed in the campaign against the sailors as proof positive that they had been tools of the Imperialist gang and that rebellion had actually been hatched in Paris. It was too obvious that this yarn was used only to discredit the Kronstadters in the eyes of the workers.

In reality this advance news was like other news from Paris, Riga or Helsingfors, and which rarely, if ever, coincided with anything that had been claimed by the counter-revolutionary agents abroad. On the other hand, many events happened in Soviet Russia which would have gladdened the heart of the Entente and which they never got to know — events far more detrimental to the Russian Revolution caused by the dictatorship of the Communist Party itself. For instance, the Cheka which undermined many achievements of October and which already in 1921 had become a malignant growth on the body of the Revolution, and many other similar events which would take me too far afield to treat here.

No, the advance news in the Paris Press had no bearing whatever on the Kronstadt rebellion. In point of fact, no one in Petrograd in 1921 believed its connection, not even quite a number of Communists. As I have already stated, John G. Wright is merely an apt pupil of Leon Trotsky and therefore quite innocent of what most people within and outside of the party thought about this so-called "link."

Future historians will no doubt appraise the Kronstadt "mutiny" in its real value. If and when they do, they will no doubt come to the conclusion that the uprising could not have come more opportunely if it had been deliberately planned.

The most dominant factor which decided the fate of Kronstadt was the N.E.P. (the New Economic Policy). Lenin, aware of the very considerable party opposition this new-fangled "revolutionary" scheme would meet, needed some impending menace to ensure the smooth and ready acceptance of the N.E.P. Kronstadt came along most conveniently. The whole crushing propaganda machine was immediately put into motion to prove that the sailors were in league with all the Imperialist powers, and all the counter-revolutionary elements to destroy the Communist State. That worked like magic. The N.E.P. was rushed through without a hitch.

Time alone will prove the frightful cost this manoeuvre has entailed. The three hundred delegates, the young Communist flower, rushed from the Party Congress to crush Kronstadt, were a mere handful of the thousands wantonly sacrificed. They went fervently believing the campaign of vilification. Those who remained alive had a rude awakening.

I have recorded a meeting with a wounded Communist in a hospital in *My Disillusionment*. It has lost nothing of its poignancy in the years since:

"Many of those wounded in the attack on Kronstadt had been brought to the same hospital, mostly Kursanti. I had an opportunity to speak to one of them. His physical suffering, he said, was nothing as compared with his mental agony. Too late he had realised that he had been duped by the cry of 'counter-revolution.' No Tsarist generals, no White Guardists in Kronstadt had led the sailors—he found only his own comrades, sailors, soldiers and workers, who had heroically fought for the Revolution."

No one at all in his senses will see any similarity between the N.E.P. and the demand of the Kronstadt sailors for the right of free exchange of products. The N.E.P. came to reintroduce the grave evils the Russian Revolution had attempted to eradicate. The free exchange of products between the workers and the peasants, between the city and the country, embodied the very *raison d'etre* of the Revolution. Naturally "the Anarchists were against the N.E.P." But free exchange, as Zinoviev had told me in 1920, "is out of our plan of centralisation." Poor Zinoviev could not possibly imagine what a horrible ogre the centralisation of power would become.

It is the *idee fixe* of centralisation of the dictatorship which early began to divide the city and the village, the workers and the peasants, not, as Leon Trotsky will have it, because "the one is proletarian . . . . . and the other petty bourgeois," but because the dictatorship had paralysed the initiative of both the city proletariat and the peasantry.

Leon Trotsky makes it appear that the Petrograd workers quickly sensed "the petty bourgeois nature of the Kronstadt uprising and therefore refused to have anything to do with it." He omits the most important reason for the seeming indifference of the workers of Petrograd. It is of importance, therefore, to point out that the campaign of slander, lies and calumny against the sailors began on the 2nd March, 1921. The Soviet Press fairly oozed poison against the sailors. The most despicable charges were hurled against them, and this was kept up until Kronstadt was liquidated on 17th March. In addition, Petrograd was put under martial law. Several factories were shut down and the workers thus robbed, began to hold counsel with each other. In the diary of Alexander Berkman, I find the following:

"Many arrests are taking place. Groups of strikers guarded by Chekists on the way to prison are a common sight. There is great nervous tension in the city. Elaborate precautions have been taken to protect the Government institution. Machine guns are placed on the Astoria, the living quarters of Zinoviev and other prominent Bolsheviki. Official proclamations commanding immediate return of the strikers to the factories . . . and warning the populace against congregating in the streets.

"The Committee of Defence has initiated a 'clean-up of the city.' Many workers suspected of sympathising with Kronstadt have been placed under arrest. All Petrograd sailors and part of the garrison thought to be 'untrustworthy' have been ordered to distant points, while the families of Kronstadt sailors living in Petrograd are held as hostages. The Committee of Defence notified Kronstadt that 'the prisoners are kept as pledges' for the safety of the Commissar of the Baltic Fleet, N. N. Kuzmin, the Chairman of the Kronstadt Soviet, T. Vassiliev, and other Communists. If the least harm is suffered by our comrades the hostages will pay with their lives."

Under these iron-clad rules it was physically impossible for the workers of Petrograd to ally themselves with Kronstadt, especially as not one word of the manifestoes issued by the sailors in their paper was permitted to penetrate to the workers in Petrograd. In other words, Leon Trotsky deliberately falsifies the facts. The workers would certainly have sided with the sailors because they knew that they were not mutineers or counter-revolutionists, but that they had taken a stand with the workers as their comrades had done as long ago as 1905, and March and October 1917. It is therefore a grossly criminal and conscious libel on the memory of the Kronstadt sailors.

In the *New International* on page 106, second column, Trotsky assures his readers that no one "we may say in passing, bothered in those days about the Anarchists." That unfortunately does not tally with the incessant persecution of Anarchists which began in 1918, when Leon Trotsky liquidated the Anarchist headquarters in Moscow with machine guns. At that time the process of elimination of the Anarchists began. Even now so many years later, the concentration camps of the Soviet Government are full of the Anarchists who remained alive. Actually before the Kronstadt uprising, in fact in October 1920, when Leon Trotsky again had changed his mind about Machno because he needed his help and his army to liquidate Wrangel, and when he consented to the Anarchist Conference in Kharkhov, several hundred Anarchists were drawn into a net and despatched to the Boutirka prison where they were kept without any charge until April 1921, when they, together with other Left politicals, were forcibly removed in the dead of night and secretly sent to various prisons and concentration camps in Russia and Siberia. But that is a page of Soviet history of its own. What is to the point in this instance is that the Anarchists must have been thought of very much, else there would have been no reason to arrest them and ship them in the old Tsarist way to distant parts of Russia and Siberia.

Leon Trotsky ridicules the demands of the sailors for free Soviets. It was indeed naive of them to think that free Soviets can live side by side with a dictatorship. Actually the free Soviets had ceased to exist at an early stage in the Communist game, as the Trade Unions and the co-operatives. They had all been hitched to the chariot wheel of the Bolshevik State machine. I well remember Lenin telling me with great satisfaction, "Your Grand Old Man, Enrico Malatesta, is for our soviets." I hastened to say, "You mean free soviets, Comrade

Lenin. I, too, am for them." Lenin turned our talk to something else. But I soon discovered why free Soviets had ceased to exist in Russia.

John G. Wright will have it that there was no trouble in Petrograd until 22nd February. That is on par with his other rehash of the "historic" Party material. The unrest and dissatisfaction of the workers were already very marked when we arrived. In every industry I visited I found extreme dissatisfaction and resentment because the dictatorship of the proletariat had been turned into a devastating dictatorship of the Communist Party with its different rations and discriminations. If the discontent of the workers had not broken loose before 1921 it was only because they still clung tenaciously to the hope that when the fronts would be liquidated the promise of the Revolution would be fulfilled. It was Kronstadt which pricked the last bubble.

The sailors had dared to stand by the discontented workers. They had dared to demand that the promise of the Revolution—All Power in the Soviets—should be fulfilled. The political dictatorship had slain the dictatorship of the proletariat. That and that alone was their unforgivable offense against the holy spirit of Bolshevism.

In his article Wright has a footnote to page 49, second column, wherein he states that Victor Serge in a recent comment on Kronstadt "concedes that the Bolsheviki, once confronted with the mutiny, had no other recourse except to crush it." Victor Serge is now out of the hospitable shores of the workers' "fatherland." I therefore do not consider it a breach of faith when I say that if Victor Serge made this statement charged to him by John G. Wright, he is merely not telling the truth. Victor Serge was one of the French Communist Section who was as much distressed and horrified over the impending butchery decided upon by Leon Trotsky to "shoot the sailors as pheasants" as Alexander Berkman, myself and many other revolutionists. He used to spend every free hour in our room running up and down, tearing his hair, clenching his fists in indignation and repeating that "something must be done, something must be done, to stop the frightful massacre." When he was asked why he, as a party member, did not raise his voice in protest in the party session, his reply was that that would not help the sailors and would mark him for the Cheka and even silent disappearance. The only excuse for Victor Serge at the time was a young wife and a small baby. But for him to state now, after seventeen years, that "the Bolsheviki once confronted with the mutiny had no other recourse except to crush it," is, to say the least, inexcusable. Victor Serge knows as well as I do that there was no mutiny in Kronstadt, that the sailors actually did not use their arms in any shape or form until the bombardment of Kronstadt began. He also knows that neither the arrested Communist Commissars nor any other Communists were touched by the sailors. I therefore call upon Victor Serge to come out with the truth. That he was able to continue in Russia under the comradely régime of Lenin, Trotsky and all the other unfortunates who have been recently murdered, conscious of all the horrors that are going on, is his affair, but I cannot keep silent in the face of the charge against him as saying that the Bolsheviki were justified in crushing the sailors.

Leon Trotsky is sarcastic about the accusation that he had shot 1,500 sailors. No, he did not do the bloody job himself. He entrusted Tuchachevsky, his lieutenant, to shoot the sailors "like pheasants" as he had threatened. Tuchachevsky carried out the order to the last degree. The numbers ran into legions, and those who remained after the ceaseless attack of Bolshevist artillery were placed under the care of Dibenko, famous for his humanity and his justice.

Tuchachevsky and Dibenko, the heroes and saviours of the dictatorship! History seems to have its own way of meting out justice.

Leon Trotsky tries a trump card, when he asks, "Where and when were their great principles confirmed, in practice at least partially, at least in tendency?" This card, like all others he has already played in his life, will not win him the game. In point of fact Anarchist principles in practice and tendency have been confirmed in Spain. I agree, only partially. How could that be otherwise with all the forces conspiring against the Spanish Revolution? The constructive work undertaken by the National Confederation of Labour (the C.N.T.), and the Anarchist Federation of Iberia (the F.A.I.), is something never thought of by the Bolshevik régime in all the years of its power, and yet the collectivisation of the industries and the land stand out as the greatest achievement of any revolutionary period. Moreover, even if Franco should win, and the Spanish Anarchists be exterminated, the work they have started will continue to live. Anarchist principles and tendencies are so deeply rooted in Spanish soil that they cannot be eradicated.

During the four years civil war in Russia the Anarchists almost to a man stood by the Bolsheviki, though they grew more daily conscious of the impending collapse of the Revolution. They felt in duty bound to keep silent and to avoid everything that would bring aid and comfort to the enemies of the Revolution.

Certainly the Russian Revolution fought against many fronts and many enemies, but at no time were the odds so frightful as those confronting the Spanish people, the Anarchists and the Revolution. The menace of Franco, aided by German and Italian man power and military equipment, Stalin's blessing transferred to Spain, the conspiracy of the Imperialist powers, the betrayal by the so-called democracies and, not the least, the apathy of the international proletariat, far outweigh the dangers that surrounded the Russian Revolution. What does Trotsky do in the face of such a terrible tragedy? He joins the howling mob and thrusts his own poisoned dagger into the vitals of the Spanish Anarchists in their most crucial hour. No doubt the Spanish Anarchists have committed a grave error. They failed to invite Leon Trotsky to take charge of the Spanish Revolution and to show them how well he had succeeded in Russia that it may be repeated all over again on Spanish soil. That seems to be his chagrin.

The Individual, Society and the State

1940.

The minds of men are in confusion, for the very foundations of our civilization seem to be tottering. People are losing faith in the existing institutions, and the more intelligent realize that capitalist industrialism is defeating the very purpose it is supposed to serve.

The world is at a loss for a way out. Parliamentarism and democracy are on the decline. Salvation is being sought in Fascism and other forms of "strong" government.

The struggle of opposing ideas now going on in the world involves social problems urgently demanding a solution. The welfare of the individual and the fate of human society depend on the right answer to those questions The crisis, unemployment, war, disarmament, international relations, etc., are among those problems.

The State, government with its functions and powers, is now the subject of vital interest to every thinking man. Political developments in all civilized countries have brought the questions home. Shall we have a strong government? Are democracy and parliamentary government to be preferred, or is Fascism of one kind or another, dictatorship—monarchical, bourgeois or proletarian — the solution of the ills and difficulties that beset society today?

In other words, shall we cure the evils of democracy by more democracy, or shall we cut the Gordian knot of popular government with the sword of dictatorship?

My answer is neither the one nor the other. I am against dictatorship and Fascism as I am opposed to parliamentary regimes and so-called political democracy.

Nazism has been justly called an attack on civilization. This characterization applies with equal force to every form of dictatorship; indeed, to every kind of suppression and coercive authority. For what is civilization in the true sense? All progress has been essentially an enlargement of the liberties of the individual with a corresponding decrease of the authority wielded over him by external forces. This holds good in the realm of physical as well as of political and economic existence. In the physical world man has progressed to the extent in which he has subdued the forces of nature and made them useful to himself. Primitive man made a step on the road to progress when he first produced fire and thus triumphed over darkness, when he chained the wind or harnessed water.

What role did authority or government play in human endeavor for betterment, in invention and discovery? None whatever, or at least none that was helpful. It has always been the individual that has accomplished every miracle in that sphere, usually in spite of the prohibition, persecution and interference by authority, human and divine.

Similarly, in the political sphere, the road of progress lay in getting away more and more from the authority of the tribal chief or of the clan, of prince and king, of government, of the State. Economically, progress has meant greater well-being of ever larger numbers. Culturally, it has signified the result of all the other achievements — greater independence, political, mental and psychic.

Regarded from this angle, the problems of man's relation to the State assumes an entirely different significance. It is no more a question of whether dictatorship is preferable to democracy, or Italian Fascism superior to Hitlerism. A larger and far more vital question poses itself: Is political government, is the State, beneficial to mankind, and how does it affect the individual in the social scheme of things?

The individual is the true reality in life. A cosmos in himself, he does not exist for the State, nor for that abstraction called "society," or the "nation," which is only a collection of individuals. Man, the individual, has always been and necessarily is the sole source and motive power of evolution and progress. Civilization has been a continuous struggle of the individual or of groups of individuals against the State and even against "society," that is, against the majority subdued and hypnotized by the State and State worship. Man's greatest battles have been waged against man-made obstacles and artificial handicaps imposed upon him to paralyze his growth and development. Human thought has always been falsified by tradition and custom, and perverted false education in the interests of those who held power and enjoyed privileges. In other words, by the State and the ruling classes. This constant incessant conflict has been the history of mankind.

Individuality may be described as the consciousness of the individual as to what he is and how he lives. It is inherent in every human being and is a thing of growth. The State and social institutions come and go, but individuality remains and persists. The very essence of individuality is expression; the sense of dignity and independence is the soil wherein it thrives. Individuality is not the impersonal and mechanistic thing that the State treats as an "individual". The individual is not merely the result of heredity and environment, of cause and effect. He is that and a great deal more, a great deal else. The living man cannot be defined; he is the fountain-head of all life and all values; he is not a part of this or of that; he is a whole, an individual whole, a growing, changing, yet always constant whole.

Individuality is not to be confused with the various ideas and concepts of Individualism; much less with that "rugged individualism" which is only a masked attempt to repress and defeat the individual and his individuality So-called Individualism is the social and economic laissez faire: the exploitation of the masses by the classes by means of legal trickery, spiritual debasement and systematic indoctrination of the servile spirit, which process is known as "education." That corrupt and perverse "individualism" is the strait-jacket of individuality. It has converted life into a degrading race for externals, for possession, for social prestige and supremacy. Its highest wisdom is "the devil take the hindmost."

This "rugged individualism" has inevitably resulted in the greatest modern slavery, the crassest class distinctions, driving millions to the breadline. "Rugged individualism" has meant all the "individualism" for the masters, while the people are regimented into a slave caste to serve a handful of self-seeking "supermen." America is perhaps the best representative of this kind of individualism, in whose name political tyranny and social oppression are defended and held up as virtues; while every aspiration and attempt of man to gain freedom and social opportunity to live is denounced as "un-American" and evil in the name of that same individualism.

There was a time when the State was unknown. In his natural condition man existed without any State or organized government. People lived as families in small communities; They tilled the soil and practiced the arts and crafts. The individual, and later the family, was the unit of social life where each was free and the equal of his neighbor. Human society then was not a State but an association; a voluntary association for mutual protection and benefit. The elders and more experienced members were the guides and advisers of the people. They helped to manage the affairs of life, not to rule and dominate the individual.

Political government and the State were a much later development, growing out of the desire of the stronger to take advantage of the weaker, of the few against the many. The State, ecclesiastical and secular, served to give an appearance of legality and right to the wrong done by the few to the many. That appearance of right was necessary, the easier to rule the people, because no government can exist without the consent of the people, consent open, tacit or assumed. Constitutionalism and democracy are the modern forms of that alleged consent; the consent being inoculated and indoctrinated by what is called "education," at home, in the church, and in every other phase of life.

That consent is the belief in authority, in the necessity for it. At its base is the doctrine that man is evil, vicious, and too incompetent to know what is good for him. On this all government and oppression is built. God and the State exist and are supported by this dogma.

Yet the State is nothing but a name. It is an abstraction. Like other similar conceptions—nation, race, humanity—it has no organic reality. To call the State an organism shows a diseased tendency to make a fetish of words.

The State is a term for the legislative and administrative machinery whereby certain business of the people is transacted, and badly so. There is nothing sacred, holy or mysterious about it. The State has no more conscience or moral mission than a commercial company for working a coal mine or running a railroad.

The State has no more existence than gods and devils have. They are equally the reflex and creation of man, for man, the individual, is the only reality. The State is but the shadow of man, the shadow of his opaqueness, of his ignorance and fear.

Life begins and ends with man, the individual. Without him there is no race, no humanity, no State. No, not even "society" is possible without man. It is the individual who lives, breathes and suffers. His development, his advance, has been a continuous struggle against the fetishes of his own creation and particularly so against the "State."

In former days religious authority fashioned political life in the image of the Church. The authority of the State, the "rights" of rulers came from on high; power, like faith, was divine. Philosophers have written thick volumes to prove the sanctity of the State; some have even clad it with infallibility and with god-like attributes. Some have talked themselves into the insane notion that the State is "superhuman," the supreme reality, "the absolute."

Enquiry was condemned as blasphemy. Servitude was the highest virtue. By such precepts and training certain things came to be regarded as self-evident, as sacred of their truth, but because of constant and persistent repetition.

All progress has been essentially an unmasking of "divinity" and "mystery," of alleged sacred, eternal "truth"; it has been a gradual elimination of the abstract and the substitution in its place of the real, the concrete. In short, of facts against fancy, of knowledge against ignorance, of light against darkness.

That slow and arduous liberation of the individual was not accomplished by the aid of the State. On the contrary, it was by continuous conflict, by a life-and death struggle with the State, that even the smallest vestige of independence and freedom has been won. It has cost mankind much time and blood to secure what little it has gained so far from kings, tsars and governments.

The great heroic figure of that long Golgotha has been Man. It has always been the individual, often alone and singly, at other times in unity and co-operation with others of his kind, who has fought and bled in the age-long battle against suppression and oppression, against the powers that enslave and degrade him.

More than that and more significant: It was man, the individual, whose soul first rebelled against injustice and degradation; it was the individual who first conceived the idea of resistance to the conditions under which he chafed. In short, it is always the individual who is the parent of the liberating thought as well as of the deed.

This refers not only to political struggles, but to the entire gamut of human life and effort, in all ages and climes. It has always been the individual, the man of strong mind and will to liberty, who paved the way for every human advance, for every step toward a freer and better world; in science, philosophy and art, as well as in industry, whose genius rose to the heights, conceiving the "impossible," visualizing its realization and imbuing others with his enthusiasm to work and strive for it. Socially speaking, it was always the prophet, the seer, the idealist, who dreamed of a world more to his heart's desire and who served as the beacon light on the road to greater achievement.

The State, every government whatever its form, character or color — be it absolute or constitutional, monarchy or republic, Fascist, Nazi or Bolshevik — is by its very nature conservative, static, intolerant of change and opposed to it. Whatever changes it undergoes are always the result of pressure exerted upon it, pressure strong enough to compel the ruling powers to submit peaceably or otherwise, generally "otherwise" — that is, by revolution. Moreover, the inherent conservatism of government, of authority of any kind, unavoidably becomes reactionary. For two reasons: first, because it is in the nature of government not only to retain the power it has, but also to strengthen, widen and perpetuate it, nationally as well as internationally. The stronger authority grows, the greater the State and its power, the less it can tolerate a similar authority or political power alongside of itself. The psychology of government demands that its influence and prestige constantly grow, at home and abroad, and it exploits every opportunity to increase it. This tendency is motivated by the financial and commercial interests back of the government, represented and served by it. The fundamental *raison d'etre* of every government, to which, incidentally, historians of former days willfully shut their eyes, has become too obvious now even for professors to ignore.

The other factor which impels governments to become even more conservative and reactionary is their inherent distrust of the individual and fear of individuality. Our political and social scheme cannot afford to tolerate the individual and his constant quest for innovation. In "self-defense" the State therefore suppresses, persecutes, punishes and even deprives the individual of life. It is aided in this by every institution that stands for the preservation of the existing order. It resorts to every form of violence and force, and its efforts are supported by the "moral indignation" of the majority against the heretic, the social dissenter and the political rebel—the majority for centuries drilled in State worship, trained in discipline and obedience and subdued by the awe of authority in the home, the school, the church and the press.

The strongest bulwark of authority is uniformity; the least divergence from it is the greatest crime. The wholesale mechanisation of modern life has increased uniformity a thousandfold. It is everywhere present, in habits, tastes, dress, thoughts and ideas. Its most concentrated dullness is "public opinion." Few have the courage to stand out against it. He who refuses to submit is at once labeled "queer," "different," and decried as a disturbing element in the comfortable stagnancy of modern life.

Perhaps even more than constituted authority, it is social uniformity and sameness that harass the individual most. His very "uniqueness," "separateness" and "differentiation" make him an alien, not only in his native place, but even in his own home. Often more so than the foreign born who generally falls in with the established.

In the true sense one's native land, with its background of tradition, early impressions, reminiscences and other things dear to one, is not enough to make sensitive human beings feel at home. A certain atmosphere of "belonging," the consciousness of being "at one" with the people and environment, is more essential to one's feeling of home. This holds good in relation to one's family, the smaller local circle, as well as the larger phase of the life and activities commonly called one's country. The individual whose vision encompasses the whole world often feels nowhere so hedged in and out of touch with his surroundings than in his native land.

In pre-war time the individual could at least escape national and family boredom. The whole world was open to his longings and his quests. Now the world has become a prison, and life continual solitary confinement. Especially is this true since the advent of dictatorship, right and left.

Friedrich Nietzsche called the State a cold monster. What would he have called the hideous beast in the garb of modern dictatorship? Not that government had ever allowed much scope to the individual; but the champions of the new State ideology do not grant even that much. "The individual is nothing," they declare, "it is the collectivity which counts." Nothing less than the complete surrender of the individual will satisfy the insatiable appetite of the new deity.

Strangely enough, the loudest advocates of this new gospel are to be found among the British and American intelligentsia. Just now they are enamored with the "dictatorship of the proletariat." In theory only, to be sure. In practice, they still prefer the few liberties in their own respective countries. They go to Russia for a short visit or as salesmen of the "revolution," but they feel safer and more comfortable at home.

Perhaps it is not only lack of courage which keeps these good Britishers and Americans in their native lands rather than in the millennium come. Subconsciously there may lurk the feeling that individuality remains the most fundamental fact of all human association, suppressed and persecuted yet never defeated, and in the long run the victor.

The "genius of man," which is but another name for personality and individuality, bores its way through all the caverns of dogma, through the thick walls of tradition and custom, defying all taboos, setting authority at naught, facing contumely and the scaffold — ultimately to be blessed as prophet and martyr by succeeding generations. But for the "genius of man," that inherent, persistent quality of individuality, we would be still roaming the primeval forests.

Peter Kropotkin has shown what wonderful results this unique force of man's individuality has achieved when strengthened by co-operation with other individualities. The one-sided and entirely inadequate Darwinian theory of the struggle for existence received its biological and sociological completion from the great Anarchist scientist and thinker. In his profound work, *Mutual Aid*, Kropotkin shows that in the animal kingdom, as well as in human society, co-operation — as opposed to internecine strife and struggle—has worked for the survival and evolution of the species. He demonstrated that only mutual aid and voluntary co-operation—not the omnipotent, all-devastating State—can create the basis for a free individual and associational life.

At present the individual is the pawn of the zealots of dictatorship and the equally obsessed zealots of "rugged individualism." The excuse of the former is its claim of a new objective. The latter does not even make a pretense of anything new. As a matter of fact "rugged individualism" has learned nothing and forgotten nothing. Under its guidance the brute struggle for physical existence is still kept up. Strange as it may seem, and utterly absurd as it is, the struggle for physical survival goes merrily on though the necessity for it has entirely disappeared. Indeed, the struggle is being continued apparently because there is no necessity for it. Does not so-called overproduction prove it? Is not the world-wide economic crisis an eloquent demonstration that the struggle for existence is being maintained by the blindness of "rugged individualism" at the risk of its own destruction?

One of the insane characteristics of this struggle is the complete negation of the relation of the producer to the things he produces. The average worker has no inner point of contact with the industry he is employed in, and he is a stranger to the process of production of which he is a mechanical part. Like any other cog of the machine, he is replaceable at any time by other similar depersonalized human beings.

The intellectual proletarian, though he foolishly thinks himself a free agent, is not much better off. He, too, has a little choice or self-direction, in his particular metier as his brother who works with his hands. Material considerations and desire for greater social prestige are usually the deciding factors in the vocation of the intellectual. Added to it is the tendency to follow in the footsteps of family tradition, and become doctors, lawyers, teachers, engineers, etc. The groove requires less effort and personality. In consequence nearly everybody is out of place in our present scheme of things. The masses plod on, partly because their senses have been dulled by the deadly routine of work and because they must eke out an existence. This applies with even greater force to the political fabric of today. There is no place in its texture for free choice of independent thought and activity. There is a place only for voting and tax-paying puppets.

The interests of the State and those of the individual differ fundamentally and are antagonistic. The State and the political and economic institutions it supports can exist only by fashioning the individual to their particular purpose; training him to respect "law and order;" teaching him obedience, submission and unquestioning faith in the wisdom and justice of government; above all, loyal service and complete self-sacrifice when the State commands it, as in war. The State puts itself and its interests even above the claims of religion and of God. It punishes religious or conscientious scruples against individuality because there is no individuality without liberty, and liberty is the greatest menace to authority.

The struggle of the individual against these tremendous odds is the more difficult—too often dangerous to life and limb—because it is not truth or falsehood which serves as the criterion of the opposition he meets. It is not the validity or usefulness of his thought or activity which rouses against him the forces of the State and of "public opinion." The persecution of the innovator and protestant has always been inspired by fear on the part of constituted authority of having its infallibility questioned and its power undermined.

Man's true liberation, individual and collective, lies in his emancipation from authority and from the belief in it. All human evolution has been a struggle in that direction and for that object. It is not invention and mechanics which constitute development. The ability to travel at the rate of 100 miles an hour is no evidence of being civilized. True civilization is to be measured by the individual, the unit of all social life; by his individuality and the extent to which it is free to have its being to grow and expand unhindered by invasive and coercive authority.

Socially speaking, the criterion of civilization and culture is the degree of liberty and economic opportunity which the individual enjoys; of social and international unity and co-operation unrestricted by man-made laws and other artificial obstacles; by the absence of privileged castes and by the reality of liberty and human dignity; in short, by the true emancipation of the individual.

Political absolutism has been abolished because men have realized in the course of time that absolute power is evil and destructive. But the same thing is true of all power, whether it be the power of privilege, of money, of the priest, of the politician or of so-called democracy. In its effect on individuality it matters little what the particular character of coercion is—whether it be as black as Fascism, as yellow as Nazism or as pretentiously red as Bolshevism. It is power that corrupts and degrades both master and slave and it makes no difference whether the power is wielded by an autocrat, by parliament or Soviets. More pernicious than the power of a dictator is that of a class; the most terrible—the tyranny of a majority.

The long process of history has taught man that division and strife mean death, and that unity and cooperation advance his cause, multiply his strength and further his welfare. The spirit of government has always worked against the social application of this vital lesson, except where it served the State and aided its own particular interests. It is this anti-progressive and anti-social spirit of the State and of the privileged castes back of it which has been responsible for the bitter struggle between man and man. The individual and ever larger groups of individuals are beginning to see beneath the surface of the established order of things. No longer are they so blinded as in the past by the glare and tinsel of the State idea, and of the "blessings" of "rugged individualism." Man is reaching out for the wider scope of human relations which liberty alone can give. For true liberty is not a mere scrap of paper called "constitution," "legal right" or "law." It is not an abstraction derived from the non-reality known as "the State." It is not the negative thing of being free from something, because with such freedom you may starve to death. Real freedom, true liberty is positive: it is freedom to something; it is the liberty to be, to do; in short, the liberty of actual and active opportunity.

That sort of liberty is not a gift: it is the natural right of man, of every human being. It cannot be given: it cannot be conferred by any law or government. The need of it, the longing for it, is inherent in the individual. Disobedience to every form of coercion is the instinctive expression of it. Rebellion and revolution are the more or less conscious attempt to achieve it. Those manifestations, individual and social, are fundamentally expressions of the values of man. That those values may be nurtured, the community must realize that its greatest and most lasting asset is the unit—the individual.

In religion, as in politics, people speak of abstractions and believe they are dealing with realities. But when it does come to the real and the concrete, most people seem to lose vital touch with it. It may well be because reality alone is too matter-of-fact, too cold to enthuse the human soul. It can be aroused to enthusiasm only by things out of the commonplace, out of the ordinary. In other words, the Ideal is the spark that fires the imagination and hearts of men. Some ideal is needed to rouse man out of the inertia and humdrum of his existence and turn the abject slave into an heroic figure.

Right here, of course, comes the Marxist objector who has outmarxed Marx himself. To such a one, man is a mere puppet in the hands of that metaphysical Almighty called economic determinism or, more vulgarly, the class struggle. Man's will, individual and collective, his psychic life and mental orientation count for almost nothing with our Marxist and do not affect his conception of human history.

No intelligent student will deny the importance of the economic factor in the social growth and development of mankind. But only narrow and willful dogmatism can persist in remaining blind to the important role played by an idea as conceived by the imagination and aspirations of the individual.

It were vain and unprofitable to attempt to balance one factor as against another in human experience. No one single factor in the complex of individual or social behavior can be designated as the factor of decisive quality. We know too little, and may never know enough, of human psychology to weigh and measure the relative values of this or that factor in determining man's conduct. To form such dogmas in their social connotation is nothing short of bigotry; yet, perhaps, it has its uses, for the very attempt to do so proved the persistence of the human will and confutes the Marxists.

Fortunately even some Marxists are beginning to see that all is not well with the Marxian creed. After all, Marx was but human — all too human — hence by no means infallible. The practical application of economic determinism in Russia is helping to clear the minds of the more intelligent Marxists. This can be seen in the transvaluation of Marxian values going on in Socialist and even Communist ranks in some European countries. They are slowly realising that their theory has overlooked the human element, *den Menschen*, as a Socialist paper put it. Important as the economic factor is, it is not enough. The rejuvenation of mankind needs the inspiration and energising force of an ideal.

Such an ideal I see in Anarchism. To be sure, not in the popular misrepresentations of Anarchism spread by the worshippers of the State and authority. I mean the philosophy of a new social order based on the released energies of the individual and the free association of liberated individuals.

Of all social theories Anarchism alone steadfastly proclaims that society exists for man, not man for society. The sole legitimate purpose of society is to serve the needs and advance the aspiration of the individual. Only by doing so can it justify its existence and be an aid to progress and culture.

The political parties and men savagely scrambling for power will scorn me as hopelessly out of tune with our time. I cheerfully admit the charge. I find comfort in the assurance that their hysteria lacks enduring quality. Their hosanna is but of the hour.

Man's yearning for liberation from all authority and power will never be soothed by their cracked song. Man's quest for freedom from every shackle is eternal. It must and will go on.

CPSIA information can be obtained
at www.ICGtesting.com
Printed in the USA
LVHW011707301221
707552LV00004B/255

9 781610 010313